British History in Perspective
General Editor: Jeremy Black

Please note that a sister series, *Social History in Perspective*, is available covering the key topics in social and cultural history.

British History in Perspective
Series Standing Order:
ISBN 0–333–71356–7 hardcover
ISBN 0–333–69331–0 paperback

You can receive future titles in this series as they are published by placing a standing order. Please contact your bookseller or, in case of difficulty, write to the address below with your name and address, the title of the series and the ISBN quoted above.

Customer Services Department, Macmillan Distribution Ltd
Houndmills, Basingstoke, Hampshire RG21 6XS, England

Politics and War in the Three Stuart Kingdoms, 1637–49

DAVID SCOTT

First published 2004 by
PALGRAVE MACMILLAN
Houndmills, Basingstoke, Hampshire RG21 6XS and
175 Fifth Avenue, New York, N.Y. 10010
Companies and representatives throughout the world

PALGRAVE MACMILLAN is the global academic imprint of the Palgrave
Macmillan division of St. Martin's Press, LLC and of Palgrave Macmillan Ltd.
Macmillan® is a registered trademark in the United States, United Kingdom
and other countries. Palgrave is a registered trademark in the European
Union and other countries.

ISBN 0–333–65873–6 hardback
ISBN 0–333–65874–4 paperback

This book is printed on paper suitable for recycling and made from fully
managed and sustained forest sources.

A catalogue record for this book is available from the British Library.

Library of Congress Cataloging-in-Publication Data

Scott, David (David A.)
    Politics and war in the three Stuart kingdoms, 1637–49 / David Scott.
        p. cm. – (British history in perspective)
    Includes bibliographical references and index.
        ISBN 0–333–65873–6 — ISBN 0–333–65874–4 (pbk.)
        1. Great Britain–Politics and government—1625–1649. 2. Great
Britain—History—Civil War, 1642–1649. 3. Scotland—History—Charles I,
1625–1649. 4. Ireland—History—1625–1649. I. Title. II. British history in
perspective (Palgrave Macmillan (Firm))

    DA395.S36 2003
    941.06′2—dc21   2003051870

10 9 8 7 6 5 4 3 2 1
13 12 11 10 09 08 07 06 05 04

Printed in China

For my father

Contents

Preface and Acknowledgements

My main purpose in this book is to provide an integrated, or holistic, narrative of events in the three Stuart kingdoms from the outbreak of the Covenanter rebellion to the execution of Charles I. As anyone familiar with recent trends in Stuart historiography will appreciate, my approach is in keeping with the current vogue for treating the Atlantic Archipelago (a convenient if rather grandiose phrase for Britain and Ireland) as the most useful framework for understanding the histories of its component peoples – a body of work known as the 'New British History'. An integrated analysis seems especially applicable to the closely intertwined histories of the Stuart kingdoms during the 1640s. It may not be able to answer all the questions that we have traditionally asked of the period, but it will certainly provide a new and revealing layer of interpretation to nation-centred histories, and this is surely to be welcomed.

The focus and framework of this book derive simply from the difficulty I encountered trying to make sense of the English Civil War without reference to the conflicts in Scotland and Ireland, and vice versa. There is ample evidence that the relationship between the kingdoms during the 1640s had a major bearing upon the pattern of events in all three. Admittedly, it would be hard to sustain this argument with regard to the kingdoms' social structures and economies, which appear to have had relatively little impact upon each other. However, it can be sustained in terms of high politics and military affairs – the fields in which most of the headline events of the 1640s occurred. Politics and war constituted the essential dynamic of 'British' history during the mid-seventeenth century, and must take centre stage in any integrated narrative of the period.

Several other consequences, besides a bias towards political history, flow from taking a holistic approach – the most obvious of which is a concentration on developments in England at the expense of those in Scotland and Ireland. The charge of Anglocentrism is perhaps the most heinous in New British History, and yet it is difficult to see how an integrated account can fail to be anything but Anglocentric. The image favoured by Conrad Russell to illustrate the way the three kingdoms interacted in the mid-seventeenth century is that of billiard balls colliding.[1] But as John Adamson has recently reminded us, in international relations, as in nature, not all balls are of equal size or collide with equal impact.[2] England was not only the seat of Charles's imperial government, it was also much the most powerful of the three kingdoms. It was inevitable, therefore, that England would exert a greater influence over Scotland and Ireland than the other way round.

To the charge of Anglocentrism can be added that of privileging the histories of ruling elites over those of groups not engaged in the pursuit or exercise of power and removed from the centres of government. This admission is really just another way of saying that a holistic approach favours the political and military over the social and economic; and clearly the exponents of 'British' history must be particularly on their guard against the assumption that political events can be understood independently of the social, economic, and cultural contexts in which they occurred. That said, it is hard to deny that the social and economic structures of all three kingdoms allowed small groups of men to exercise a disproportionately large influence over the lives of their respective communities. Indeed, one of my aims in this book has been to explore how ruling groups in each kingdom, having courted the common people and involved them in the political process to an unprecedented degree in the period 1637–42, were then able to shut up shop and impose their will in harsher and more peremptory fashion than the supposedly tyrannical Charles I would ever have dreamed possible.

The case for focusing on the powerful rather than the powerless becomes stronger still in light of the imbalances between the scholarly canon on each kingdom. Thanks to recent work by Tadhg Ó hAnnracháin, Allan Macinnes, Micheál Ó Siochrú, and John Young, we now have a clearer picture of the structure of high politics in Scotland and Ireland during the 1640s than we possess for Westminster, and certainly for the royalist headquarters in Oxford. As Adamson has rightly observed, 'it is this world of the "centre" [and he is referring here to Westminster] which currently appears to be the most puzzling and confused: how do the varying monograph accounts of the moments of climacteric – 1642, 1645–7, 1648–9 – relate to one another? How are their differing analyses of the workings of politics during the period to be reconciled?'[3] These are some of the questions that this book hopes to address.

Our familiarity with the political landscape at the centres of English power in the 1640s also suffers by comparison with our knowledge of the provincial dimension to the Civil War. Recent studies by John Morrill, Martyn Bennett, and a host of local historians have given us a good understanding of how the English localities experienced and responded to war and the general unpleasantness that accompanied it. As for Scotland and Ireland, much more research is needed on the local impact of the upheavals there before we can attempt an authoritative history of the Stuart peoples (as distinct from the Stuart kingdoms) in the mid-seventeenth century. But this is a huge task in itself, and not one that I feel qualified to undertake.

My final excuses relate to the book's somewhat idiosyncratic time-frame. Perhaps the most logical period for a holistic account to address is that covered by the 'wars of the three kingdoms', or roughly 1637–53. My reason for cutting the story short at the regicide is partly practical – Ronald Hutton's contribution to this series, *The British Republic*, takes up the running from 1649 – but also because I feel that there was a signifi-cant change in political direction in all three kingdoms in the six months from September 1648. A starting date of 1637 and the outbreak of the Covenanter rebellion is more readily comprehensible, although in fact the opening chapter takes all of early Stuart history in its stride. It covers some of the ground explored by Ann Hughes's preceding volume in the series, *The Causes of the English Civil War*, but with greater emphasis on developments in Scotland and Ireland.

My debts to colleagues and friends in writing this book are numerous. I am grateful to John Adamson, Lloyd Bowen, Ian Gentles, Sean Kelsey, Patrick Little, John Morrill, Jason Peacey, Stephen Roberts, David Smith, and Arthur Williamson for reading and commenting on part or all of the first draft; to my colleagues on the 1640–60 section at the History of Parliament Trust for helping me to make sense of the 1640s; and to directors of the History, past and present, for having given me the oppor-tunity to make a living from an obsession. My thanks are also due to Robert Armstrong, Phil Baker, Alexia Grosjean, Ann Hughes, Chris Kyle,

Keith Lindley, Allan Macinnes, Steve Murdoch, Elliot Vernon, Scott Wheeler, and John Young for making free with their advice, research, and unpublished work. I am especially indebted to John Adamson for allowing me to read chapters from his forthcoming book *The Noble Revolt* (Weidenfeld & Nicolson). On those occasions where I cite his work but provide no endnote, it is to this book I am referring. On a more personal note, I would like to thank Steve Parks for his unfailing generosity; Claire Cross for having inspired me as an undergraduate; and Andrew and Frances for their help with the maps. Among those of my friends not vitally interested in Stuart history but who had to put up with this book anyway, I am particularly grateful to Monique Morris, Michael Orme, Yasmin Rafiq, Gizelle Rahman, James Smith, and Alison and John Tyzack. Finally, I would like to thank my father, to whom this book is dedicated, for having got me this far.

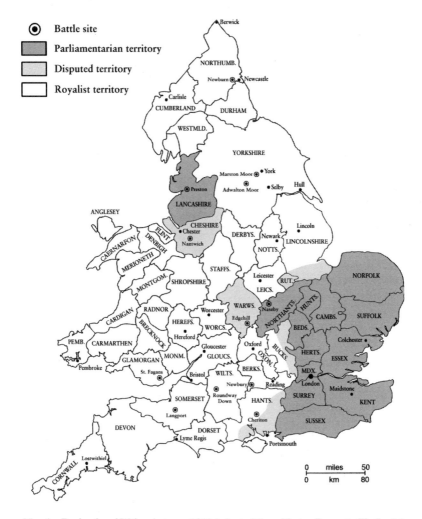

Map 1 England and Wales, Autumn 1643 (adapted from Martyn Bennett, *The English Civil War*, London: Longman, 1995, p. 48).

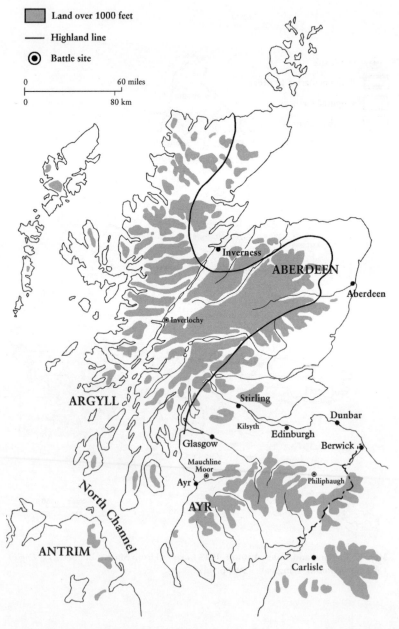

Map 2 Scotland (adapted from David L. Smith, *A History of the Modern British Isles, 1603–1707*, Oxford: Blackwell, 1998, p. 13).

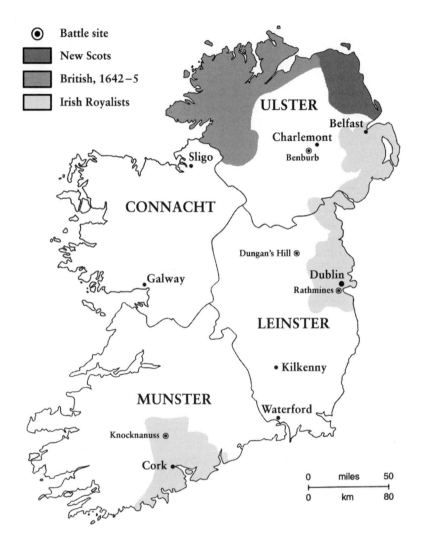

Legend:
- ◉ Battle site
- New Scots
- British, 1642–5
- Irish Royalists

ULSTER

Belfast

Charlemont

Benburb ◉

Sligo •

CONNACHT

Dungan's Hill ◉

Galway •

Dublin •
Rathmines ◉

LEINSTER

• Kilkenny

MUNSTER

Waterford •

Knocknanuss ◉

Cork •

0   miles   50
0   km   80

Map 3   Ireland, Summer 1643 (adapted from Martyn Bennett, *The Civil Wars in Britain and Ireland, 1638–1651* (Oxford: Blackwell, 1997).

Chapter 1: Society, War, and Allegiance in the Three Kingdoms, 1637–42

The State of the Stuart Nations

England

Looking back on the England he had known in the 1630s, the statesman and historian Sir Edward Hyde observed a familiar English trait: 'the truth is, there was ... little curiosity either in the Court or the country to know any thing of Scotland, or what was done there ... nor had that kingdom a place or mention in one page of any gazette, so little the world heard or thought of that people'.[1] Since 1603, when the Scottish king, James Stuart, had succeeded Elizabeth Tudor, England and Ireland had been joined with Scotland through the person of the monarch (and little else). James's son Charles had inherited this 'union of crowns' in 1625, and though he had been born in Scotland, and even spoke with a Scottish accent, the English thought of him first and foremost as king of England. If he chose to rule other kingdoms 'in his spare time' it was no concern of theirs. Little wonder then that when rebellions in Scotland and Ireland precipitated civil war in their own country, the English were generally at a loss as to how this calamity had come about.

The English blind-spot when it came to the king's 'other' kingdoms arose partly from chauvinism – a belief in the superiority of England, her people and institutions, over other countries. Yet it also reflected a fundamental truth about the relative power and importance of the constituent parts of the Stuart dynastic agglomeration. England was the wealthiest and most powerful of Charles's domains. Its population on the eve of civil war numbered close on five million, which was almost twice that of Scotland, Wales, and Ireland put together. Although the vast majority of the English lived in rural settlements, reflecting the predominantly agrarian nature of the economy, England was a more urbanised society than most of its neighbours. Bristol, Newcastle, York, and several other provincial capitals could boast populations of over 10,000; while London, with its 400,000 or so inhabitants, was the largest metropolis in western Europe. A large slice of the kingdom's rapidly expanding overseas trade passed through the City, which also made it one of Europe's principal money markets.

Fittingly for a city of such disproportionate size and wealth, London was the centre of what, by contemporary standards, was a highly centralised state. All government, civil as well as ecclesiastical, derived from the person and authority of the king; and access to this font of power and patronage was through the royal court at the Palace of Whitehall, in London. It was here that Charles and his queen, Henrietta Maria (sister of Louis XIII of France), normally resided, and that royal government was conducted. The king, aided by his privy council (which comprised the principal ministers of state) and other executive bodies, exercised a wide range of prerogative – that is, discretionary – powers, including the appointment of bishops, judges, and county officials such as JPs.

The crown's most prized prerogatives were the right to call and dissolve Parliaments, and to veto legislation passed by the two Houses – the so-called negative voice. Parliament, pre-1640, had several functions: it represented the people's grievances to the monarch; cooperated with the crown in passing laws (statutes); and voted the king taxes (subsidies). Parliament's role as the king's great council, which he could summon and dissolve at will, and the fact that it neither possessed nor sought executive powers, meant that it had no direct involvement in governing the country. Nevertheless, the Westminster Parliament was far more influential than its Scottish and Irish counterparts. The authority of king-in-Parliament, as represented by statute law, carried the greatest legislative force in the land. Indeed, there was a strong body of opinion that statute and the mass of accumulated legal precedents it elaborated – known collectively as the common law – defined and limited the royal prerogative. English identity itself was interwoven with an acute sense of England's constitutional and legal exceptionalism; an unshakeable belief in the antiquity, superiority, and sovereignty of her laws.

Despite the restricted nature of the electoral franchise – women, servants, and the indigent poor being denied the vote – Parliament had become identified in an almost mystical sense with the entire nation. At a time when the power of princes was thought to be growing at the expense of their subjects' rights, Parliament was regarded as the guardian of English 'liberties' such as habeas corpus and the principle of no taxation without consent. The preservation of these liberties, moreover, had become indelibly associated with the defence of English Protestantism and national autonomy against 'popery' (international Catholicism), which was synonymous in popular perception with tyranny over body and soul. Thus Parliament was a focus for patriotic feeling and zeal for 'the true Protestant religion'. Above all, regular Parliaments were thought to act as lightning conductors for domestic discontent – an important role in a realm where, in the absence of a trained police force, large salaried bureaucracy, or standing army, government depended upon the consent of the governed and the voluntary cooperation of local office-holders.

The English reverence for Parliaments was the product of a politically well-informed and engaged public – a phenomenon related to deeper trends such as increasing social differentiation and rising literacy levels. Improvements in agriculture and trade in the century before 1640 had created an industrious 'middling sort' that was keen to join the fight against popery and disorder at all levels, from common drunkenness to the presence of 'evil counsellors' at court. Some of the kingdom's 15,000 or so gentry felt threatened by the increasing assertiveness of the lower orders, and looked for ways to promote hierarchy and deference. Others, however, sought to harness the concerns of the middling sort to further local campaigns for moral reform or to pressure the crown for an aggressively anti-Catholic foreign policy. Even great aristocrats were not above courting popular support. The Earl of Warwick, for example, could rally large numbers on his home soil of Essex as the champion of liberties and true religion. He and his circle believed that civil liberties must be earned through strenuous public service – a notion that chimed perfectly with the urge towards active citizenship among the middling sort. This state of political symbiosis between commoners and elites illustrates the dynamism yet stability of English society. The majority of peers, however, sustained their political pre-eminence by more traditional means. They dominated high office at court and in their counties, and many derived additional influence as great landowners. Noblemen such as the earls of Newcastle and Northumberland were regional magnates, whose estates dwarfed those of most gentry.

The very vibrancy of English society was a source of political tension. Rising prices, together with the demands of war against Spain and France in the 1620s, obliged the crown to seek additional funds in the form of parliamentary subsidies. Yet, Parliaments, mindful of popular concerns over popish influences at court and perceived mismanagement of crown revenues, proved reluctant to vote for subsidies until the people's griev- ances had been redressed (a formula that prevented the crown from tapping all but a fraction of the nation's wealth). Some of this reluctance, moreover, was couched in the language of the subjects' liberties and com- mon law limitations upon the royal prerogative. Insecure in his person and authority, Charles did not react well to any sign of non-compliance from his subjects. Seen through his eyes, the unsettling changes that were occurring within English society became a populist conspiracy against monarchy and the social order. His response, as Richard Cust and Ann Hughes have shown, was to ' "close down" the political system; to avoid Parliament if possible, to emphasise hierarchy, order, and honour, and to insist on absolute obedience'.[2]

Charles's over-compensating desire for order in the face of 'popular- ity' coloured all aspects of his rule. It encouraged him to adopt 'new counsels' that pronounced him answerable to God alone, and thus justi- fied in resorting to prerogative taxation. It strengthened his resolve to do without Parliaments from 1629, and to deny their more fervent advocates a foothold at court. Most importantly perhaps, it shaped his religious views. Charles advanced clerics such as William Laud (whom he made archbishop of Canterbury) who shared his passion for ceremony and order in church worship, as well as his exalted notions concerning the royal supremacy in religion. Not since Edward the Confessor had England had such a pious monarch, nor one so dedicated to church reform. The problem was that in religion, as in much else, Charles stood outside the mainstream of English opinion. A significant section of the political nation believed that the ultimate arbiter in church matters should be king-in-Parliament rather than royal prerogative. The gentry resented the Caroline trend towards greater clerical involvement in tem- poral affairs. And many people were wedded to the familiar liturgy of the Book of Common Prayer, and could muster little enthusiasm for Laudian innovations. Moreover, to the 'hotter sort of Protestants', and particularly to the Puritans – those members of the Church of England eager to cleanse it of Catholic vestiges – Laudian ceremonies smacked of outright popery. Although relatively few in number, and subject to increasing state harassment from the late 1620s, the Puritans were an influential group- ing. They were represented at almost every social level, and by promot- ing a preaching ministry and godly magistracy they hoped to realise their vision of the English as an elect nation under God. Laudianism they regarded as a stalking-horse for the restoration of papal authority in England, and rather than suffer the attentions of the 'Romish whore' some of them emigrated to the American colonies.

Wales

Wales had been joined with England formally in the 1530s and 1540s, when English law and administration had been extended throughout the principality and the Welsh were granted the right to send MPs to Westminster. The majority of Wales's 400,000 or so inhabitants were monoglot Welsh-speaking, although there were enclaves of English-speakers in south Pembrokeshire and the Gower. Because of the language barrier, and the country's relative poverty and difficult terrain, Wales had not been evangelised by Protestant reformers to anything like the degree that parts of lowland England had. But the Welsh were none the less a Protestant people. Care had been taken in Tudor times to translate the liturgy of the Church of England into the native tongue, and the majority of Welsh were sincerely attached to Prayer Book worship and the communal pastimes that accompanied it.

In a fresh and stimulating look at the Welsh and their Celtic cousins the Cornish during the Civil War, Mark Stoyle has attributed to both peoples a strong sense of ethnic and national identity, and depicted their Royalist allegiance as partly an expression of 'national independence'.[3] Racially and culturally, the native Welsh (and, for their part, the Cornish) certainly formed a distinct body of people within the Stuart realm. And given the paucity of peculiarly Welsh institutions, religious creeds, or legal codes, it would seem that the only solid basis for Welsh 'nationalism' was indeed a sense of ethnic separateness. Unfortunately, we know too little about the native Welsh in this period to say whether they defined themselves primarily by blood, language, and other ethnic traits. Their gentry leaders, of whom they rarely acted independently, certainly did not. In terms of government, politics, and religion at least, the Welsh were entirely 'jointed in' to the English state, making it very difficult – as Peter Gaunt and John Morrill have argued – to identify a dimension to the Civil War in Wales that is not mirrored in parts of England.[4]

Stoyle's focus on the 'dark forces of ethnic hatred' in the wars of the three kingdoms – or as he prefers, 'a war of five peoples': English, Scots, Irish, Welsh, and Cornish – is least convincing when applied to the English. The English people's ethnic identity was not central to their sense of Englishness, which they defined primarily in regnal, juridical, and confessional terms. If they thought of the Welsh, Irish, and Scots at all, it was not as irredeemable racial 'others' – as the Spanish regarded the Jews and Moors, for example – but as benighted outlanders in need of the civilising influence of English laws and customs.

Ireland

Tudor rhetoric that the kingdom of Ireland was 'united and knit to the Imperial Crown of the realm of England' had been essentially that – rhetoric. Not until the very last year of Tudor rule, when Elizabeth's forces defeated the Ulster Gaelic leaders in the Nine Years War (1594–1603), did the crown succeed in bringing all of Ireland under its control. Before then, the full exercise of royal authority had been limited mainly to the Pale – a narrow strip of land around Dublin in the eastern province of Leinster. Much of the territory in the three other provinces – Munster, Ulster, and Connacht – had been under the sway of powerful overlords, some of whom paid little heed to the Dublin administration.

In the four decades of peace that followed the Elizabethan conquest, Ireland's population grew to between 1.4 and 2 million. The Irish economy too was expanding during the early seventeenth century, although from a very low base. Industry was limited to rudimentary woollen manufacture, small-scale urban artisanry, and a few iron-smelting ventures in Leinster and Munster. Large parts of the country, particularly in Ulster and Connacht, remained covered in forest and bog, and the majority of the people lived directly off the land in conditions that to English eyes appeared primitive. Overseas trade was dominated by the export of cattle, wool, and hides to England, and was concentrated in the ports of the eastern seaboard. Dublin, which enjoyed about a third of this export trade, was easily Ireland's largest town, with a population of about 20,000 by the 1630s.

The growth of the Irish economy was underpinned by the gradual extension of the common law system throughout Ireland. English-style property rights and tenurial relations were already spreading beyond the Pale by the late sixteenth century, as Gaelic chiefs began to take out legal title for their land from the crown, and to impose leases and levy rents on their retainers in place of the traditional obligation of military service in return for protection. The collapse of resistance to English power after the Nine Years War strengthened the crown's juridical authority, as indeed did the accession of James, who unlike the Tudors could claim descent from the ancient royal houses of Ireland. Certainly the Stuarts inspired more loyalty among the Irish than their predecessors had.

The ultimate source of power in Ireland was the monarch. However, for practical reasons he delegated authority to a lord deputy or lieutenant – usually an English-born courtier – and the Irish privy council in Dublin. The limitations upon the Dublin administration were few, but significant. First, the crown reserved to itself the right of appointment to high office and the summoning and dissolving of the Irish Parliament. Secondly, the Irish privy council was subordinate to its English equivalent at Whitehall. And thirdly, by virtue of Poynings's Law, all legislation submitted to the Irish Parliament had first to be approved by the crown, and it alone. Ireland was a dependency of the English crown, not of the state of England and much less its Parliament. If any group in Irish society failed to secure satisfaction from Dublin then it could appeal directly to the crown.

Reverence for the king and his prerogative authority was one of the few things that Ireland's disparate peoples had in common. The kingdom was composed of four main – and, to varying degrees, mutually antagonistic – ethnic groupings. By far the largest of these, comprising at least three-quarters of Ireland's population, was the Gaelic or native Irish, otherwise known as the Old Irish. Again, we know too little about the Old Irish to say whether they defined themselves primarily in terms of clan, region, *fír Erenn* (men of Ireland), or as part of the *Gaedhil* – the Gaelic peoples of Ireland and Scotland. That they were overwhelmingly and self-consciously Catholic was another major component in the intricate weave of Old Irish identity.

The second largest group, the Old English, were the descendants of Anglo-Norman colonists who had settled in Ireland during the Middle Ages. They too were predominantly Catholic, although a few of their number, including one of Ireland's leading magnates, James Butler, Earl (and from 1642, Marquess) of Ormond, were Protestants. The Old English were concentrated in the Pale and the more anglicised parts of Munster and Connacht, and until the reign of Elizabeth they had been the principal political force in Ireland. In the decades after the Reformation, however, the crown had come to equate loyalty not just with Englishness but with being *Protestant* and English. Despite insisting that their religious attachments did not compromise their long record of temporal allegiance to the crown, the Old English had been removed from high office during the second half of the sixteenth century and replaced by English-born Protestants. Excluded from power and denigrated for

their religion, the Old English found themselves in much the same boat
as their traditional enemies the Old Irish, and it is this shared fate as
second-class subjects that explains the increased political collaboration
and intermarriage between the two groups during the early seventeenth
century. Another corrosive of old barriers was the spread of Counter-
Reformation Catholicism in Ireland during the early seventeenth century.
It is true that there were tensions within the Irish Counter-Reformation
movement, but as Nicholas Canny has argued, they stemmed less from
ethnic divisions than from differences in the types of communities in which
Catholic clergy worked.[5] Those who operated in the Pale, for example,
where the Catholic elite was well established, tended to favour a seigneurial, household-based form of worship; whereas those who carried the fight
into Protestant settler areas such as west Ulster became convinced that
Catholicism could only survive if papal jurisdiction was restored and ordinary Catholics were allowed free practice of their religion.

The third largest group were the English Protestant settlers who had
come to Ireland in the wake of the Reformation. There were perhaps as
many as 80,000 of these New English by the 1630s, mostly living in Ulster
and Munster. With the backing of the crown they had supplanted the Old
English as the most powerful group in the Dublin administration and the
Irish Parliament, and were dedicated to 'civilising' (that is, anglicising)
the Gaelic elements of the population by getting them to adopt English
religion, law, and customs. The main weapon of the New English in this
cultural war was the plantation scheme, whereby land was expropriated
from the Catholic Irish and given to Protestant settlers, whose presence,
it was believed, would increase agricultural production and promote civil-
ity among the native inhabitants. The largest and most controversial plantation occurred in the aftermath of the Nine Years War, when the estates
of the defeated Ulster warlords were parcelled out among English settlers,
'deserving' Gaelic leaders, and Protestant colonists from Scotland – the
fourth largest of Ireland's distinctive cultural groupings.

By the 1630s, Scots made up perhaps two-thirds of the 40,000 or so
adult Protestant settlers in Ulster, a group known collectively as the 'British'.
The crown had encouraged Scottish migration to Ulster in the hope that
it would drive a wedge between the province's most powerful clan the
MacDonnells and their Gaelic cousins in Scotland, the MacDonalds of Clan
Ian Mor. Both branches of this family were strongly Catholic, and both were
committed to the re-establishment of a MacDonnell–MacDonald lordship
across the North Channel (the narrow stretch of water separating Ulster
from Scotland).

The Nine Years War and the Ulster plantation helped to swell the numbers of Catholic Irish who quit their homeland for Britain or the Continent during the early seventeenth century. The majority of these migrants were economic refugees – vagrants and the dispossessed fleeing harvest failure and the injustices of the plantation system. At least 32,000, however, were 'idle swordsmen' and other undesirables who volunteered for, or were conscripted into, foreign military service. Many of these men ended up in the Irish regiments of Spain's army in Flanders, where Catholic volunteers from all over Europe fought against the Dutch and their Protestant allies, among them the English. The Irish regiments in Spanish service were nurseries not only of military professionalism, but also of Counter-Reformation devotions and the cause of re-establishing the Catholic Church in Ireland.

Scotland

When James VI of Scotland hurried south in 1603 to be crowned James I of England and Ireland, he left behind a stable if not exactly unified kingdom. To say that there were about 750,000 Scots by the early seventeenth century is to imply that they were a united people, and this was not the case. Ethnically, Scotland was divided between the Anglo-Scots-speaking Lowlands and the *Gaidhealtachd* – the area of Gaelic speech that was broadly coterminous with the Highland regions that extended north and west of Edinburgh. The need for unity in the face of English aggression had encouraged Lowland Scots to think in terms of one Scottish nation and people. Nevertheless, they derided their Highland neighbours as lawless savages, given to feuding and raiding, and more akin to the 'barbarous' Irish than true Scots. One Lowland poem described how God had created the first Highlander from a horse turd! Similarly, some Highlanders thought of Lowlanders as a different race, the *Gall* (non-Gael or foreigner), and resented them for having driven the Gaels from the fertile Lowlands. Like 'the Irish' therefore, 'the Scots' is a problematic label, and in this present study it usually refers to those in Scotland who took their lead from Edinburgh.

But there is a danger in making too much of the Lowland–Highland divide. Significant cultural and social variations can be found within as well as between the two parts of Scotland – just as there were in England between arable regions and the pastoral uplands, forests, and fens. The Clan Ian Mor of the western Highlands, for example, was closer in terms of lineage and literary culture to the Ulster MacDonnells than to the clans of the central Highlands. Similarly, the confessional division between Catholics and Protestants in Scotland did not conform to any simple Highland–Lowland dichotomy. Irish Franciscan missionaries created pockets of Counter-Reformation Catholicism in the western Highlands during the 1620s and 1630s; and many Highlanders were at least nominally Catholic. On the other hand, the main clan enemies of the MacDonalds, the Campbells of Argyllshire in the south-west Highlands, were enthusiastically Protestant. Lowlanders too were split on religious grounds. Ayrshire and the surrounding region – the so-called 'radical south-west' – was the heartland of 'reformed' Protestantism, or Presbyterianism (which we shall discuss below), whereas Aberdeenshire was noted for its episcopalian sympathies. Too much emphasis on the differences between Lowlands and Highlands can also obscure the fact that in terms of basic social structure the two parts of Scotland were much alike. Kinship reinforced feudal and client networks on both sides of the Highland Line (the line is shown in Map 2), although the role of the family in buttressing landed authority was declining during the seventeenth century as inflation and a vigorous land market led to the increasing commercialisation of tenurial relations.

Perhaps the main difference between the two parts of Scotland cen-tred on their relationship to the crown. Lowland magnates participated in and attempted to manipulate central government. Highland chiefs, by contrast, although they acknowledged themselves subjects of the Stuart monarchy, preferred to ignore royal authority altogether. It was only when fighting between the MacDonalds and neighbouring clans got out of hand in the late sixteenth century that the crown and Scottish privy council began to apply concerted pressure on clan chiefs to conform to the standards of the rest of Scotland's elite. The one major clan that sup-ported the crown's 'civilising' mission in the Highlands, and profited accordingly from the feuding among its rivals, was the Campbells.

Although the power of the Scottish crown increased during the early seventeenth century, Scotland remained a highly decentralised state. Indeed, it could hardly be otherwise – the monarch and royal court had decamped to England in 1603; the central legal courts were limited in competence; and there was no standing army. The most powerful organ of royal government was the Scottish privy council; and it relied for local enforcement not upon crown officials but on the landed elite. The administration of justice over much of the country was divided into a patchwork of regalities and baronies – heritable courts (that is, tied in with land ownership) that were controlled by the nobility and the greater lairds (gentry), or barons. Some regalities, like that of Argyll, extended across an entire region, and were effectively 'petty kingdoms outside the jurisdiction of central authority'.[6] The Scottish Parliament did little more than clarify and systematise the laws on which the heritable courts operated. It was a unicameral body comprising four political estates – the nobility (titled aristocrats), clergy (bishops), shire commissioners (barons), and burgesses (borough representatives). As in England, Parliaments were occasional events, summoned at the monarch's pleasure. Unable to raise taxes by prerogative, the king relied on Parliament or a similar body, a convention of the estates, to obtain additional revenue. However, it took strenuous parliamentary management by the crown to make substantial increases in Scotland's minimal tax burden.

One of the most effective agents of central authority in England, the bishops, had been reintroduced into Scotland by James VI in the late sixteenth century. The Scottish national church, or Kirk, was thus a hybrid system of ecclesiastical government in which episcopacy (the rule of the church by bishops) had been grafted onto Calvinist structures such as the kirk sessions – parochial church courts that operated throughout lowland Scotland, enforcing a strict moral discipline that augmented the social control exercised by the heritable courts. Presiding over the kirk sessions with the ministry were lay elders – mainly lairds, professional men, and other prominent members of the parochial community. Coordinating the work of the kirk sessions were a series of clerical assemblies, or presbyteries (hence Presbyterianism), modelled on the government of the 'best reformed' Calvinist churches on the Continent. Although the power of calling General Assemblies of the Kirk lay with the king, a small but committed group of radical Presbyterians asserted the Kirk's complete independence from the crown.

Apart from the vagrant poor, the only groups that lay beyond the power of the Kirk to discipline were the nobility and the greater lairds. The kingdom's 2000 or so heads of aristocratic families dominated all aspects of public life. Only the affairs of the largest towns – Edinburgh, Glasgow, and the few other burghs with populations of over 5000 – lay outside their direct control. Aristocrats comprised a majority on the privy council, were a commanding presence in Parliament, and exerted a powerful influence over the Kirk as patrons and ruling elders. The crown could not rule effectively without their cooperation. Similarly, in a country where the principal sources of wealth were agriculture and mining, economic power inevitably lay with the larger landowners. Scotland's overseas commerce, which was concentrated in the hands of Edinburgh's mercantile elite, accounted for a tiny fraction of national output. Most of this trade was limited to the North Sea and the Baltic, and was worth about 4 per cent of England's in value.

Economic hardship in Scotland, as in Ireland, resulted in an exodus of the poor, the enterprising, and the adventurous. Between 1603 and 1638 more than 100,000 people left Scotland – some as colonists to Ulster; others to fight in the armies of the Protestant powers on the Continent. Scottish soldiers figured prominently in most of the campaigns against the Spanish and German Habsburgs during the Thirty Years War (1618–48). Indeed, the many Scots who served in the Swedish army in the 1630s were at the very cutting edge of Protestant resistance to Counter-Reformation Catholicism.

Scotland and Britain

It was a commonplace of contemporary statecraft that any prince who failed to impose uniformity in religion upon his subjects was asking for trouble. James I recognised that the existence, in each of his three kingdoms, of significant groups that preferred the climate of worship in one of the other two was a potential source of political instability. His efforts to bring the Kirk and the episcopal churches of England and Ireland more into line with each other were thus a logical response to the problems inherent in ruling multiple kingdoms. From north of the border, however, royal policy came to be viewed in a more sinister light, as a process of creeping anglicisation that threatened to reduce Scotland to the status of an English province. James himself did not help matters. He returned to his native country just once after 1603, preferring instead to rule Scotland by pen from Whitehall. Furthermore, although he aimed at a broad congruence between his churches, the longer he remained in England the more he came to favour English episcopacy, liturgy, and royal supremacy in religion as models for reform in Scotland. No people, especially one as proud of its autonomy and its 'purity of religion' as the Scots, would happily tolerate this state of affairs.

James's pragmatic policy of congruity was jettisoned by Charles in favour of a programme of uniformity between his dominions – the creation of a Caroline imperial monarchy. Whether this change of direction was a considered response to the challenges of ruling multiple kingdoms seems doubtful. What spurred Charles on was his own desire for order and obedience. The most powerful agency of Caroline author-itarianism in the three kingdoms would be a revitalised, and decidedly Laudian, episcopate. But where Scotland was concerned, Charles concentrated initially on making central government more efficient and more responsive to royal diktat. His approach was the same as in England – the bare assertion of monarchical authority without recourse to wider consultation; the closing down of the political system.

It was no accident that most of Charles's initiatives served as a demon-stration of prerogative at the expense of aristocratic power. The king purged many leading nobles from high office, replacing them with more pliable men such as lawyers and bishops. He made a concerted effort to increase royal authority at local level by buying up heritable jurisdictions. He acted to quash dissent in Parliament. And he introduced a scheme for revoking all grants of church land since 1540 – a move intended to improve the income of the Church, but which the landed community saw as a threat to property rights in general. Yet regardless of the intent behind Charles's policies, their net effect was actually to increase the influence of the aristocracy, at least in the localities. The Scottish people were unused to the abrasive impact of unfettered prerogative power, and lined up willingly behind disgruntled noblemen and lairds to frustrate most of the king's reforms. The ranks of the disaffected were swelled by the crown's pursuit of economic uniformity, which brought higher taxes and a recession. But most alarming of all was the realisation by the mid-1630s that Charles was preparing to use the prerogative to reform – and, from most Scots' perspective, to anglicise – Scottish church life. As well as boosting popular support for the dissident nobility, therefore, the king's actions allowed militant Presbyterian ministers – who had been marginalised under James – to pose as the true champions of the Kirk. In the face of Charles's determination to exercise his supremacy in religion without consulting the Scottish people, the causes of preserving Scotland's legal liberties, its religious integrity, and national identity would merge, with revolutionary results.

Ireland and the Imperial Crown

The Caroline programme of uniformity was not extended to Ireland until the appointment of Viscount Thomas Wentworth as lord deputy in 1632. Wentworth was as keen on strengthening royal authority as Charles was himself, and in a kingdom like Ireland, in which the executive was less hedged about by custom and law than was the case in England, he found the perfect environment for his brusque, uncompromising style of government. Like his predecessors, he attached great importance to civilising the Irish, but his priority was to make Ireland pay its own way (it had been a drain on the English exchequer for years). In his search for new sources of revenue he proposed a major plantation scheme for Connacht, which he anticipated would earn the crown £5000 a year. In the normal course of events, any lord deputy who embraced the plantation option would receive the full backing of the New English. But in his zeal to subordinate all interests to those of his prince, and to make Ireland financially solvent, Wentworth was just as liable to offend the New English as the Catholics. In fact, the wealthiest Protestants became his most high profile targets – their very riches being evidence in his eyes that they had defrauded the crown. By making an example of these men, Wentworth intended to send a message to all the peoples of Ireland – that lese-majesty of any kind would not be tolerated.

Money was not the only source of tension between Wentworth and the New English. The lord deputy was a friend and ally of Laud, and was determined to convert Protestants as well as Catholics to the kind of worship favoured by Charles and his archbishop. The Connacht plantation was intended not just to raise revenue or to anglicise the Irish, but to pave the way for the Laudianisation of all Ireland's peoples. Ireland, like Scotland, was to serve as a laboratory for Charles's imperial church policy. A vital step in this 'vast work' was to re-endow the established ministry in Ireland, and to this end Wentworth used the ecclesiastical and prerogative courts to divest landowners (Protestant as well as Catholic) of alienated church property – a cruder, if more effective, version of the revocation scheme in Scotland. Committed like Laud to strengthening the episcopate, he was particularly affronted by the Presbyterian Scots in Ulster. In his eyes they were insubordinate fanatics, and he made sure that their ministers were denied church livings.

If Wentworth's attack on Protestant interests was an unsettling new departure in royal policy towards Ireland, the suspicion and contempt in which he held Catholics was far otherwise. He found the idea of an ecclesiastical authority not derived from the crown insufferable, and used the prerogative courts to clamp down on the semi-clandestine operations of the Catholic Church hierarchy. But discrimination and persecution had been part and parcel of Catholic life in Ireland for generations. Perhaps more worrying for lay Catholics was Wentworth's determination to deny them redress at law, and to prevent their leaders appealing over his head to the king. In a country where a settler mentality – Ireland as mere colony, ripe for exploitation – constantly threatened to undermine its status as a legally-constituted kingdom, recourse to the common law and access to the king's favour were perhaps even more cherished liberties for Ireland's Catholics than for its Protestants.

Wentworth's rule impinged relatively little upon the common people, who were more affected by the recession that hit Ireland in the 1630s. A series of bad harvests, outbreaks of cattle disease, and narrowing markets in the other two kingdoms all took their toll of the Irish economy. Times were hardest in Ulster, where an influx of Scottish economic migrants and an increase in the settler population generally made life difficult for everyone, but particularly the native Irish. Against this background of hardship and misfortune, Wentworth's remarkable success in uniting previously antagonistic groups in common opposition to his rule was a particularly ominous development. Nevertheless, it was the impact of the crown's imperial policies in Scotland and England that would decide the timing and to some extent the nature of the crisis that engulfed Ireland in the 1640s.

The Covenanter Rebellion

The immediate cause of the wars in the three Stuart kingdoms was the crown's attempt to foist a new prayer book upon the Scots. The book was the work of Charles, Laud, and a select group of Scottish bishops, and was given its première on 23 July 1637 in St Giles Kirk, Edinburgh, where it caused a riot. The Scots objected to the new prayer book on several counts – it had been introduced by royal prerogative alone, without consulting the people through a General Assembly or a Parliament; it represented an importation of Anglican practices into Scottish worship, contrary to the perceived national interest; and its contents – which were deemed popish – threatened to sully the purity of the reformed religion in Scotland.

Although the public demonstrations against the prayer book reflected genuine popular concern, they were not spontaneous. The Earl of Loudoun, Lord Balmerino, and a knot of militant Presbyterian ministers (some of whom had been victims of Wentworth's Laudian offensive in Ulster) had been organising resistance for months. The introduction of the prayer book – touching, as it did, so many raw nerves in Scotland – gave them the ideal opportunity to rally the people against Caroline authoritarianism. In the face of further rioting, a petitioning campaign against the prayer book and the bishops, and a take-over of local government by dissident noblemen and ministers, the dithering and divided Scottish privy council abandoned Edinburgh in the autumn of 1637. By early 1638 the protesters had set up what amounted to a provisional government, consisting of commissioners elected from the four political estates. Their aim at this stage was to press for 'free assemblies' that would limit the exercise of the royal prerogative and replace the bishops and other evil counsellors with members of the traditional ruling elite. Assuming that the king would be more likely to compromise if the entire nation was arrayed against him, the disaffected leadership sought, in February, to broaden the movement's appeal by introducing a National Covenant to be subscribed by every adult in Scotland.

The Covenant was a revolutionary document – a radical redefining of the relationship between crown and subject in which loyalty was reserved to a 'covenanted king'; that is, a monarch who would agree to defend 'the true reformed religion' (in effect, Presbyterianism) and to rule according to the laws of the realm. Implicit in its terms was an attack upon the royal prerogative generally, and Charles's supremacy in religion, and hence episcopacy, in particular. The cornerstone of this new contract between ruler and ruled was a religious covenant with God. If the king failed to defend the reformed tradition in the Kirk or to govern according to law, the people were morally required to resist him in fulfilment of their covenanted obligation. Last, but not least, the Covenant enjoined an oath of allegiance and mutual association, binding the subscriber to defend a covenanted king and his authority, and to assist other subscribers in the same cause. The Covenant was essentially a national constitution underwritten by a religious compact.

The Covenant raised political consciousness in Scotland to unprecedented heights. All those who subscribed it, irrespective of rank, became parties to its implementation and thus legitimate actors in the political process. Perhaps even more significant, however, was the sense of national destiny the Covenant imparted. To those Scots – and there were many – who believed that Scottish Protestantism was purer than any practised elsewhere, the Covenant offered a momentous opportunity to perfect Scotland's Reformation, and to realise their vision of themselves as a chosen people. The Covenant heightened feeling that the Scottish nation, under a covenanted king, had a special role in God's providential design to overthrow popery and establish Christ's rule on earth. Some Scots went even further, and extended this reading of the Covenant's apocalyptic significance to envisage a shared destiny for all the British nations – a development that, as we shall see, was closely linked to the reaction of the king and his leading English opponents, to the Scottish troubles.

The Covenant, although touted as an exercise in national bonding, was a divisive document. Where it did not merely paper over the cracks in Scottish society it widened them. The disaffected leadership, for example, used it as much to identify and coerce its opponents as to rally supporters. It is unlikely that much coercion was needed in the heartland of the movement – the central and southern Lowlands. Likewise, the Covenant proved popular with the people of Edinburgh and Glasgow. However, less than half the Scottish nobility, and virtually no Catholic aristocrats or those the king had advanced to high office, were actively in favour of it. Glasgow's civic leaders were at first reluctant to commit themselves to the Covenant, and the inhabitants of Aberdeen and Inverness were lukewarm at best. Loyalty to the king was particularly strong in and around Aberdeenshire, although it lacked an effective leader. The region's most powerful nobleman, the Marquess of Huntly, was hamstrung by his Catholicism and his taste for the English courtly fashion of aloofness and formality in dealing with inferiors – a most un-Scottish trait. The driving force behind armed if not intellectual resistance to the Covenanters came from the Highlands. Broadly speaking the majority of the clans, and particularly those threatened by Campbell expansion in the central and western Highlands, were hostile to the covenanting movement. This is not to say that they shared Charles's religious or political convictions. Their support for the king was founded largely on the belief that he was less likely to meddle in their affairs than a centralising Covenanter regime.

An Uncounsellable King

Despite warnings from the Scottish privy council that it was powerless to resist the Covenanters, Charles refused to back down. His tendency to interpret disagreement with his views as disloyalty, even sedition, deterred royal counsellors from speaking the unpalatable truth – that simply demanding blind obedience to his sovereign will was not enough, and that genuine compromise was necessary. Yet even when he realised the extent of Scottish opposition to the new prayer book, he refused to accept any limitation upon his prerogative. From the start he showed little interest in a political solution to the problem. Instead, he quickly began to entertain the idea of using the military resources of England

and Ireland to crush the 'rebels' in Scotland. In having tried and failed to impose his religious reforms on the Scots however, he was then limited in how much he could concede without sending a dangerous message (push me and I compromise) to the English Puritans – who were watching events in Scotland very closely.

In order to buy himself time, Charles appointed the leading Scottish nobleman, James, Marquess (and from 1643, Duke) of Hamilton, as his emissary to the Covenanters. The general impression of Hamilton, until recently, has been that of a talentless, self-interested individual. But as John Scally has argued, Hamilton could be a subtle and effective politician.[7] He was certainly a figure of considerable influence both at court and in Scotland, possessing a large network of kinsmen and allies among the Scottish elite. Hamilton realised the need for a quick solution to Scotland's troubles in order to avoid destabilising the other two kingdoms, and that this meant compromise. Charles's response, however, was assuming a pattern that would become all too familiar in the years ahead – the offer of (minimal) political concessions and the marshalling of military force.

The king's intransigence, made evident to the Covenanters by his military preparations, destroyed Hamilton's attempts to reach a compromise. In the General Assembly that met in November, radical Presbyterian ministers and Covenanter nobles worked together to reform the Kirk – the first group to complete Scotland's Reformation, the second to destroy the bishops as a political force. The nobility's concern to re-establish the foundations of secular and aristocratic power, and the aim of the radical Presbyterians to fashion a new and godly society around a fully independent Kirk, were fundamentally at odds, and would prove a constant source of friction within the covenanting movement. But for the moment the two groups were united by 'common perils and common antipathies'.[8] With little ado, the assembly abolished episcopacy and remodelled the Kirk along thoroughly Presbyterian lines. Charles could not accept this usurpation of his prerogative in the area where he valued it most, his supremacy in religion, and war became inevitable.

Oligarchic Centralism

The king's resolve to prevail in Scotland by force gave the Covenanter leadership the impetus to effect a radical restructuring of Scottish civil government. The drive to reform was inherent in the movement's core principles, but was also necessary to mobilise the kingdom's resources for war. The Covenanters' central executive body drew up a new constitutional blueprint in 1638–9, and used the Scottish Parliament that sat intermittently between 1639 and 1641 to ratify its programme as well as the Presbyterian church settlement worked out in the General Assembly. The key reforms were the expulsion of the clerical estate from Parliament; parliamentary control over appointments to high office; the abolition of the king's negative voice; and the regular calling of Parliament. Power in the intervals between parliamentary sessions devolved upon a new executive organ, the Committee of Estates, and a host of subordinate commissions. Some of these measures were inspired by the resolve among lay Covenanters, and particularly the nobility, to increase parliamentary control over the Kirk. But the main thrust of the reforms was to strip the crown of its prerogative powers and vest them in Parliament, reducing the king's personal authority in Scotland to that of a mere figurehead – a 'Duke of Venice' as Charles himself put it.[9] This was a radical remodelling of government – several years in advance of similar developments in England – and it was intended to be permanent.

The Covenanters' grip on power was strengthened late in 1638, when they were joined by Archibald Campbell, Earl (and from 1641, Marquess) of Argyll. Argyll was an enigmatic figure – a consequence, in part, of his anomalous position as both a Presbyterian in religion and a Gaelic Highland chief. As head of the Campbells, he controlled large areas of the western Highlands, including many estates that his family had seized, often by unscrupulous means, from their main clan rivals the MacDonalds. He had leaned towards the Covenanters from the beginning of the troubles. However, it was the king's willingness to consider using the MacDonalds and MacDonnells, under their leader the Catholic Earl of Antrim, to suppress the Covenanters that decided Argyll's allegiance. Argyll exploited his clan's territorial power and support for Presbyterianism to claim a leading role for himself in what Allan Macinnes has dubbed 'the radical mainstream', or the broad mass of committed Covenanters in Parliament and Kirk.[10] It was through Argyll's adroit leadership that his own following, or 'Argyll's party', had come to dominate the radical mainstream by 1642.

The leading role of men like Argyll in covenanting politics highlights the fact that this was no social revolution. The lords of the Covenant were determined to sustain the power and pre-eminence of the noble estate against all challengers – monarchical, clerical, or popular. In order to circumvent those noblemen who took the Covenant merely to gain admittance to Parliament, and who regarded any further encroachment upon the king's authority as a threat to the established order, the Covenanter leadership allowed the voting strength of the nobility to decrease relative to that of the shire commissioners and burgesses, the majority of whom were firmly within the radical mainstream. Nevertheless, in terms of parliamentary management, and the formulation of policy in key areas such as military and diplomatic affairs, the initiative seems to have been retained by an oligarchic inner core in which Argyll and other nobles exercised a decisive role. The dominance of Argyll and his allies was sustained partly by their innovative use of parliamentary executive committees – a lesson in the exercise of power that would not be lost on their future allies at Westminster. Allan Macinnes has termed the structure of Covenanter rule 'oligarchic centralism'.[11]

The huge increase in parliamentary and central power under the Covenanters was made possible by their reorganisation of provincial government. A series of gentry-dominated local committees was set up for conscripting, training, and provisioning a national army. For experienced soldiers and arms, the Covenanters looked to the Scottish military and mercantile diaspora in northern Europe. Veterans from the Protestant armies on the Continent flooded home in the late 1630s, and command of the Covenanter forces was given to Alexander Leslie – formerly a senior officer in the Swedish army. In addition, Scottish merchants purchased munitions in Holland and the Baltic and shipped them home with the connivance of sympathetic foreign powers. In order to fund this military expenditure, the local committees oversaw a massive increase in the tax burden. By the efficient exploitation of available resources, the Covenanters were able in part to offset Scotland's weakness in men and money relative to England. This in turn is testament to the remarkable power of the Covenant in unleashing human potential at all levels of Scottish society. With a powerful executive and Britain's first professional standing army at its disposal, the Covenanter leadership would not just reverse the tide of anglicisation, but bid for a share in imperial government throughout the three kingdoms.

The First Bishops' War, 1639

The Scots' military preparations were more than matched by the king's own – at least on paper. Over the winter of 1638–9, Charles and his advisers drew up plans for an integrated, four-pronged assault on the rebels. Hamilton was to lead an amphibious force against the east coast of Scotland; Antrim was to deploy his clansmen to pin down Covenanter troops in the western Highlands; Wentworth was to raise 10,000 men in Ireland to reinforce Antrim's expedition; and Charles himself was to march an English army up to the border, and, if necessary, to invade Scotland. This was an ambitious plan; indeed, given the available time and resources (only £200,000 was allocated for the entire campaign) it was too ambitious. Antrim habitually promised more than he could deliver, and his expedition never got off the ground. Wentworth was unable to mobilise his levies in time. Hamilton's offensive needed a bridgehead in Scotland – in other words, a strong Royalist party – to succeed, and Charles's intransigence had put paid to that. Which left just the king's English army, and this proved difficult to assemble and of debatable quality. Early Stuart England was a demilitarised society. Most Englishmen neither owned combat weapons nor were proficient in their use. The same could be said of many Lowland Scots, but then the Covenanters had a larger reservoir of Continental veterans to draw upon than the English did.

The shortcomings in the royal war-effort must also be seen in the context of a general dissatisfaction (or at least unease) in England with many aspects of the Personal Rule – Charles's experiment in government without Parliament. In order to balance the books in the absence of parliamentary subsidies, the king had introduced a range of taxes purely on the basis of his prerogative, in direct challenge to the principle of taxation by consent. Likewise, the Laudian 'new ceremonies' had apparently alienated many people besides the Puritans. Admittedly, opposition to the king's policies had been muted, but this may simply have been because without Parliament it lacked an effective forum.

There can be no doubt that domestic resentments, and to a lesser extent pro-Scottish feeling, did indeed retard the king's military preparations. Nevertheless, by June 1639 he had marshalled an army of about 15,000 men, which at least equalled that of the Covenanters and was stronger in cavalry. Moreover, most of the king's troops were probably as well armed and better provisioned than their opponents. Morale could have been higher, but it was improving, and there was a determination, certainly among the northern regiments, to acquit themselves well in battle. A chauvinistic dislike of the Scots, rooted in centuries of border conflict, was particularly strong in northern England. Whatever misgivings leading northern landowners such as the Earl of Northumberland and his friend Sir Ferdinando Fairfax had about the direction of royal policies, they were apparently outweighed by a desire to serve loyally against 'the common enemy'. If the Covenanters had a military advantage over the English it was that their commanders were more experienced and had better intelligence of the enemy's strength and movements.

In the event, the First Bishops' War, as it came to be known, ended with hardly a shot fired. On 6 June the Scots invited the king to treat, and Charles accepted. A negotiated settlement was a victory in itself for the Covenanters, who doubted their ability to sustain a long-term campaign against the English. For the king, however, it was a disaster, brought on by what can only be described as a loss of nerve among the royal high command. Charles seems to have believed that merely by marching an army to the border he would intimidate the Covenanters into submission. To then be faced with what seemed a stronger and more determined Scottish force was chilling proof in his eyes of an Anglo-Scottish Puritan plot against the crown. In some respects, he was right to think this way, but with an army at his back he at least had the opportunity to confront his demons head on. His decision to negotiate with the Covenanters rather than risk battle was one of the greatest mistakes of his life. The enormity of his error quickly became clear to him, which was why the treaty worked out at Berwick in June was not worth the paper it was written on. Within six months of its signing, Charles, and perforce the Covenanters, were preparing for a second campaign.

The Second Bishops' War, 1640

The Second Bishops' War was the pivotal conflict of the entire period. The consequences of the king's defeat in this war contributed powerfully to the Irish Rising of 1641 and the outbreak of civil strife in England a year later. The conflict was also remarkable in itself in that it witnessed the Scots' first major military victory against the English for over 300 years, and, just as significantly, a virtual *coup d'état* in England. John Adamson has argued convincingly that Charles's defeat in 1640 owed as much to the activities of an English fifth-column as to anything the Scots did. By highlighting the English contribution to the collapse of the Personal Rule, Adamson has challenged the view of Conrad Russell and other 'revisionist' historians that England of itself lacked sufficient combustible material to ignite civil war in 1642, let alone in 1640. According to this line of argument, only Scottish intervention and the divisions it created injected enough heat into English society to make it explode.[12] And it was not until the late 1630s that English dissidents began to make common cause with the rebellious Scots, galvanised into action by Covenanter propaganda and the unfolding events north of the border. For the next three years at least, they remained wholly reliant upon the Scots for a military power-base, and were thus forced to let the Scots set the political agenda with the king. On this reading, the Covenanters virtually created an English opposition. It was they who occupied the driving seat of British politics, and who forced the English down a road that they would not otherwise have thought or dared to travel.

There can be no doubt that the Scots played a major role in destabilising England in 1638–40. Nevertheless, the facts of the Second Bishops' War suggest that responsibility for the downfall of the Personal Rule should be apportioned more equally among the king's enemies in the two kingdoms.

The guiding force behind the king's second campaign against the Scots was Wentworth, whom Charles made Earl of Strafford early in 1640. Strafford had quashed all opposition tendencies in Ireland, and was confident he could do the same in England and Scotland. He urged Charles to 'go on with an offensive war as you first designed, loosed and absolved from all rules of government'.[13] But such a strategy required money, and the only way of raising the necessary amount quickly was on the back of parliamentary subsidies. In March 1640, Strafford had wrung money from the Irish Parliament for a new army against the Covenanters, and was again confident he could perform a similar feat at Westminster. He therefore advised the king to summon a Parliament in England – the first in eleven years.

The Short Parliament – so called because it sat for only three weeks – met in April 1640, and quickly confounded Strafford's expectations. MPs would not vote the king supply before he had made substantial offers towards the redress of their constituents' accumulated grievances. Yet some of the grievances raised included the very taxes and infringement of civil liberties necessary for a viable military campaign. True to form, the king perceived a Puritan design against his sovereignty, and angrily dissolved Parliament. Parliament's refusal to vote supply was a financial setback for the crown but also a political one. It sent a powerful message to the people that their representatives were dubious as to the wisdom and legality of the king's war. The response over the summer was predictable. There was a taxpayers' strike; county leaders pleaded inability to raise men or money for the war-effort; and conscripts on their way to the front mutinied. Resentment was compounded by the fact that the counties had made a herculean effort to support the 1639 campaign only to see their resources squandered at Berwick.

An empty exchequer and passive disobedience in the provinces would have been bad enough in themselves. However, as Adamson has demonstrated, the king's will, indeed his very authority, was being openly challenged by some of his leading English subjects. For several months, a group of disaffected peers and gentlemen centred upon the Earl of Warwick, Viscount Saye and Sele, and John Pym had been plotting with the Covenanters to effect a Scottish invasion. With a Covenanter army encamped in northern England, Charles would be forced to call a Parliament – one that he could not readily dissolve, and that would end the disaffected faction's exclusion from power as well as reform the 'abuses' of the Personal Rule. If this strategy was to work, however, the conspirators had to ensure that the king's army did not present a serious military obstacle. Public sympathy would quickly evaporate if there were heavy English casualties. To prevent any 'effusion of blood' therefore, they encouraged localist opposition to the mobilisation of Yorkshire's militia, which made up almost half the king's fighting strength, and they suborned units of the royal army. Even more provocatively, they organised a display of military power in London, thereby obliging the privy council to withdraw to Hampton Court, and sending a clear message of defiance to Charles.

If the Scottish army was the disaffected peers' most potent weapon for coercing the king, it was clearly not their only one. Nor was their collaboration with Scottish malcontents in 1640 the work of a few years. Jason Peacey has found evidence that suggests there had been high-level contact between the king's Puritan opponents in all three kingdoms for over a decade.[14] Similarly, the knot of disaffected men around which English opposition coalesced in 1640 had been a tightly organised group, with a coherent political programme, since the 1620s. They had met regularly both in private and as members of the Providence Island Company and the Saybrook project – two zealously Puritan colonial ventures; they had published propaganda (both Scottish and English); and had generally done their best, in the restrictive environment of the Personal Rule, to sway public opinion against the king's policies. They were not the fortuitous beneficiaries of a rebellion 'exported' from Scotland; rather, they were part of a three-kingdoms Puritan network that shaped as well as exploited the Scottish troubles. It seemed obvious to contemporaries that the Covenanter leadership would not have dared to rebel 'had they not been sure to have as good friends in England as they had in Scotland ... for some of the chiefest Inconformists [sic] here [in England], had not onely Intelligence with them, but had been of their Cabinet-counsells in moulding the Plot'.[15]

And the plot succeeded. On 28 August the Covenanters routed a numerically inferior royal force at Newburn, in Northumberland, and two days later they occupied Newcastle. It might have been a very different story if the Yorkshire militia had been deployed in the town's defence, but their mobilisation had been deliberately retarded. On 5 September, having mounted a show of military strength in London, the dissident peers presented a petition to the king (who was then at York), demanding that he summon Parliament. With Northumberland and County Durham in Scottish hands, his exchequer empty, and a powerful party in London arrayed against him, Charles had no choice but to comply. It was a victory for his majesty's *dis*loyal opposition, but it was bought at a high price. Instigating an invasion by a foreign army was an act of treason; and Charles knew exactly who the guilty parties were, though for the moment he lacked the power to prosecute them. Moreover, by coercing the king, his opponents had committed themselves to seeking a stringent settlement – one that left him powerless to do them harm. To make matters worse, they had started a cycle of violence in domestic politics that would be very hard to reverse, for it would take a monarch of greater statesmanship than Charles to resist using the tactics of threat and coercion against his enemies that they had used against him.

The Long Parliament

The Long Parliament assembled on 3 November 1640, and was to sit more or less continuously for over twelve years. It was secure against a precipitate dissolution by the need to pay off the English and Scottish armies raised over the summer, for only parliamentary taxation could meet the enormous expenditure involved. With the king defeated in war and for the moment bankrupt, both politically and financially, the Long Parliament effectively assumed the reins of government in England. In short order the two Houses swept away many of the perceived abuses of the Personal Rule – extra-parliamentary taxation, Laudian innovations, etc. – and introduced legislation for the regular calling of Parliaments. Laud and Strafford, the most hated and feared of Charles's evil counsellors, were arrested and executed – Strafford in May 1641; Laud early in 1645.

But while Parliament-men were more or less united in what they disliked about the Personal Rule, they were split over how to prevent a similar state of affairs developing again. No issue was more divisive in this respect than the settlement of the church. A strong constituency at Westminster and throughout the country wanted merely a return to pre-Laudian episcopacy and Prayer Book worship 'by law established'. On the other hand, the Laudian project had so scandalised Puritan MPs that they would settle for nothing less than a thorough purge of anything they deemed popish or prelatical. A vocal minority even pressed for the total abolition of episcopacy. The pressure on Parliament for godly reformation was also sustained by a vigorous lobbying and petitioning campaign by Puritan networks in London and across the country.

The problem of reconciling competing agendas for church settlement was rendered even more intractable by the influence of the Covenanters. A Scottish delegation was resident in London from the autumn of 1640 to negotiate a treaty with Parliament (to be ratified by the king) for remedying the causes and recompensing the victors of the Bishops' Wars. Agreement with Parliament, if not necessarily with the king, would have been relatively simple if the Covenanters had confined themselves to seeking confirmation of their gains in Scotland. But their vision for a durable settlement now extended to cover all of Charles's kingdoms. The Covenant and its undreamt of success had created a sense of apocalyptic expectancy in Scotland that sought expression in a British and European context. Excitement at the prospect of a covenanted Britain carrying the fight to the popish Antichrist in Europe was particularly strong in Argyll's party, which at the same time had sound practical reasons for a British programme of settlement. Argyll and his confederates had compromised themselves in plotting the king's defeat in 1640, just as their English co-conspirators had, and they now sought firmer guarantees for their continuance in power than they had in 1639. There could be no long-term security for Scotland or for themselves unless prelacy – which to their eyes lay at the root of the quarrel between the two kingdoms – had been eradicated. And for some of the more zealous Covenanters, the surest way of achieving this was by establishing one form of church government throughout the king's dominions. The churches of England and Ireland, like the Scottish Kirk, should be subordinate to autonomous Presbyterian assemblies – a form of government the Scots regarded as *jure divino*: that is, divinely warranted. In place of Charles's Laudian uniformity, the Covenanters were determined to impose a covenanted uniformity; and with English power temporarily in abeyance there seemed no better opportunity.

The Scots were doubtless encouraged in their plans by the fact that the parliamentary leadership at Westminster, dubbed 'the junto', was largely composed of the very men who had conspired with them during the Personal Rule – the earls of Essex and Warwick, Viscount Saye, John Pym, John Hampden, Oliver St John, etc. Yet even the Scots' closest allies balked at their demands. Although the two groups saw eye to eye on a number of broad issues – the need for strong representative assemblies in both kingdoms, the prosecution of the king's evil counsellors, the extirpation of popery in Britain and abroad – their views on the proper constitution of the Church differed markedly. The likes of Saye and Pym had made common cause with the Covenanters not from any admiration for the Kirk, but out of a sense of godly fellowship in the face of the cosmic struggle between Christ and Antichrist being played out across Europe. Their preferred method for curbing Charles's ceasaro-papism was not to make the clergy independent of the crown – as the Covenanters had – but to subordinate both the clergy and the royal supremacy to parliamentary control. Indeed, many future Parliamentarians were not vitally concerned about the precise form of church government adopted so long as it sustained a national preaching ministry and left Parliament the ultimate arbiter in religion.

But it was not just Scottish church government that the English found objectionable. Despite the Scots' claims that a covenanted uniformity was their chief desire, they were equally concerned to prevent Charles mobilising the military resources of England and Ireland against them. The Irish (and largely Catholic) army that Strafford had raised in 1640 had been poised to offer powerful support to the king's English forces during the Second Bishops' War. The Scots could not intervene directly in Ireland because it was a dependency of the English crown. However, they could and did attempt to control English power as a way of neutralising the threat from both England and Ireland. To this end they proposed an Anglo-Scottish alliance, based upon cooperation between the Edinburgh and Westminster Parliaments – a redefinition of the constitutional relationship between England and Scotland that Allan Macinnes has termed 'confederalism'.[16] The Scots hoped that a confederal settlement would establish the two kingdoms as equal partners in the formation of a British diplomatic and military agenda, and thus banish any prospect of Scotland being reduced to the status of an English province. No one at Westminster, however, including the junto, was enthusiastic about such a settlement. It ran counter to English legal and institutional exceptionalism, not to mention an ingrained pride in England's ancient claim to suzerainty over Scotland. So long as the junto-men relied upon the Scots' army to coerce the king into granting them courtly office – still the best guarantee of power over the long term – and so long as that army continued to occupy northern England, the Covenanters could exert enough leverage at Westminster to obtain at least half their desires. But where they failed to make much headway was on the religious front. Some English people were as eager as the Covenanters for a Puritan overhaul of the Church, but not its replacement by a Scottish-style Kirk.

By demanding the abolition of episcopacy and pressing the case for religious uniformity, the Covenanters heightened English divisions. It was during the debates early in 1641 over the future of the Church that an embryonic Royalist party first emerged. Proto-Royalists such as Sir Edward Hyde and Sir John Culpeper believed that episcopacy and the royal supremacy in religion were an integral part of English constitutional arrangements. Any attempt to abolish the one and vest the other solely in Parliament would undermine both the crown and the rule of law, which in turn would pose a threat to the entire social order. Fears of this sort were also beginning to emerge in Scotland. Although Argyll's party favoured a confederal settlement, some leading Covenanters, notably Argyll's rival the Earl (and from 1644, Marquess) of Montrose, wanted to limit any further encroachments upon the royal prerogative in either kingdom.

The junto's demands regarding church reform and restraints upon the popish presence at court proved the main sticking points in their negotiations with the king. Parliamentary leaders could envisage no alternative to a settlement with Charles, but the longer they failed to secure his agreement the harder a settlement became. The growing unpopularity of the Scots, particularly in northern England where Leslie's army was quartered, was bound to weaken the junto. And the longer the Covenanters remained in power in Scotland the more enemies they would make there too. All the king had to do was to bide his time, court the discontented in both kingdoms, and wait for the Scots to withdraw their army, as they must. Once the Scots were gone he could dissolve Parliament and proceed against his English enemies at will. Not for the last time, however, Charles played right into his opponents' hands. Goaded by the junto's withholding of royal revenues, and its aggressive stance towards the queen and other highly placed Catholics, the king sanctioned several half-baked plots to use the English army in the north to expel the Scots and overawe Parliament. He seems to have conceived a similar role for Strafford's Irish army – that is, until it was disbanded at Parliament's insistence in the spring of 1641. Scottish resentment at the niggardly response to their demands at Westminster offered Charles a good opportunity to play his two British kingdoms off against each other. But when he visited Scotland in the autumn of 1641 he overplayed his hand again, approving an abortive plot, known as 'the Incident', to imprison, and possibly even to murder, Argyll and Hamilton. Hamilton had been drifting towards the Covenanters ever since Charles had turned the war over to the anti-Scottish Strafford; and the Incident accelerated this process.

The king's various plots were a public relations disaster in both kingdoms. They retarded the development of a Royalist political interest. More specifically, they helped convince parliamentary leaders that a policy of simply intruding themselves into courtly office was no longer sufficient to keep Charles in check. From the summer of 1641 the junto began to press for reforms designed to reduce the king's power to a cipher. This was more than simply 'functional radicalism' – the pragmatic adoption of radical policies to keep pace with political events. It seems that Viscount Saye and his circle had been thinking wishfully about a redistribution of the respective powers of king and Parliament for several years, possibly longer. Once the majority of Parliament-men had come to think likewise, however, which was apparently the case by the end of 1641, then a political settlement became all but impossible. Charles preferred a fight to the death before life as a puppet monarch. Yet though the junto and the king were mentally prepared for armed confrontation, there was no similar readiness among the people generally – the majority of whom, regardless of their religious sympathies, still hoped for an accommodation.

The Irish Rising

The Irish Rising of October 1641 was intimately linked to the emergence of an aggressive Covenanter party in Scotland, and the forging of an Anglo-Scottish parliamentary alliance for extirpating popery throughout the three kingdoms. Irish Catholics' awareness of their religious isolation within the Stuart dominions heightened their sensitivity to events in Britain. Their apprehension of a Protestant plot to destroy Catholicism and to appropriate Irish land was possibly even more pervasive than corresponding Scottish and English fears of a popish plot. A host of alarming rumours circulated in Ireland during 1641 – that the Covenanters were preparing to invade Ulster; that the 'Puritans' were planning a massacre of Catholics; even that the king had been executed.

Yet the complicated inter-relationship between the three kingdoms gave some Irish Catholics cause for optimism even in the face of the threatening developments in Britain. Catholic political leaders saw the meeting of the Long Parliament as an opportunity first to bring down Strafford, and secondly to wring concessions from a beleaguered king. It is a measure of the fear that Strafford had inspired in Ireland that Catholic members of the Irish Parliament colluded with their Protestant colleagues in supplying evidence against the lord deputy to his enemies at Westminster. The Protestant contribution to this bipartisan attack on Strafford was managed by an Ulster planter, Sir John Clotworthy, and represented the Irish dimension of the Puritan 'Plot' discussed above. Yet by making it possible for the Long Parliament to prosecute Strafford on charges relating to his Irish administration, his enemies in Dublin encouraged his enemies at Westminster to push for the extension of English parliamentary authority over Ireland. Any such move would represent the subjection of Ireland and its Catholic population to outright colonial rule, and not surprisingly its strongest proponents were the Covenanters and the English Puritans. Irish Catholic politicians responded to this threat by seeking the king's support for measures that would affirm the autonomy of the Irish Parliament (under the crown), revoke the Connacht plantation, and restore their access to the benefits of the common law and royal favour. Desperate for allies against the junto, the king was ready by the summer of 1641 to make these concessions, but was effectively blocked by the Long Parliament and the Covenanters.

The crown's inability to protect Ireland's Catholics from the 'Puritan party' in Britain encouraged a number of disaffected Ulster natives to press ahead with plans for an uprising. Like Catholics elsewhere in Ireland, they feared for the future of their religion, but most of their grievances were rooted in the peculiar circumstances of post-Plantation Ulster. Many of the conspirators were 'broken men' – sufferers either financially or politically through the influx of Protestant settlers and the Irish recession of the 1630s. Not without cause, they perceived an ongoing design by Protestant interlopers, supported by the Dublin administration, to deprive them of their land and liberties. In seeking a remedy for these injustices they concurred with the Catholic leadership in Dublin in believing that their best hope lay in preserving the king's authority against his British enemies. However, they put little faith in securing a settlement by purely political means. Their strategy, in Aidan Clarke's words, was to present the king 'with a pre-emptive coup which would place him far enough in their debt to establish a firm claim for the redress of their long-standing grievances'.[17]

The Rising began on 23 October 1641, and within a few days much of central Ulster was in Irish hands. A plan to seize Dublin Castle was betrayed at the last minute, however, thus denying the insurgents a valuable bargaining counter. Although the conspirators had envisaged a bloodless military coup, their actions triggered a mass uprising as ordinary Catholics exploited the breakdown in authority to vent their fear and frustration upon the settler community. Economic distress, alarm at the growing Puritan menace in Britain, and generations of bitterness born of religious discrimination and enforced social and tenurial subordination, combined to create a wave of popular unrest that quickly spread from Ulster into the other three provinces. However, it was only after savage military reprisals by the Protestants that both sides began to commit the atrocities for which the Rising is infamous. In all, roughly 5000 Protestants were killed in the first months of the Rising; the number of Catholic dead is not known. Frightened at the prospect of mob rule, Catholic gentry and clergy tried to suppress the violence or to channel it towards godly purposes. The clergy acquired a particularly influential role, for the majority of insurgents were motivated at some level by the desire to make Ireland a Catholic (or at least more Catholic) kingdom.

The reaction of the Protestant zealots who now dominated the Dublin administration merely served to heighten the violence. They made no attempt to distinguish between the insurgents and those Catholic gentry who were willing to cooperate with Dublin in stemming the crisis. Instead, they gave free rein to Protestant commanders like Sir Charles Coote senior, who believed that the only good Catholic was a dead one. Caught between a runaway popular uprising and Protestant aggression, the Catholic political leadership had little choice by December 1641 but to make common cause with their Ulster counterparts. As Micheál Ó Siochrú has argued, this coming together was made easier by the fact that the leaders of both camps were closely related by marriage and shared the common concerns of all landowners.[18] Their meeting did not represent an historic rapprochement between the Old English and native Irish communities, therefore, but an alliance of landed interests for preserving and expanding their role within the existing order. The majority of Catholic leaders depicted their cause in very conservative terms, as a struggle to 'vindicate the honor of our sovereigne, assure the liberty of our consciences, and preserve the freedom of this kingdom under the sole obedience of his sacred majesty'.[19] It was the pretensions of the English Parliament and its Puritan allies that worried Irish Catholics, not those of the crown: hence their insistence that the king's authority in Ireland was independent of his authority in England, and thus of any change in the distribution of power there. The Covenanters' example in using force to redefine their relationship with England was consciously imitated, but for very different ends. Irish Catholics sought to preserve their liberties not by fettering the royal prerogative but by upholding it as the only executive link between Ireland and England.

Not all the insurgents, however, were as committed as the leadership to preserving the existing landed order and framework of government in Ireland. Nor was there a united front behind the leadership's resolve to seek merely the toleration of Irish Catholicism under an official Protestant Church. Leading Ulster insurgents, for example, were in close contact with their compatriots in Spanish service on the Continent, many of whom belonged to families that had been disinherited as a result of the Ulster plantation. These Ulster exiles, under their commander Owen Roe O'Neill, were eager to return to Ireland to challenge the claims of Catholics as well as Protestants to the land redistributed by the state since the Nine Years War. Likewise, many Irish exiles had been heavily influenced by Counter-Reformation culture, and shared the zeal of the Catholic clergy (themselves Continentally-trained) for the official restoration of Catholicism in Ireland. The Catholic bishops' efforts to exercise their jurisdiction had been severely restricted under Strafford, and they were determined to prevent the same situation developing again. Furthermore, their main source of income – donations from the Catholic laity – had been badly hit by the Protestant settler influx. Consequently, many of the clergy, besides demanding the public exercise of worship and the recovery of church property and revenues, backed the exiles' demands for a reversal of the Ulster plantation. For tactical reasons – the need to forge an understanding with the landed elite – the exiles and the clergy were obliged to pledge allegiance to Charles. But they did so in the belief that his situation in all three kingdoms was so desperate by 1641–2 that they could drive a much harder bargain with him than the limited package of concessions the landed elite was seeking. They certainly showed little interest in upholding his prerogative power in Ireland, particularly in matters of religion.

An appeal to the emotive claims of land and religion played well among ordinary Catholics. Nevertheless, it is hard not to regard the expectations of the exiles and clergy as unrealistic in the wider context of three-kingdoms politics – for the more Charles conceded to the Irish Catholics the more support he would lose among Protestants, who formed by far the largest and most powerful constituency within his dominions. Whereas the strategy of the Irish leadership was at least broadly calibrated to the tangled relationship between the Stuart monarchies, that of the clergy and exiles was at once more Hibernocentric and

Continental. These contradictory impulses at the heart of the Irish Catholic cause would prove impossible for its leaders to resolve.

Patterns of Allegiance

The Irish Rising upped the tempo in the 'intricate war dance of the three kingdoms'.[20] The need to raise money and troops to subdue Ireland meant that Charles no longer had the option of dissolving the Long Parliament. Instead, the Rising left him and the junto yoked together, which given their unwillingness to settle their differences by negotiation did not augur well. Moreover, the Rising placed them on a collision course over control of the forces to suppress the 'rebels', for neither side would trust the other with an army. In an attempt to get round this impasse, the Long Parliament asked the Covenanter regime for assistance. The Scots, eager to protect and strengthen their colony in Ulster, were happy to oblige, and by the summer of 1642 had sent 10,000 troops to Ireland. But allowing the Covenanters (of all people) to intervene in a kingdom where they had no rightful constitutional interest amounted to a declaration of war against every Catholic in Ireland, and undoubtedly strengthened Irish resistance. No less provocative was the Long Parliament's decision to fund an invasion of Ireland by selling land that would be confiscated from Irish Catholics once the Rising had been suppressed. Charles, without forces of his own to quell the Rising, had no choice but to assent to the Adventurers' Act, and by so doing established Parliament's right to exercise the crown's law-making and war-making powers in Ireland. Anglo-Irish policy had been officially handed to those eager to turn Ireland into one vast Protestant plantation.

The severity of Parliament's reaction to the Irish Rising reflected a readiness in England to interpret such cataclysmic events in the context of long-standing, divisive political prejudices. Many people saw the Rising as just the latest horrifying instalment in a century-old popish plot to extirpate English Protestantism and liberties. From early November 1641, when news of the Rising first broke in London, the press was awash with lurid tales of barbarous Irish Catholics murdering, raping, and torturing defenceless Protestants. The reported number of Protestant dead eventually escalated in most accounts to well over Ireland's entire Protestant population. But then exaggerated stories of Catholic atrocities against the godly had been a staple of Protestant propaganda in England since the Reformation. On the other hand, to those more concerned by the fracturing of civil and religious authority at home, this kind of yellow press journalism smacked of rabble-rousing and was seen as yet another Puritan and populist attack on the established order. The Rising's capacity to polarise the English was enhanced by the willingness of leading politicians to manipulate the media for partisan ends. There is strong evidence that Pym and his friends sought to manage the flow and content of news in order to widen support for their assault on Charles's authority. Similarly, leading figures in the king's party used press reports on the Rising to deliver a homily on the evils of disobedience to constituted authority – a theme with obvious significance in light of the junto's challenge to the king.

Propaganda was one weapon in the junto's armoury of coercion; another was the London crowd. By rallying concerned Londoners against the king's supporters at Westminster, in particular the bishops, the junto and its allies in the City were able to provoke Charles into committing major political blunders. The most glaring of these was his attempted arrest early in January 1642 of Pym and five other junto-men on charges of treason – a violation of parliamentary privilege that affronted people across the political spectrum. Charles compounded this folly a few days later when he allowed his fear of the mob to drive him out of London, thereby surrendering the capital and its resources to Parliament without so much as a fight. Victory for the Puritan interest in the December 1641 elections to the Common Council, London's governing body, handed the junto an even more potent weapon, the City's 8000-strong militia.

The massive increase in newsprint following the collapse of censorship in 1640, and the petitions that flooded into London in support of godly reformation of the established church, were part of an unprecedented exchange of information between centre and localities that helped transform a crisis in high politics into civil war. The dominant discourse in popular parliamentarianism, for example, was anti-popery – a political vocabulary that drew heavily on the fictions constructed (with licence from the Westminster junto) around the Irish Rising to encourage and legitimise all kinds of civil unrest, from ransacking the houses of Catholic gentry to fighting in Parliament's armies. One of the most potent of these fictions was that Charles and his papist queen had been complicit in the Rising. This was enough to convince some people, particularly Puritans, that he had abrogated his royal responsibility in the most vital area of its application, and that it was lawful to resist him. The clothing districts of Essex, the West Country, and Yorkshire – where socio-economic conditions lent themselves to the spread of Puritanism – provide dramatic evidence of the way such propaganda helped to nerve ordinary people into taking up arms for Parliament. Intriguingly, while anti-popish paranoia fuelled support for Parliament in England, in Wales it seems to have fed, by processes as yet unexplained, into popular royalism. The Welsh were therefore unique among the Stuart peoples in 1642 in feeling threatened by English Parliamentarians and Irish Catholics alike.

If 'Parliamentarian', at one level, is simply another term for those who systematically identified popery as the main threat to order, then Royalists were those who thought in identical fashion about Puritanism. The king's propaganda machine took longer getting started than the Parliament's, but by early 1642 proto-Royalists were well on their way to developing a demonology to rival that of popery. The emergence of a Royalist party was intimately bound up with the fear that the established church, Prayer Book worship, and with them the whole fabric of society, were under attack from a puritanical faction led by 'King Pym'. Again, there was nothing new about this hatred of Puritanism. The godly and their crusade against moral disorder had been making enemies in English parishes for generations. What was novel in 1641–2 was the heightened menace that anti-Puritans attached to 'sectaries' – extreme Puritans who had abandoned public worship for private conventicles; or nests of sedition, to Royalist eyes. Like the anti-popish reflex, fear of the sectarian menace had little basis in fact. A breakdown in ecclesiastical authority since 1640 had encouraged a modest rise in separatism, or at least allowed it to emerge into the open, but the numbers involved were tiny.

Loyalty to the person of 'his sacred majesty' was added relatively late to the amalgam of ideas that went to make up royalism. As a result of some well conceived royal propaganda in the spring and summer of 1642, and the increasing odium that attached to Parliament as its military preparations forced it to encroach ever more on the people's liberties, Charles succeeded in partially re-inventing himself as the champion of the rule of law and what for many Royalists was its keystone, the pre-Laudian church.

Wars of Religion?

The cause of defending true religion (however defined) had been central to the new compacts forged between rulers and ruled in all three kingdoms by 1642. The fracturing of authority had allowed unprecedented freedom of political choice for the ordinary people – a choice that often presented itself as a duty to fight for God's people or church against His enemies. Religion is generally seen as the most important factor in determining popular allegiance in all three kingdoms; and in Scotland and Ireland there were powerful groups that justified the resort to arms partly in terms of a holy war against Antichrist. The English were certainly no strangers to the concept of a holy war, but it sat uneasily with their ideas about religion as one of the subject's liberties that crown and Parliament – in other words, civil institutions – had a legal authority to defend and amend. Many English people, including future Royalists, were worried not so much by Charles's preference for 'popish' religious forms as by his self-proclaimed authority to make changes in religion without recourse to Parliament or due legal process. The Covenanters, by contrast, based their defiance of Charles largely upon the duty of a covenanted nation to fulfil God's design and preserve itself from spiritual corruption. This difference in modes of opposition was rooted in the contrasting political cultures of the two kingdoms. Statute and customary law carried more authority among the broad mass of people in England than they did in Scotland (or in Ireland). English jurisprudence and politics had established the principle that 'it was the law that guaranteed to Englishmen the Christian Faith'.[21] In Scotland it was more a case of godly religion underpinning the law than vice versa.

It was only when the English looked to the struggle in Ireland that they habitually thought in terms of a war of religion. Without the constraints imposed by a common national identity and shared ideas about the interdependence of customary law and religion (as applied in England, and to a lesser extent in Scotland), the conflict in Ireland conformed more closely to the wars in the Low Countries and Germany, where Protestantism and Counter-Reformation Catholicism collided head on, with little in the way of civil containment to prevent the free play of religious passions.

Chapter 2: The Outbreak of the English Civil War: August 1642–September 1643

The Road to Edgehill

The English Civil War took an inordinately long time to get started considering that by January 1642 both Charles and the junto were determined to settle their differences by force. Of course, civil war was only possible if each side had a committed popular following; and Charles's bungled attempt to arrest the six junto members had temporarily discredited his cause. Not that Parliament was any more capable of raising an army at this stage. The people were deeply divided on certain issues, notably the settlement of religion, but they were neither prepared for war materially, nor ready to accept that the breach between king and Parliament was irreparable. They would be gradually disabused of this notion during the first half of 1642, as the pursuit of rival claims to the kingdom's military resources generated controversy and a series of armed stand-offs. The fact that the nation still clung to the ideal of consensus and the rule of law made both sides anxious not to forfeit the constitutional high ground and thus hampered their military preparations. Nevertheless, while Charles and Parliament engaged in paper skirmishes over the spring and summer aimed partly at wooing moderate opinion, their enthusiasts in the counties battled (sometimes literally) to raise men and to seize arms and places of strategic importance. By the time Charles raised his standard at Nottingham on 22 August, sporadic fighting had broken out in a number of counties, and two of the kingdom's major ports, Hull and Portsmouth, were under siege.

The very outbreak of civil war represented a victory of sorts for the king. The dubious legality surrounding his chosen instrument for raising troops, the Commission of Array, and the military excesses of some of his more zealous supporters, had tarnished his newly acquired image as a law-abiding monarch. Even so, by the autumn of 1642 he had gained a sufficient party to fight a war. In the struggle for military resources, however, Parliament had clearly emerged the victor. London, the south-east, East Anglia, most of the south and east Midlands, and all but one of the major outports (Newcastle-upon-Tyne) – in other words the richest and most populous parts of the kingdom – were, broadly speaking, under parliamentary control, leaving the king with the counties north of the Trent (although with sizeable parliamentarian enclaves in Yorkshire and Lancashire), Wales and the border counties, and most of the west Midlands and the south-west.

Control of London gave Parliament a huge advantage in the initial scramble to assemble field forces. The London citizenry constituted a large reservoir of generally enthusiastic manpower on which Parliament could draw; the Tower was well stocked with munitions; and money was to hand in the form of loans – secured against anticipated taxation revenue – from wealthy City merchants. In the space of a few weeks in July and August, Parliament was able to recruit a large army under the command of the Earl of Essex – a proud and reserved man, whose popularity, particularly among Londoners, outweighed his military abilities.

While Essex was assembling his army, Parliament's lord admiral (and Essex's cousin) the Earl of Warwick seized control of almost the entire royal navy. This was a massive coup for Parliament. Using the fleet, Warwick quickly secured Hull and Portsmouth, thus providing Parliament with vital bridgeheads behind enemy lines. In the longer term, control of the navy gave Parliament the means to out-do the Royalists logistically and to ensure a steady stream of customs revenue.

But Parliament's triumph was far from assured. Charles may have had to rely on the more despised sections of the population – the Welsh, Catholics, etc. – to bring his army up to scratch; nevertheless, by October he had raised about as many troops as Essex, or roughly 14,000 men, which by English standards was a formidable force. Made up largely of volunteers raised by gentlemen bearing royal commissions, it was main-tained by a variety of financial expedients, including confiscation of par-liamentarian estates and the sale of titles. Indeed, if raising horse and foot was no easy task in a society as demilitarised and generally reluctant to take up arms as England, then maintaining these forces proved even harder. Military organisation on both sides was makeshift and rudimentary, and often hampered by the deeply felt desire of local communities to preserve their money and arms for their own defence. The *ad hoc* nature of the rival war machines reflected the widespread belief that the whole sorry business would be settled by one pitched battle.

The two armies met at Edgehill, in Warwickshire, on 23 October 1642. In what was to become a familiar pattern as the war progressed, the king's cavalry, under his dashing 23-year-old nephew Prince Rupert, swept the parliamentarian horse from the field. But instead of then rallying his victorious troopers to attack the exposed enemy foot, Rupert was happy to let them waste their energies plundering Essex's baggage train. It was thus left to the infantry to fight it out 'at push of pike', and the better-armed Parliamentarians were soon rolling back the Royalist foot, and would have won the day for Essex if the Royalist cavalry had not eventually returned to halt their advance. In terms of casualties, Edgehill was a draw: each side losing about 1500 men. Strategically, the honours went to Charles, who marched his army down the Thames Valley to threaten London itself, before being checked at Turnham Green in mid-November by the massed ranks of the City militia. Both armies then retired to winter quarters, the king establishing his court and military headquarters at Oxford.

War and Peace at Westminster

The realisation that Essex's army was not going to carry all before it as many, even on the king's side, had believed, changed the whole face of the conflict. For Charles, the events of October and November had been an epiphany. Seemingly against all odds he had raised a formidable army, seen it hold its own against a better equipped Parliamentarian force at Edgehill, and then commit 'great slaughter' on Essex's troops during the advance on London. Having had one offer to treat dismissed by Parliament late in August he was in no mood to make fresh overtures after Turnham Green when the military advantage seemed to have swung in his favour. During the winter of 1642–3, his forces consolidated their hold on Cornwall, Wales, and the border counties, while the commander of his northern army, the Earl (and from 1643, Marquess) of Newcastle, overran much of Yorkshire and established a vital bridgehead in the Midlands at Newark. For Parliament on the other hand, the lacklustre performance of Essex's army in the Edgehill campaign came as a nasty shock, and led to a major shift in the balance of power at Westminster.

The exodus of Royalist peers and MPs from Parliament during the course of 1642 had strengthened the junto's grip at Westminster. In the Commons, Pym and his friends enjoyed the backing of the 'fiery spirits' – hard-line MPs who favoured the vigorous prosecution of the war – and by early 1642 the junto had been joined by some of the greatest peers of the realm, notably the earls of Northumberland, Pembroke, and Holland. Although deeply distrustful of the king, these former courtiers did not share the enthusiasm for further reformation in religion of the Commons' militants. They had supported the raising of an army under the Earl of Essex only because, like almost everyone else at Westminster, they had believed the Royalists would be crushed at the first time of asking, with Charles being forced to accede to what, by later standards, were still moderate parliamentary terms. After the Edgehill campaign, however, they were faced with the awful prospect of total defeat by the king, or, not much better (in fact to some peers and MPs, not better at all), a long drawn out civil war that would threaten both property and the established order. At the end of October a number of peers began to push for a peace settlement, and were strongly seconded by a faction in the Commons. For the first time since December 1641, the junto faced determined political opposition in its own backyard.

The Commons debates over the winter of 1642–3 about Parliament's war aims and how best to achieve them were the focus of Jack Hexter's influential analysis of Westminster politics in the year after Edgehill.[1] In addition to the recognised Commons factions that comprised the fiery spirits – the 'war party' – and those desperate for a swift, negotiated settlement – the 'peace party' – Hexter discerned a third force, which he labelled the 'middle group'. Led by Pym, the middle group consisted of a small but critical number of swing voters, who tried to steer a middle course between the extremes of all-out war and a sell-out peace. It was their determination to remain true to Parliament's core objectives, to negotiating only from a position of strength, that in Hexter's view accounted for the seemingly contradictory policies of the Houses during 1642–3 of pursuing peace talks while strengthening the Parliamentarian war-effort.

Hexter's account of political structure at Westminster is now over 60 years old, and is beginning to look its age. There is nothing, for example, to support his portrayal of Pym as a war leader to rank alongside Churchill. Nor does the existence of a middle group stand up to close scrutiny. Above all, Hexter virtually ignored the Lords as an institution, and the peers as politicians, even though a number of them were every bit as influential as the most prominent MP.

A more persuasive and sophisticated model of politics in the Long Parliament has recently been developed by John Adamson. In his interpretation, the play of events at Westminster was strongly influenced by the machinations of rival, bicameral 'interests', that vied with each other for control of Parliament in order to impose their own national political agendas.[2] Adamson developed this model mainly with reference to the period 1645–9, but he clearly sees something very similar operating by 1642–3. Indeed, the post-Edgehill crisis at Westminster evidently marked the beginning of an important stage in the development of this bicameral party politics.

The string of military setbacks that Parliament suffered after Edgehill put severe strain on the partnership between the junto and the Northumberland group of peers, and by the end of 1642 it is possible to identify two main interests, two differing agendas, at Westminster. The more powerful of these interests (certainly in the Lords) centred upon the earls of Northumberland, Pembroke, and Holland, plus Denzil Holles, Sir John Evelyn, William Pierrepont, and a few others in the Commons. Aristocratic rivalry played a part in the formation of this group. Several of the peers 'thought themselves as much overshadowed by the greatness of the earl of Essex and the chief officers of the army as they could be by the glory of any favourite or power of any [royal] counsellors, [and] were resolved to merit as much as they could of the King by advancing an honourable peace'.[3] The Northumberland–Holles interest sought a quick, negotiated settlement with the king – one that left him with most of his prerogative powers and that stopped short of the total abolition of episcopacy. It was this group that was primarily responsible for Parliament's first set of peace terms, which were presented to the king at Oxford in February 1643.

Ranged against the Northumberland–Holles group was an interest associated with the most godly of the peers – the Earl of Manchester, Viscount Saye, and Lord Wharton – and John Pym, Sir Henry Vane junior, and Oliver St John in the Commons. The Earl of Essex was also part of this network, as were his most trusted staff officers, the MPs John Hampden and Sir Philip Stapilton. Most of these men had been complicit in the 1640 Scottish invasion, which had brought down the Personal Rule. They knew that if the king regained the throne on the easy terms proposed by the Northumberland–Holles group it would leave them exposed to his vengeance. Consequently, they were desperate not to conclude a peace from the position of weakness in which the two Houses found themselves in the winter of 1642–3: 'For the Lord Say, Master Pym, and others of the leading Members were exceeding sensible ... that they had no hopes of safety in peace, or any other course then the way of power.'[4] Since most people did yearn for peace, however, and they themselves did not want to be branded the enemies of a settlement, they had to proceed cautiously. Rather than openly frustrating the peace process, they tried to stiffen Parliament's terms to the point where they were sure Charles would reject them. At the same time, they launched a propaganda offensive over the winter of 1642–3 against an 'unsafe and unworthy' accommodation. That some of this literature put the case for parliamentary sovereignty probably says a lot about how the Saye–Pym group was thinking at this juncture.

In seeking a much more stringent settlement, the Saye–Pym group pinned most of its hopes on a Scottish alliance. It had been preparing the ground for such an alliance since the spring of 1642, and in July had organised a declaration to the Covenanters giving vague assurances of Parliament's willingness to pay the necessary price of Scottish support – namely, closer ties between the two kingdoms 'as well spiritual as civil'. On 2 November, the same day that the Commons voted to open talks with the king, the House made its first direct appeal to the Scots for military assistance – the Scots were to be invited to enter England to crush the Earl of Newcastle's northern Royalist army. Much effort was put into depicting Newcastle's troops as a pack of papists intent on reducing the two kingdoms to 'the base and unnatural slavery of their monarch, the Pope'.[5] Aimed primarily at a Scottish audience, this propaganda was so effective that Newcastle's army became known simply as 'the popish army'. Similarly, Pym's persistent efforts to introduce a Scottish-style Covenant, or at least a declaration 'that this warre was for Religion & that his Ma[jes]ties armie consisted for the most part of Papists & was raised for the extirpation of the true religion', were part of a campaign to portray the war not merely as a struggle for the reform of English government, but as a crusade to defend Protestantism in all three kingdoms.[6] The threat to both kingdoms from the Irish rebels was also invoked to further the policy of bringing in the Scots.

To the extent that the advocates of a quick peace did not oppose this policy of allying with the Scots, it was only because they saw it as a way of pressuring Charles to moderate his terms before it was too late. Otherwise, they regarded the idea of involving the Scots in the war as a potentially ruinous escalation of the conflict. If Parliament brought in the Scots it would encourage the king to bring in Irish and other foreign troops. Besides which, asking for help from 'that beggarly nation', as the Earl of

Northumberland referred to Scotland, was considered an affront to English honour. Few even among the Saye–Pym group were immune to this kind of anti-Scottish chauvinism. But their desire for military assistance, and the prospect of a settlement to which both kingdoms were party – and which would therefore be doubly difficult for Charles to break – temporarily overrode their dislike of the Scots' confederalist agenda.

The Rise of the Grandees

The MP Sir Simonds D'Ewes was moved to keep a parliamentary diary in order to lay bare the 'secrett workings & machinations of each partie as well of the Two Howses of Parliament, cheifelie ledd & guided by some few members of either Howse, as of the Kings partie'.[7] Although D'Ewes used the word 'party', it should be emphasised that neither of the main bicameral interests at Westminster were parties in the modern sense. They had no manifesto, no party whip. Each consisted of a small number of dedicated politicians, or 'grandees', with a shared vision as to the ideal settlement and how it could be achieved. This political bond was often reinforced by ties of kinship, friendship, or patronage. Some of the grandees were adept speakers or enjoyed great personal prestige. But to turn policy into legislation required more than just charisma; it demanded the constant attention of a well-primed body of friends in both Houses. Outspoken hard-liners such as Henry Marten (the only openly republican MP in the early years of the war) might dominate a debate, but they had little actual power because they were not plugged into a bicameral network that could implement their agenda.

The grandees' power at Westminster was far from being absolute, however. If the twenty or so peers who sat in the Lords during the war were fairly consistent in their party allegiance, the majority of MPs supported one or other of the 'engaged' factions only as their reason or self-interest dictated. Those MPs eager to take the fight to the king, for example, tended to support the Saye–Pym group on the Scottish alliance or in introducing the coercive taxation and sequestration machinery necessary to fund the war-effort. Likewise, the crypto-Royalists at Westminster, or those members who feared a total breakdown in the social and political order if the war continued, generally backed the Northumberland–Holles interest on the question of peace talks. There were also regional caucuses at Westminster – transitory, single-issue groups that came together in the interests of their particular locality. The majority of the 'northern gentlemen' at Westminster, for example, backed the Saye–Pym group on the Scottish alliance. Northern MPs were naturally eager to have their estates liberated from the clutches of the Royalists, and they saw a Scottish invasion as the quickest way of achieving this end. Religious preferences, by contrast, had little bearing on factional alignment, at least before 1644. For the first two years of the war, the question of what kind of church government and liturgy should replace episcopacy and the Prayer Book was left to Parliament's ecclesiastical talking-shop – the Westminster Assembly. Besides, there was a large degree of common ground at Westminster on church matters. Most Parliament-men can be classed as Puritan erastians – that is, they favoured a godly national church under state control.

The presence of a non-aligned majority at Westminster was due in large part to the revulsion that many Parliament-men felt for a political system based upon 'party' and 'faction'. A party was seen as a corrupt political group that eschewed decision-making by free debate in favour of imposing its own predetermined course of action – which to contemporaries implied the pursuit of self-interest against the common good. As Mark Kishlansky has pointed out, the procedures and rules governing conduct in either House were intended specifically to promote consensus through open debate.[8] In order to impose their own agendas, therefore, the grandees had to devise methods of circumventing or managing this cumbersome political system.

In investigating these methods of management, as Adamson has argued, we inevitably step outside the analytical framework of the Whig historians, with their focus on the 'great debates' in the Commons and the guiding genius of Puritan heroes such as John Pym and Oliver Cromwell. One of the grandees' principal mechanisms for managing the Houses was the executive standing committee. During the course of 1641 the Long Parliament had taken over many of the executive and administrative functions of royal government. The outbreak of war had imposed a whole new set of burdens, and Parliament's response was to set up permanent bicameral committees to handle the extra workload that would otherwise have overwhelmed its proceedings. Oratory and a forceful personality were useful assests for any would-be parliamentary manager, particularly in the Commons. However, the development of executive committees had the effect of sidelining proceedings on the floor of the Houses. It was in the back-room workings of these committees that real power in terms of political patronage and policy-making often resided.

The Long Parliament's first major executive committee was the Committee of Safety, set up in the summer of 1642. Both main interests made use of this committee – the Pym–Saye group to forward their policy of bringing in the Scots; the Northumberland–Holles group to rein in Essex's army – and both defended it against the attacks of those who disliked their oligarchic practices. As the war progressed, more and more of these bodies were established, and almost all of them became dominated by the grandees and their placemen. Using these committees, the grandees were able to side-step or manipulate the potentially fickle, non-aligned majority of Parliament-men. Control of Parliament's financial committees, for example, gave massive scope for grandee patronage in terms of rewards, bribes, and offices. 'These Committee men are so powerfull', observed one commentator, 'that they over-awe and over-power their fellow members, contrary to the nature of a free Parliament.'[9]

The influence wielded by the grandees helped to undermine Parliament's pre-war role in integrating local and national interests. The fact that MPs in the 1640s did not have the immediate prospect of parliamentary dissolution and re-election hanging over them as their predecessors had, and that the war had divided many of them from their constituents both physically and politically, meant that they were less accountable to their localities than the members of any other seventeenth-century Parliament. Equally, the fact that many MPs had either had their estates destroyed in the fighting or seen their rents slashed as a result of economic dislocation and heavy taxes made them more susceptible to grandee blandishments in terms of office and reward. The establishment of local parliamentary committees in 1642–3 may have broadened access to central politics for Parliament's supporters in the provinces. Nevertheless, it is significant that large-scale county petitioning ceased after 1642. In fact, by the mid-1640s petitions had come to represent a tacit admission of political impotence at Westminster: of an inability to 'cog in' with grandee and factional interests in the two Houses.

Grandee-dominated executive committees came to control Parliament's military affairs – the movement and maintenance of its armies; and there was no more powerful instrument of political will than an army. Although the forces raised during the 1640s may not have been strong enough to allow Parliament to override popular and localist sentiment with impunity, they certainly shifted the balance of political power dramatically in favour of the centre. Control of an army enabled the grandees not only to defy public opinion but to overawe Parliament itself. Nevertheless, the use of armed force to settle political scores at Westminster, though effective, came at a high price in terms of bad publicity. If the grandees wanted a more subtle way of putting pressure on their opponents in Parliament then they turned to their friends in the City. The Northumberland–Holles group probably encouraged, and certainly exploited, petitions from the peace movement in London, urging the Houses to reach an accommodation with the king. Similarly, the Saye–Pym interest collaborated with a powerful group of godly citizens, headed by the lord mayor and City MP, Isaac Pennington, to advance its own political programme. On regular occasions throughout the winter of 1642–3, the City 'godly party' presented petitions to Parliament demanding as well as offering greater commitment to the war-effort. There was more than a little truth in D'Ewes's assertion that 'these fierie spirited citizens ... weere the maine instruments w[hi]ch Hampden & the other violent men of the Howse of Commons [used] to blow upp the flame of our present civill warrs'.[10] It was no coincidence that Pennington and the Saye–Pym grandee Oliver St John sat next to each other in the Commons. But D'Ewes was wrong to imply that the City militants were the mere instruments of the grandees. The militants were strongly represented on the Common Council and on its various finance and militia committees; without their backing the Saye–Pym group could not tap London's resources of men and money that were so vital for sustaining the war-effort. Thus on certain issues such as military strategy and godly reform the Saye–Pym group had to meet the City militants at least half-way.

The Oxford Treaty

Parliament's peace terms were presented to the king at Oxford on 1 February 1643 by a delegation headed by the Earl of Northumberland. Although the treaty owed much to the Northumberland–Holles grandees' desperate desire for peace, Charles was convinced that 'No lesse power than His, who made the worlde of nothing, can drawn peace out of thease articles.'[11] The Saye–Pym group had done its work well.

In truth, it is likely that the king would have rejected Parliament's terms even if the Saye–Pym grandees had not contrived to make them quite so unpalatable to him. His armies seemed poised for victory on all fronts, and, as he informed the queen, the 'distractions of the rebels are such that so many fine designs are laid open to us we know not which first to undertake'.[12]

In behind-the-scenes meetings and secret communications with moderate Royalists at Oxford, the Northumberland–Holles grandees conceded the 'tyranny and unreasonableness' of the peace terms, and 'perfectly abhorred ... the power and superiority of the earl of Essex'.[13] Yet they were confident that a mere gesture from the king of his willingness to treat would so boost their power at Westminster that all support for continuing the war would melt away. Without Essex and his army in their camp, however, the peace grandees lacked the power to make good such assurances, and the king knew it. In an effort to undermine the treaty and alienate moderate opinion at Oxford, the Saye–Pym group and its Westminster allies chose February and March to launch a series of controversial initiatives – weekly assessments to fund the war-effort; defensive fortifications around London; and the sequestration of Royalists' property. The talks dragged on fruitlessly until mid-April, when Parliament recalled its delegation from Oxford. The collapse of the Oxford treaty bought the Saye–Pym grandees a little time, nothing more. Their survival in the longer term still depended upon securing an alliance with the Covenanters.

The Covenanters in the Balance

The English Civil War had begun with both sides looking nervously over their shoulders in fear or hope that the Covenanters would weigh in as they had in 1640. In order to understand why the Covenanters took so long to commit themselves to intervention it is necessary to go back to the spring of 1642 and the first serious attempts by king and Parliament to secure Scottish support. In the case of Parliament, this consisted of a declaration of intent to reform the government and liturgy of the English church, and the introduction of legislation for the Westminster Assembly. The king, for his part, sent a letter to the Scottish privy council forbidding the Scots from meddling in English politics, but hinting that their military assistance would be welcome. The factional balance between Royalists and Covenanters in Edinburgh was too close for the council to declare firmly in favour of either side. Nevertheless, the Covenanters on the council, led by Argyll, were strong enough to make it clear to Charles that the best he could hope for was Scottish neutrality.

On the face of it, the king's prospects of preventing the Covenanters coming to Parliament's assistance did not look good. By the summer of 1642, the Kirk was close to backing intervention, insisting that until the churches in England and Ireland had been thoroughly reformed along Scottish lines, there could be no security for Presbyterianism in Scotland. If the Royalists managed to overthrow the English Parliament, then, in the words of the Scottish Presbyterian minister Robert Baillie, all the work of reformation in both kingdoms would be 'not worth a figg'.[14] So long as Charles retained the capacity to use the resources of the English crown against Scotland it would be impossible to preserve the large measure of autonomy that the Scottish Parliament and Kirk had gained since 1637. For its own safety, Scotland must be given a greater say in the government of its more powerful southern neighbour – in other words, there must be closer union between the two kingdoms. And since Charles showed no inclination to relinquish either episcopacy or his prerogative powers, and the Edgehill campaign had suggested that the English Parliament was not strong enough to compel him to do so, Scottish intervention against the king seemed the only sure means of forging this greater Britain.

Given the presence of powerful factions, in both kingdoms, pushing for an Anglo-Scottish alliance, it might seem strange that it took them until August 1643 to tie the knot. Part of the reason for this delay was the strength of the anti-alliance interest at Westminster, particularly in the Lords. But the main impediment emerged in Scotland, from a faction centred upon the Marquess of Hamilton.

Following the Incident in the autumn of 1641, Hamilton had formed a fragile alliance with Argyll. Although distrusted by the more extreme Scottish Royalists as well as the more radical Covenanters, he remained an influential figure in Scotland, and his support-base was augmented during the early 1640s by those noblemen who resented Argyll's supremacy. By the summer of 1642, he had emerged as the leader of what David Stevenson and other Scottish historians have termed the 'conservative' or 'pragmatic' Covenanters – moderate Royalists who accepted the Covenant and most of the constitutional and religious changes since 1637, but were unwilling to see the crown's authority further eroded.[15] Yet despite his links with the Covenanters, Hamilton did not entirely lose the confidence of the king, and in the summer of 1642 Charles sent him to Edinburgh to rally support for keeping Scotland neutral. Hamilton was reasonably confident that he could frustrate or at least delay the interventionist agenda of the radical mainstream, leaving the king a free hand to defeat the English Parliamentarians – but only so long as Charles did nothing to offend or alarm moderate opinion in Scotland. It was at Hamilton's urging that Charles shelved plans by the Earl of Montrose – who had abandoned the Covenanters to lead Scotland's royalist hard-liners – for an armed uprising against the Covenanter regime.

The King and the Scots

Ironically, it was the very success of Charles's armies in England, and particularly in the northern counties, that did much to undermine his prospects of victory. The more likely he looked to win the English Civil War the stronger the forces in both kingdoms became for a Parliamentarian–Covenanter alliance. It was in the wake of the Edgehill campaign that the English Parliament made its first direct request for Scottish military assistance – the November declaration organised by the Saye–Pym group. As an 'antidote to that poison' the king sent an open letter to the Scottish privy council in which he tried to calm the Scots' fears that he intended using Catholic or foreign forces against his enemies in England.[16] He stressed that the English Civil War was a purely domestic dispute between himself and a corrupt faction in London, and that the Scots should not interfere. The letters sparked a power-struggle in the council, and although the first round went to Hamilton it strained to breaking point his uneasy friendship with Argyll. Hamilton's influence was further eroded by the Earl of Newcastle's admission that his army did indeed contain many Catholics, but that since the war was (in his view) not one of religion it hardly mattered. Hamilton too plugged the line that 'The quarrell betweene King and Parliament is not religione ... why should we meddle in it?'[17] But the cry from the Edinburgh pulpits was for 'takin[g] up of armes for rescueing his Ma[jes]tie from that captivity wherein papists hold him'.[18] By early 1643, Argyll's party was in the ascendant, though it still had Hamilton's mediation policy to contend with.

In January 1643, Charles granted safe conduct for commissioners to come to England for talks. The Argyll grandees could not ignore this royal gesture, so instead they turned it to their own advantage. In February, four Scottish commissioners, including Argyll's kinsman the Earl of Loudoun, arrived at Oxford with instructions not only to mediate a peace but to supplicate the king for a covenanted uniformity in religion and the calling of a new Scottish Parliament. The terms of this mission put Charles in a difficult position. He had no choice but to reject the commissioners' requests – to do otherwise would have alienated his friends in all three kingdoms – yet in doing so he risked handing a propaganda coup to Argyll's party. Nevertheless, a diplomatic and respectful response to the mission might have given Hamilton something to work with back in Scotland. Instead, after allowing the Oxford populace to insult and threaten the commissioners, Charles bluntly informed them that they had no right to interfere in English affairs. His one success was to string out the talks until April, thereby further delaying the negotiation of a Westminster–Edinburgh alliance.

Gratuitously offending the Scots ran entirely counter to Hamilton's strategy, but by the spring of 1643 Charles was beginning to lose confidence in it anyway – perhaps reasoning that Covenanter intervention was inevitable. What would certainly make it so was his readiness to explore an alternative option for winning the war – namely, doing a deal with the Catholic 'rebels' that would allow him to import troops from Ireland. Charles had apparently persuaded himself, as he had in the Bishops' Wars, that bringing Irish forces into England would be easier than keeping the Covenanters out, even though his cause was still far from hopeless at Edinburgh. He further calculated that he could bring over enough soldiers from Ireland to clinch victory before the Covenanters could come to Parliament's rescue. Again, this was a doubtful proposition. Above all, any compromise with the Catholic Irish risked offending British and Irish Protestants, including many on his own side. But then Charles had never fully attuned himself to the anti-popish reflex of his Protestant subjects; nor had he shown much preference for conciliation over coercion. His decision to explore the Irish option rather than stick single-mindedly with Hamilton's strategy was evidence of both these traits.

Protestant Ireland Besieged

The king's Irish policy was a grim reminder to Ireland's Protestants of their loss of power since the Catholic Rising of October 1641. The only sizeable chunks of territory left to the Protestants by the spring of 1642 consisted of a narrow coastal strip running from northern Ulster down the east coast to Dublin, and an enclave in County Cork in Munster. Many settlers had been so badly traumatised by the Rising that they had fled back to England or Scotland. And yet the position of those that had managed to weather the initial Irish onslaught was far from hopeless. Units of the king's regular army in Ireland garrisoned the key ports of Leinster and Munster, including Dublin; while British forces held Belfast and other fortified towns in Ulster and Connacht. With the arrival in Leinster of 3000 troops from England in March 1642, and the landing in Ulster in April and July of 10,000 men under Robert Monro, the Protestants were able to go onto the offensive. Monro's army of 'New Scots' was the most powerful field force in Ireland by the summer of 1642 and was able to traverse Ulster and north Leinster with relative impunity. Less than a year after the Rising had begun, a Protestant reconquest seemed a real possibility. All that was needed to sustain Protestant momentum was a steady stream of men and supplies from Britain. But just as the Irish Rising had intensified the crisis in England, so the outbreak of the English Civil War ended any prospect of a speedy resolution of the conflict in Ireland.

The war in England consumed the attention and resources of the combatants. Though Protestant leaders in Ireland pleaded with both sides to send them supplies, men and money allocated for the Irish war were diverted to the home front. At Westminster the discussion of Irish affairs was either pushed down the agenda or suspended altogether. As one Irish Protestant lamented, the English were 'soe involv'd in theyr owne danger that a word of Ireland will not be heard'.[19] Starved of supplies, the Protestants in Ireland withdrew to their strongholds, and the war degenerated into a desultory stalemate of raid and counter-raid.

The supply problem exacerbated the localised and fragmented nature of the Protestant war-effort in Ireland. The dominant figure among the Leinster Protestants was the Marquess of Ormond, whom Charles was to make lord lieutenant of Ireland in November 1643. Although raised a Protestant, Ormond was head of a prominent Old English family, and had many relations and former clients among the insurgents. Ormond and the Irish privy council represented the severed head of royal government in Ireland, and their writ ran only within Dublin and those parts of the Pale they still held from the insurgents. Ormond had a staunch ally in the Ulick Burke, Earl of Clanricarde, who did his best to maintain royal authority in County Galway, in Connacht; but his anomalous position as both a leading Catholic and loyal king's man left him politically isolated.

Overall command in Munster was assumed by the vice-president of the province, Murrough O'Brien, Lord Inchiquin. He was generally respectful of Ormond's authority but his priority was to defend the Munster Protestants, and he was prepared to switch allegiance between king and Parliament depending on which offered the best solution to his supply problems.

The situation in Ulster was particularly complicated (see Map 3). Under the terms of the Anglo-Scottish treaty concluded in the wake of the Rising, the 10,000 Scottish troops sent to Ulster were to be maintained by Westminster and were ultimately at the disposal of the lord lieutenant. In practice, however, Monro recognised no authority but that of the Covenanter leadership in Scotland. His concern to advance Scottish political and religious interests in Ulster caused considerable tension between himself and the leaders of the British forces – the regiments raised by English and Scottish settlers.

The Civil War in England widened the divisions among and between these Protestant groupings. Westminster's inability to meet its financial commitments to the New Scots army meant that most of what little supplies Monro's men received came from Scotland, thereby increasing their dependence on Edinburgh. The result was to heighten distrust of the New Scots among the British forces; and distrust turned to anger as a result of Monro's unwillingness to stray too far from his bases in eastern Ulster. Monro pleaded lack of supplies, but the growing threat of a Royalist victory after Edgehill obliged him to preserve his army lest it be needed to invade England in support of Parliament.

The Confederate Catholics of Ireland

The Protestants faced an added difficulty by the autumn, and that was the growing strength and confidence of their Catholic adversaries. By forcing the Protestants onto the defensive, the onset of war in England gave the Catholics breathing space in which to organise themselves. Much of the initiative in giving order and direction to the insurgents came from the clergy, who saw the uprising as a God-given opportunity to secure freedom of worship for Ireland's Catholics. Alarmed by a string of Protestant victories in the early months of 1642, the Catholic bishops held a series of meetings at Kilkenny, in Leinster, in May and June 1642, to devise some means of coordinating the war-effort. At the end of their deliberations they invited the Catholic nobility and gentry to join them in drawing up plans for an interim national government until they could negotiate a settlement with the king. Thus was conceived the government of the Confederate Catholics of Ireland.

The Kilkenny meetings also saw the introduction of an 'oath of association', pledging the insurgents to 'bear true faith and allegiance' to the king, and to maintain 'the free exercise of the Roman Catholic faith and religion throughout this land'.[20] The oath followed the Scottish National Covenant (perhaps consciously) in linking obedience to the king's authority with defence of 'true religion'. The problem here, of course, as with the Covenant, was that Charles's most cherished prerogative power was his supremacy in religion, and he could no more accept a Catholic Church in Ireland than he could a Presbyterian church in England or Scotland.

The new government was officially established on 24 October 1642, when the first General Assembly of the Confederate Association was held at Kilkenny. Composed of elected representatives from all four provinces, the General Assembly was the ultimate authority within the Association. When the General Assembly was in recess, the functions of government were to be exercised by a Supreme Council elected by the assemblymen. Every General Assembly, except one, was held at Kilkenny, which became the Confederates' headquarters.

The main challenge facing the Association was to turn its political authority into military power; a task made easier by the return to Ireland in 1642 of Owen Roe O'Neill and Thomas Preston, both veteran commanders in the Spanish armies. O'Neill was assigned command of the Confederate army in Ulster; Preston that of Leinster. With the help of modest, but – in the context of Ireland's chronic lack of ready money and military resources – vital supplies of money and arms from France, Spain, and the papacy, O'Neill and Preston recruited and trained the Confederate forces. Gradually, as lack of supplies from England began to cripple the Protestant war-effort, the Confederates tightened the noose on their enemies. During the course of 1643, O'Neill and Preston gained ground in Ulster and the Pale, while in Munster the Confederate forces began to make life very difficult for Inchiquin.

To the extent that the Rising had been an expression of popular grievances, the establishment of the Confederate Association shifted its centre of gravity decisively towards the elite. In Ireland, just as in Scotland and England, the exigencies of war and the power vacuum left by the collapse of royal government led to the creation of complex new political and administrative structures. The demand for cash to sustain the Confederate war-effort resulted in the appointment of a 'multitude of officials, assessors, collectors etc.'[21] – despite the fact that Ireland's commercial and manufacturing base was too weak to sustain a heavy tax burden. And again, just as in the other two kingdoms, the development of this war-machine served to buttress oligarchic rule while at the same time stifling the expression of popular feeling. Although the Association claimed to represent and act for all of Ireland's Catholics, in practice there was no widening of the electoral franchise during the 1640s. The General Assembly and the Supreme Council were dominated by the same strata of the landed elite that had represented Catholic interests in the pre-war Parliaments at Dublin. Certain sections of Catholic society, in particular the clergy and merchants, enjoyed greater political influence after the Rising. But the views of the vast mass of the Irish population were scarcely more consulted at Kilkenny than they had been at Dublin.

The Structure of Confederate Politics

Although the creation of the Association represented an impressive display of Catholic solidarity, in fact the Confederates were as divided as their Protestant opponents. A potentially major source of disunity among leading Confederates was the ethnic divide between the Gaelic Irish and the Old English. Racial distinctions were certainly commented upon at the time, and it is hard to deny that they contributed to political tensions within the Association. But with the Confederates, as with the native Welsh, we must be careful not to attach too much significance to race as a determinant of political allegiance. As Dónal Cregan has noted, there is no clear correlation between racial differences and Confederate political divisions.[22] In fact, the very idea of separate racial groups is something of a red herring as far as the upper levels of Irish society are concerned. The Old English and native Irish nobility and gentry had been intermarrying for generations and were of 'mixed stock'. Among this landed elite, a concern to maintain the established order generally took precedence over issues of ethnic identity.

There were many other determinants of political allegiance within the Association that cut across the racial fault line. The two most influential elements within the Association after the great landowners were the bishops and lawyers. Their contrasting educational backgrounds – the lawyers in English common law; the episcopate in Roman canon law – tended to push them in different political directions regardless of their ethnic backgrounds. Several bishops of Old English descent supported the so-called Old Irish faction in demanding the re-establishment of the church and papal authority. Similarly, those of Old Irish descent who owned former monastic property, or land confiscated in plantation schemes, often shared the supposedly Old English preoccupation with a limited settlement. Provincial rivalries were another solvent of ethnic allegiance. Many Ulster Confederates were distanced from the Gaelic community in the other three provinces by their affinity with the Gaels of western Scotland. The fact also that they had suffered greater dispossession and persecution than their countrymen meant that they had less of a stake in preserving the existing religious and landed order. These distinctions tended to make them seem either 'barbarous' or 'haughty and ambitious' in the eyes of other Confederates.[23]

Micheál Ó Siochrú's recent study of the Association has confirmed Cregan's findings. It reveals that the fundamental division among the Irish, as Confederates, was not ethnic but religious and economic in nature, and related closely to their minimum terms for assisting the king in Britain. The Confederates were only too aware of the dire consequences for Catholic Ireland that would follow from a Parliamentarian victory in England. In some ways their problem was the same as that of the Covenanters – how to prevent their enemies using the power of the English state against them. But the Covenanters' solution of seeking a closer union with England was not open to the Confederates. Their status as Catholics rendered them incapable of exerting any lasting influence within Protestant England. Rather than adopt a confederalist approach, they sought a settlement that would *reduce* their ties with the English state, and make Ireland independent of any external authority except the royal prerogative. The surest way of securing such a settlement was to send an army to help the king win the English Civil War, thereby ensuring that the crown's powers were exercised by Charles, not a Puritan faction at Westminster. The problem was that the Confederates found it impossible to agree on what religious and constitutional concessions they should obtain from Charles before intervening on his behalf. This was a political quarrel, and the two factions it gave rise to were political groupings. Thus rather than use their traditional names – the Old Irish and Old English – Ó Siochrú prefers the 'peace' and 'clerical parties'.

The leadership of the peace party was drawn mainly from those sections of the Catholic nobility that had best adapted to the pre-war Protestant ascendancy. Their seigneurial form of worship and, in many cases, ownership of former monastic lands made them suspicious of the clericalist pretensions of the church hierarchy. The common lawyers had also fared reasonably well in pre-war Ireland, and they too tended to gravitate towards the peace party. Both of these groups looked to the crown to preserve their estates and influence, and thus had a strong vested interest in defending the king and his authority against his British opponents, even if it meant compromising Catholic freedom of worship. The imperative of assisting Charles as soon as possible meant limiting Confederate demands to what he could reasonably grant in conscience and political prudence. If the price of maintaining the English connection on which their interests depended required jettisoning the clergy's demands for the full re-establishment of the Catholic Church in Ireland, then it was a price they were prepared to pay. A majority of leading figures within the peace party could claim Old English descent, and because some of them were kinsmen or former associates of Ormond, the members of this faction became known as the Ormondists.

The clerical party was dominated by the bishops and the Irish who had returned from exile on the Continent after 1641. Like their rivals, they appreciated the need to help the king defeat his Puritan opponents in Britain. Yet because the church hierarchy and the exiles had suffered much greater losses in land and influence than the peace party, and had been more exposed to Counter-Reformation influences, their terms for settlement were more exacting. Before they would consider assisting the king they demanded full and public exercise of religion (not merely the pre-war 'tacit licence' of Catholicism that the peace party would be content with), restoration of papal authority, retention of the church property seized since 1641, and the restitution of confiscated land. The clerical party too was defined primarily on the basis of shared religious and proprietorial interests. For historical reasons, these interests were associated with the Ulster exiles, yet by no means exclusively. Both Confederate factions had the same oligarchic structure as their Westminster and Edinburgh counterparts – 'loose groups of individuals, dominated by one or two personalities, sharing a common goal'.[24]

The King and the Irish

The creation of the Confederate Association was conceived as a temporary expedient until a settlement could be reached with the king, and to this end the Irish Catholic leadership wrote to Charles in July 1642 suggesting a cessation of arms between their own forces and the Irish Protestants. Charles responded on 11 January 1643 by granting a commission to Ormond, Clanricarde, and several other Irish Royalists, to hear the Confederates' grievances. Not that he was vitally interested in what the Confederates had to say; it was the Irish Protestants that he was concerned with at this stage. The diversion of English resources from Ireland to the home front during the course of 1642 had caused considerable discontent among the Protestants, and Charles now saw a way of channelling this to his own advantage. His plan was to arrange a cessation of arms with the Confederates on the cheapest terms possible and so release Protestant units in Leinster and Munster for service in England. Charles knew that he could not supply these troops in Ireland. This way he could win over the soldiers by satisfying their material grievances (pay and plunder being easier to come by in England), ease the burden of Ireland's Protestants, and boost his military fortunes in England. His desire for Irish troops was given added urgency by the Saye–Pym group's overtures to the Covenanters, and the increasing influence of Argyll's party in Scotland.

The drawback in Charles's plan was that it opened him to charges of treating with Catholics and of undermining the suppression of the Rising. Not only that, it widened the cracks within the Protestant community. The outbreak of the English Civil War, but more parti-cularly Charles's cessation scheme, 'tugged at two corners of [the Irish] Protestant self-perception'[25] – on one hand, as the king and crown's most loyal subjects in Ireland; on the other, as the defenders of 'true religion' and the English national interest against Irish popery. The chasm that had seemingly opened up in England between defence of godly religion and of royal authority made rival claims on the loyalties of Irish Protestants, and in response opposing parties began to form around these two strands in Protestant identity. Ormond and Clanricarde emerged as leaders of a group keen to draw distinctions between loyal Catholics and rebels; which accorded well with Charles's desire to build a party for him-self in Ireland based solely upon allegiance to his service. This Irish Royalist interest was opposed by the rabidly anti-Catholic Sir William Parsons and his friends on the Irish privy council. To those of Parsons's mind, true loyalty to the English crown was inseparable from Protestantism. They saw the Confederates not just as rebels but as intractable enemies of the New English mission to protestantise and angli-cise Ireland. The Parsons group found the king's commission to treat with the Confederates unacceptable, and with the tacit support of Westminster tried to detach the Dublin army from Ormond early in 1643. Ormond and his party responded by having the king remove Parsons and his fellow Parliamentarian sympathisers from office. Ormond's ascen-dancy in Dublin and as the head of the Irish Royalists was now assured.

The failure of the Oxford treaty encouraged Charles to press ahead with his Irish design, and in April 1643 he ordered Ormond to conclude a truce with the Confederates. By this time, Charles had probably received the latest loyal protestation from the Confederates, in which they had offered him 10,000 soldiers for service in England. The king had been ready to use Catholic Irish troops against the Scottish Covenanters since 1638. Whether he was now prepared to deploy a Confederate army in England is not clear, but the queen and other leading Royalists took his willingness to treat with Kilkenny as a green light to proceed down just such a path. In the spring of 1643, the queen gave her approval to a design hatched by the Earl of Antrim for a three-kingdoms Royalist offensive against the king's British opponents. The 'Antrim plot' envisaged the negotiation of a cease-fire between the Confederates and Ormond's Irish Royalists, following which their combined forces would invade western Scotland and link up with a Highland army raised by Antrim, Montrose, and other Scottish Royalists, and an English invasion force led by the Earl of Newcastle. Once Scotland had been subdued it was hoped that the Irish army would then march south against the Parliamentarians. As with Antrim's previous variations on this scheme, not the least of his objectives was to revive the MacDonnell–MacDonald lordship in Ulster and the western Highlands.

Charles knew about the plot, and his failure to prevent the queen and Antrim setting the wheels in motion was doubly foolish, for not only was it impractical to begin with, but if news of it leaked out then those Covenanters and Parliamentarians who were still unsure as to the legitimacy and wisdom of an Anglo-Scottish military alliance would be driven straight into the arms of the Saye–Pym group and Argyll's party. Hamilton was a friend of Antrim, but mindful of the earl's unpopularity with Argyll and the Covenanters, he had washed his hands of him from the autumn of 1642. Unfortunately for Hamilton, his royal master showed no such tact.

War and Peace at Oxford

It was not just Parliamentarians and Covenanters who were alarmed by Charles's treating with the Confederates. The court at Oxford contained a number of influential figures who were worried by this trend, in particular a group of the king's leading advisers associated with the Marquess of Hertford, Sir John Culpeper, and the chancellor of the exchequer, Sir Edward Hyde. The commitment of these so-called 'Constitutional Royalists' to the king's cause was tempered by their reverence for the established government and laws of England in church and state. Their preference, like that of the Northumberland–Holles interest at Westminster, was for a swift, negotiated settlement. A total victory by either side, especially if it was gained using Irish, Scottish, or other foreign troops, threatened the subversion of English honour and forms of government. Competing with the Hertford–Hyde group for the king's ear were less fastidious Royalists, however, for whom the prime objective was to win the war outright by whatever means available. The queen and George Lord Digby, who many saw as Charles's evil genius, fell conspicuously within this category, as did most of the leading Catholics and Catholic sympathisers at court.

Some of the Hertford–Hyde group had tried to use the Oxford treaty as a platform for peace, but they had been frustrated by the lack of trust on both sides, and above all by the king's refusal to accept anything short of almost total capitulation by Parliament. Their ability to influence the king was further eroded by his dislike of taking advice through formal channels, such as his privy council. Instead, he preferred to formulate policy by informal discussions with favoured advisers, around whom small cabals of politicians then formed. This situation would not have been so bad if the king's counsellors had been united among themselves, but they were deeply divided along personal as well as political lines. The most corrosive of these rivalries was that between Digby and Rupert. In policy terms the two men were very close – both preferring outright victory to a negotiated settlement. But Rupert and his clique of professional soldiers, the 'swordsmen', thought they alone were competent to run the war, and were contemptuous of civilian attempts to determine military policy. The queen's return in 1643 from her fund-raising mission on the Continent exacerbated these rivalries. Keen to make a party for herself at Oxford, she used her intimacy with Charles to advance her own favourites (Digby was made a secretary of state at her suggestion) – disrupting existing court networks and arousing new jealousies.

The emergence of factions at court hindered military operations at both strategic and field level. Ian Roy's work on the Royalist war-effort has revealed that the king's main field armies were about equal in hitting-power to Parliament's during the first two years of the war; and that in terms of command structure the Royalists enjoyed a distinct advantage.[26] Until the Saye–Pym grandees had won their political struggle to develop and strengthen the Parliamentarian war-machine, Parliament's military administration remained ramshackle and cumbersome. Yet the Royalists, despite possessing a unified command, failed to come up with any big ideas about how the war should be fought. There is certainly little evidence of the grand strategy – the two- or three-pronged attack on London – that many historians have discerned in Royalist military dispositions in 1643–4. The king's forces made significant gains across the Midlands and in the West Country during 1643, most notably in capturing Bristol – the second city of the realm, and a vital centre for the manufacture and import of arms. But in the long run the Royalist war-effort was vitiated by opportunism and lack of coordination – weaknesses that had their root in Charles's unwillingness or inability to quell the 'discomposures, jealousies, and disgusts' that raged among his courtiers and senior commanders.[27] In the words of Ian Roy:

> If he had chosen his counsellors wisely, listened judiciously, and acted firmly, he would have brought all the advantages he enjoyed – a centralised command based on his own authority, the advice of experienced generals – to fruition; and the outcome of the war would never have been in doubt. But his favourites were wayward; individually brilliant, they were incompatible as a group.[28]

Hamilton Eclipsed

Royal counsellors such as Hamilton and Hyde who saw the danger in treating with Irish Catholics were to have their misgivings confirmed by developments in Scotland over the summer. In order to limit the damage done by his mishandling of the Scottish delegation to Oxford, Charles addressed several open letters to the Scots assuring them that their religion and liberties were safe in his hands. Argyll's party responded by procuring votes in the Scottish executive for summoning a Convention of Estates, the unstated purpose of which would be to raise support for an Anglo-Scottish military alliance. This was a blow to Hamilton's party, and to the king, but the situation was still not entirely hopeless. The general feeling in Scotland was that the time for intervention had not quite arrived. But whatever chance Hamilton had of rallying this constituency in the convention was dashed late in May, when the Covenanters captured Antrim in Ulster and extracted details of his plot from one of his servants. Revelation of the Antrim plot made a mockery of Hamilton's assurances that the king could be trusted. As Baillie put it, the plot 'wakened in all a great fear of our safetie, and distrust of all the fair words that were or could be given us'.[29]

The convention assembled on 22 June, and although Hamilton commanded a majority among the nobility, the barons and burgesses lined up almost unanimously behind Argyll. Outvoted at every turn, Hamilton withdrew from the convention, leaving the king's party leaderless and in disarray. The way was now clear for Argyll and his supporters to prepare the ground for military intervention in England – the question was: could the Saye–Pym group impose its will in similar fashion upon the anti-alliance majority in the House of Lords?

Much of the blame for the king's failure to thwart Argyll's party has traditionally attached to Hamilton. Charles himself certainly blamed the duke and was to have him imprisoned in December 1643 on charges of treason, thereby completing the eclipse of the Hamiltonian interest that had begun in the winter of 1642–3. Yet it is difficult to see how Hamilton could have prevailed given the threatening situation in England and the king's own political miscalculations. Only Charles could have allayed the Covenanters' fears and bolstered the non-interventionist middle ground in Scotland; and his cavalier treatment of the Scottish commissioners in Oxford and sanctioning of the Antrim plot achieved precisely the opposite.

Parliament's Summer of Discontent

The Saye–Pym grandees, like Argyll's party, were able to make considerable capital out of Charles's dealings with the Irish, but they faced tougher domestic opposition than their Scottish allies. The collapse of the Oxford treaty between the king and Parliament, far from convincing the more peace-minded Parliamentarians of the necessity of a Scottish alliance, had heightened their resolve to prevent the Covenanters interfering in English affairs. Bringing in the Scots would simply encourage the king to import Irish or French troops to redress the balance, thus threatening to drag England into the carnage of the Thirty Years War on the Continent. No less worrying perhaps was the threat from below. The Covenanters' Confederalist demands would make it even harder to reach an accommodation, and the longer the fighting continued, the greater the risk that 'the necessitous people of the whole kingdom will presently rise in mighty numbers and ... set up for themselves to the utter ruin of all nobility and gentry'.[30]

Discontent at the failure of the peace process and the increasingly militant counsels at Westminster was particularly strong in London. Acting on a secret commission issued by the king in March, a group of conspirators, headed by the crypto-Royalist MP Edmund Waller, devised a plan for seizing the Tower and other metropolitan strongpoints as a prelude to a general rising by the king's supporters among the citizenry. The 'Waller plot' was discovered by the Committee of Safety late in May, however, and was used by the Saye–Pym group to discredit the advocates of peace in Parliament and the City. The fact that the conspirators targeted the Saye–Pym grandees (who were to be seized in their beds), and that the Earl of Northumberland was made privy to the design, suggests that the plot had been intended not to topple Parliament but to allow the Northumberland–Holles interest a free hand to conclude a soft peace with the king. In the wake of the plot, Pym was able to introduce the 'vow and covenant' – a new test of loyalty aimed largely at satisfying the Scots of Parliament's commitment to fighting popery. The convening of the Westminster Assembly a month later served a similar purpose: to convince the Covenanters that reformation in religion was high on Parliament's agenda.

Within a month of the Waller plot the Saye–Pym group was handed another propaganda coup when Argyll's party sent down the information extracted from Antrim's servant. Parliament had known for months about Charles's commissioning Ormond to treat with the Confederates, but the Antrim plot seemed to confirm Parliamentarians' worst fears about what such overtures really portended. 'This plot', wrote D'Ewes, 'did more work upon most men than anything that had happened during these miserable calamities and civil wars of England, because it seemed now that there was a fixed resolution in the popish party utterly to extirpate the true Protestant religion in England, Scotland, and Ireland.'[31] Hard on the heels of this news came a report that Parliament's northern forces under Sir Ferdinando (now Lord) Fairfax and his son Sir Thomas had suffered a crushing defeat by the Earl of Newcastle's 'popish' army at Adwalton Moor, near Bradford. Two weeks later Parliament learnt that its western army, commanded by Sir William Waller, had been utterly destroyed at the battle of Roundway Down, near Bath – a defeat that allowed the Royalists to consolidate their grip on Wales and the West Country (for battle sites, see Map 1). The Saye–Pym group exploited these various plots and defeats to push through orders for sending parliamentary commissioners to Scotland, despite much foot-dragging by the anti-alliance majority in the Lords. But whereas the Antrim plot had swept away opposition at Edinburgh to an alliance, the Waller plot failed to do the same at Westminster. Although the Northumberland–Holles grandees had apparently lost the battle in the Commons and the City, the deteriorating military situation allowed them to attack a third and vital source of power for the Saye–Pym group – the trust of the Earl of Essex.

Essex the Conqueror

Parliament's introduction of bold new fiscal measures in 1642–3 to fund the war-effort – assessments, sequestrations, the excise, etc. – was not matched by similar improvements in the supply and command structure, and the result was that Essex's army was periodically short of men and money. After taking Reading in April, his forces began to waste away through disease and desertion, and these losses were not made good. The army's weaknesses were cruelly exposed in a series of cavalry engagements on the approaches to Oxford in which Hampden was killed. The problem was not only one of infrastructure but also of Essex himself. Although he could inspire dogged loyalty in his troops, he possessed neither the strategic insight nor the tactical flair to inflict any serious damage on the Royalists. Essex's shortcomings led to unfavourable comparisons being made between his own performance and that of more decisive generals. Sir William Waller's daring martial exploits earned him the nickname 'William the Conqueror', and it was with some justice that he and his London supporters blamed the defeat at Roundway Down on Essex's failure to prevent the king sending reinforcements from Oxford into the West Country.

Essex's inability to deal the king a decisive blow made him the butt of criticism and mockery in London. Under pressure from the City militants and the fiery spirits at Westminster, the Saye–Pym group rebuked Essex in mid-June for his dilatory generalship. This criticism, and Parliament's failure to keep his army well supplied, angered Essex so much that he offered to resign his command. The deterioration in Essex's relations with the Saye–Pym group became abundantly clear on 8 July, when he wrote to Parliament suggesting that in light of his own army's weaknesses the two Houses should sue for peace. When this letter was read out in the Commons some of the fiery spirits were observed to 'pluck their hats over their eyes' in frustration.[32]

Essex's 'cold affections' encouraged the City and Commons militants to press ahead with a scheme for channelling London's resources into a new army under Waller that would fight wholeheartedly for victory. Anxious not to offend the City, the Saye–Pym group supported this initiative, but at the cost of further alienating Essex, who saw Waller's 'independent' army as an affront to his honour and authority. The Earl of Manchester's appointment to head up another new command – the Eastern Association Army – for preserving Lincolnshire and East Anglia against Newcastle's forces was also badly taken by Essex.

What Essex lacked as a general, however, he made up for as a politician. After Roundway Down, and until the recruitment of Waller's and Manchester's forces, Essex commanded Parliament's only sizeable field army in southern England. He could effectively hold Parliament to ransom – a temptation that in light of his beleaguered position was to prove irresistible. 'Abused in Pictures, censured in Pulpits, dishonoured in the table-talke of the common people',[33] and generally neglected by his supposed friends at Westminster, he began to lend a favourable ear to the Northumberland–Holles grandees, who were keen to detach him from the Saye–Pym group and to use his army to force Parliament into accepting a soft, exclusively English settlement before it could conclude an alliance with the Covenanters. As part of a deal worked out between the new allies, Essex sent propositions to Parliament late in July demanding legislation to strengthen his army and to re-establish his authority as commander-in-chief. The Lords promptly agreed to every one of his demands, as indeed did the Commons, where Pym and his friends hoped that by gratifying Essex they could prevent him forcing a sell-out peace. Seemingly assured of Essex's support, Northumberland and his allies in the Lords drew up the softest of peace terms, allegedly in concert with a faction at Oxford opposed to Prince Rupert and the swordsmen. The plan was that if the Commons failed to accept these terms then the Northumberland–Holles grandees would use Essex's army either to force the lower House's compliance or simply to make their own treaty with Oxford.

When the terms were sent down to the Commons on 5 August, they received the backing not only of Holles's interest but also of Essex's officers. To counter this powerful new alliance, the Saye–Pym grandees and their friends in the City resorted to strong-arm tactics. Lord Mayor Pennington and the Common Council petitioned against the Lords' terms as 'destructive to our Religion, Lawes, and Liberties';[34] and a citizen mob of '5 or 6000 of the usual hacksters, which had beene alwayes ready for such purposes at a minutes warning', surged around Westminster threatening the supporters of peace in both Houses.[35] The Commons duly rejected the proposed treaty, citing among its reasons the fact that Parliament had agreed not to conclude a peace without the consent of the Scots. The Northumberland–Holles group responded by drumming up several thousand women demonstrators, who virtually laid siege to the Commons, shouting threats against Saye and Pym and demanding 'peace presently and our king', before being dispersed by troops loyal to the City militants.

After this clear demonstration that the Saye–Pym group still controlled London, Essex decided to distance himself from the Northumberland–Holles interest. He had achieved all he could reasonably have hoped for – his authority had been confirmed, and he had ensured that his army would have first claim upon the resources of the City and the support of the dominant party at Westminster. Abandoned by Essex, the peace peers fled London – lords Bedford, Clare, Conway, Holland, and Portland quickly making their way to Oxford; Northumberland and Pembroke withdrawing and waiting to see how their colleagues would be received there before deciding whether to follow them. Many pacific MPs likewise abandoned their seats, handing undisputed control of both Houses to the Saye–Pym group.

Essex's renewed partnership with the Saye–Pym grandees quickly bore fruit. With the help of the City militia, the lord general relieved Gloucester early in September, fought the king's army to an honourable draw at the battle of Newbury, and then returned in triumph to London. The Royalists' decision to besiege Gloucester had been a major blunder. After Roundway Down and Adwalton Moor, there had been little to prevent the king's Oxford, western, and northern forces converging on London. In that eventuality, the Royalists alone, or in concert with the Northumberland–Holles interest, might have been able to force a Parliamentarian climb-down. But the opportunity was missed, and Essex's Gloucester campaign underlined Parliament's military re-vitalisation. Moreover, the Royalists now faced the prospect of fighting not just Essex's army, but also Waller's and Manchester's new commands, and above all, a Covenanter invasion force.

Covenant and Cessation

Parliament's commissioners for negotiating a treaty with the Covenanters arrived at Edinburgh on 7 August. Most of the talking on the English side was done by the Saye–Pym grandee Sir Henry Vane junior, who had instructions to secure Scottish military assistance without paying the Scots' full asking price – namely, a covenanted uniformity in religion. Most Parliament-men accepted that the English church should be brought closer into line with that of Scotland. What they did not accept was the Scots' insistence that their Presbyterian church discipline was divinely warranted and therefore the only proper model for further reformation in England. It was not so much Presbyterianism itself that the English objected to, as the fact that the Scottish church claimed an authority independent of the state. But the two sides' eagerness to forge an alliance, and the long-standing contacts between the Saye–Pym group and Argyll's party, made for swift negotiations, and by mid-August a draft had been agreed of a solemn [i.e. sacred] league and covenant. Vane had ensured that the wording of this draft did not commit England to any specific form of church government, and subsequent amendments by the Commons and the Westminster Assembly fudged this issue still further.

This new Covenant bound its subscribers to preserve the Scottish church, to reform those of England and Ireland, and to bring all three 'to the nearest conjunction and uniformity in religion'. Further clauses enjoined the extirpation of Catholicism and episcopacy, and the preservation of the king's person and authority so far as they were consistent with maintaining 'the true religion' and the liberties of the kingdoms.[36] Like the Scottish National Covenant, which it superseded, the Solemn League and Covenant proclaimed the interdependence of the crown and British Presbyterianism. Any attack on the one was inherently an attack on the other. In 1643 the Covenanters still regarded Charles as the greatest threat to their imperial church vision. Within little over a year, however, they would begin to perceive a threat to both crown and church from a new quarter, the English Independents.

Under the terms of the treaty accompanying the Covenant, the Scots agreed to send an army into England under the command of Alexander Leslie (now Earl of Leven), and the English Parliament pledged to contribute £30,000 a month towards its maintenance. The Scots realised that the vagueness of the Covenant had left a door open in England to an erastian church settlement, but they were confident that Leven's army would defeat the king in such short order that Parliament would be in no position to deny them anything.

The absence of the peace lords and many of their allies in the Commons made the Saye–Pym grandees' task of securing acceptance of the Covenant much easier. But the most important factor in overcoming resistance to the Covenant both in London and in Edinburgh was the continuing fear of inundation by papists. Newcastle's army was making inroads in the Midlands, and by September it was common knowledge that the king was engaged in treating with the Irish Confederates. Charles had indeed sent letters to Ormond urging him to conclude a cessation with the Confederates. A truce in Ireland would enable the king to siphon off Protestant troops for service in England; it might also, he hoped, frustrate a Scottish invasion. Charles was convinced that the Covenanters could not raise an army under Leven without recalling Monro's New Scots. A cessation, by allowing the Confederates to pin down Monro's forces in Ulster, would thus foil the Covenanters' invasion plans.

The Confederates were indeed eager to concentrate their resources against the New Scots, who represented the greatest challenge to their domination of Ireland. But above all they hoped that a cessation would create a favourable climate for negotiating a long-term settlement with the king. On the Protestant side, there were strong economic inducements for calling a truce. The harvest of 1643 had proved disastrous, and trade with England had been disrupted by the Civil War. The cessation was signed on 15 September and was renewed annually until 1646.

The Covenant and cessation were perhaps inevitable responses to the breakdown of unitary authority in a multiple monarchy. They reflected the king's tendency, when threatened in Britain, to turn to Ireland for support; and that of his English and Scottish opponents, when threatened at home or from Ireland, to turn to each other. But there was a more personal dimension to the origins of the Covenant and cessation, and that was the fear and loathing that the *coup d'état* of 1640 had generated between the belligerents, particularly in England. Neither Charles nor the Saye–Pym group would trust the other to observe the terms of a negotiated settlement, and yet neither was strong enough to secure outright victory. The resort to 'foreign' arms was the only logical alternative.

Chapter 3: The Wars of the Three Kingdoms: September 1643–August 1645

Covenant and Cessation: the Reaction at Westminster

The cessation and the Covenant helped to transform what had been a number of largely discrete, if causally interlinked, conflicts, into something not far short of a single archipelagic war. The king received his first shipment of troops from Ireland in October 1643; a Covenanter army under Leven entered northern England in January 1644; and six months later a party of 'Scotch Irish' embarked from Ireland for the western Highlands and a blood-soaked campaign that its leader, the Marquess of Montrose, hoped would topple all of Scotland into the king's hands. In time these developments would change the face of the English Civil War. But it was at Westminster that the cessation and, more especially, the Covenant had their most immediate impact.

Between them, the Covenant and cessation broke and recast the political mould at Westminster. To the Northumberland–Holles grandees, the intervention of the Scots portended the utter ruin of England, and several of them contemplated going into exile rather than witness the spectacle. Yet for others, the actions of the king and his advisers represented an even more alarming prospect. The defection of the Earl of Holland and the other peace peers in August had presented the court with the perfect opportunity to put on a statesmanlike show of magnanimity and moderation. But instead of welcoming the peers as lost sheep returned to the fold, Charles and his courtiers had either cold-shouldered or openly reviled them, obliging those such as the earls of Northumberland and Pembroke who had been contemplating going

68

to Oxford, to reconsider. Then came news of the king's cessation with the Confederates' Catholics, which to some of the peace grandees had even more dreadful implications than Parliament's Scottish alliance – the Scots were at least Protestants – and ruled out any prospect of a negotiated settlement. With Northumberland himself among their number, they threw in their lot with Saye and the man who replaced the ailing John Pym (who died that December) as the perceived leader of the pro-Scots interest in the Commons, Oliver St John.

Travelling in the opposite direction that autumn were several groups that had been closely aligned with the Saye–Pym interest, notably Essex and his staff officers. Essex's victories at Gloucester and Newbury had raised his stock to its old height, giving him the authority and confidence to revive the scheme he had toyed with in the summer – that is, of using his army to broker a moderate peace. The main threat to his plans was the imminent arrival of the Scots. Essex disliked the Scots' religious demands as much as any man at Westminster. Moreover, once the Scots had entered the war, he would no longer command Parliament's largest field army, nor, in consequence, the clout to impose a settlement. The goal of a moderate, and exclusively English, settlement was of course shared by Holles and other stalwarts of the peace interest, and during the autumn the two groups – Essex's and Holles's – rapidly converged in common opposition to the Saye–St John faction and the Scots. Joining the Essex–Holles interest were Sir John Clotworthy and other Anglo-Irish MPs, angered that the supporters of the Scottish alliance had conceded supreme command of the British forces in Ireland to the Scots. It was here in reaction to the Covenant and cessation – not, as is generally assumed, in the reversal of alliances that was to occur a year later – that the future leaderships of the Independent and Presbyterian factions coalesced.

The new factions differed in important respects from their prior incarnations. Whereas most of the more peace-minded members had formerly questioned all military expenditure, they now tended to support the upkeep of Essex's army as the best means to 'command a peace' against the war-mongers at Westminster or Oxford. On the other hand, the heirs of the Saye–Pym group, having supported Essex's army in the past, were now eager to join the City militants in clipping its wings. Distrusting its ambitious yet irenic commander, they preferred to re-direct Parliament's resources to the armies of Waller, Manchester, and above all the Scots, which would fight for outright victory. But both factions remained small, bicameral groups with an uncertain following among the mass of non-aligned members. Like the old Northumberland–Holles interest, the

Essex–Holles faction usually enjoyed the backing of the more pacific members and those who were especially squeamish about overriding the ancient constitution to advance the war-effort; while the Saye–St John group, like its predecessor, was able to rally those MPs who feared the consequences of a Royalist victory more than the destabilising effects of the war itself. The voting strength of each faction varied according to the issue under consideration, but in many areas of policy the Saye–St John group had the edge over its rivals.

The Committee of Both Kingdoms

The re-drawn battle-lines at Westminster hardened late in 1643 with heated debates over the Earl of Holland, who had returned to Parliament in disgust at his treatment at Oxford. The Essex–Holles group battled to have Holland re-admitted to the Lords; the Saye–St John interest, to keep him out. But the starkest confirmation of the new factional alignment came early in 1644 with the struggle to set up the Committee for Both Kingdoms – the first, indeed only, Anglo-Scottish executive body of the Civil War period. The committee was justified by its authors – the Saye– St John grandees and the Scots commissioners at Westminster – on military grounds. With the Scots' entry into the war, a joint executive to coordinate the two nations' forces was clearly necessary; and there was also the problem of Parliament's own disjointed commands to consider. Factional rivalry at Westminster had resulted in a fractured command structure, and some form of central executive was urgently needed to gather the reins of military authority.

Exploiting the very real need for greater strategic coordination, the Scots and their allies pursued what was perhaps their main objective in setting up the committee – to thwart Essex's military and political ambitions. Despite protests from Essex's friends, the new body was given large powers not only to manage the war but also to draw up terms for peace – policy areas in which the lord general claimed a special interest. Essex's enemies also ensured that the committee's membership was weighted in their own favour. Subsequent attempts by the Essex–Holles grandees to undermine or limit the committee's authority were all frustrated. When they tried to revive the peace process in the spring of 1644, for example, the Saye–St John group succeeded in turning the issue over to the committee, where the Scots had drawn up such terms as they hoped to obtain 'in the end'. An immediate peace was out of the question. Scottish intervention had put the Saye–St John group in the driving seat at Westminster – a situation that would remain largely unchanged until the autumn.

The Oxford Parliament

Parliament's Scottish alliance presented the Royalists with their greatest propaganda opportunity of the war. If even Parliamentarians thought bringing in the Scots a slight to national honour, then Royalists were outraged at yet another invasion by 'the Authors of soe much mischiefe and miserie to this Kingdome'.[1] The Covenant may not have swelled the ranks of the king's party, but it probably consolidated popular support for the Royalists in the areas they already held – particularly the northern counties, where the common people 'abhorred to hear of the coming in of the Scots'.[2] But Royalist polemicists were prevented from playing the anti-Scots card to full effect by reason of the king's own Scottish background. Besides which, no amount of propaganda point-scoring could have made up for the advantage that Parliament derived from a powerful Covenanter army.

The reaction among Royalists to the cessation was mixed. According to Parliamentarian propagandists it provoked a wave of desertions from the king's party. But though the cessation may have alienated some lukewarm Royalists, there is no evidence of any serious haemorrhaging of support for the king. Rather than weaken the Royalists in their convictions, the cessation's main effect was to strengthen the Parliamentarians in theirs. Most Royalists apparently had no major problem with Charles using English soldiers who had fought in Ireland against the Confederates. However, it was generally believed that the deployment of such troops would lead in time to the bringing over of native Irish soldiers, and indeed by November 1643 Charles had approved just such a policy. Enlisting the help of foreign troops, especially Irish Catholics, was a different matter altogether, and upset a good many Royalists. In court circles, the strongest opposition to the king's Irish policy came from the Hertford–Hyde group. Although court politics present a very confusing picture by 1644, with personal rivalries often obscuring wider political divisions, there are signs that the strategy of seeking a military alliance with the Irish increased the tension between those courtiers who favoured a negotiated settlement and hard-liners such as lords Digby and Jermyn, who were quite happy to enlist Catholic support.

The role of Catholics – English as well as Irish – in the Royalist war-effort was one of the issues raised when the Oxford Parliament assembled in January 1644. This convention of Royalist MPs and peers had been summoned by Charles in the hope that it would vote taxes to help repel the Scottish invaders. Instead, the first day's debate almost ended in fighting between some of the queen's circle and those MPs uneasy at the Irish cessation and opposed to the employment of papists in the royal armies. Like their former colleagues at Westminster, many members of the Oxford Parliament were desperate to head off any foreign military intervention by reaching a swift, negotiated settlement.

The king's efforts to steer the Oxford Parliament away from thoughts of peace and onto raising money for his armies received a major boost from Westminster. The Scots' hostility to negotiating with the king before Leven's army had won them a controlling influence in English affairs meant that the Oxford Parliament's peace overtures got short shrift at Westminster. The Scots commissioners and their allies responded by sending a copy of the Covenant to Oxford along with several declarations 'inspired with the Scotch dialect and spirit'.[3] As Parliamentarian moderates had feared, the intervention of the Scots had raised a major barrier to a negotiated settlement. Its olive branch flung back in its face, the Oxford Parliament voted to raise more troops and introduced a levy of £100,000 and an excise tax to help pay for them.

Where the cessation really damaged Charles was not at Oxford but at Westminster, by creating a majority in favour of a Scottish alliance. The corresponding military benefit to the Royalist cause was less than the king had anticipated. Between October 1643 and April 1644 between 6000 and 10,000 Protestant troops were shipped over piecemeal from Ireland to ports up and down the west coast, where they were absorbed into existing Royalist armies. With them they brought plenty of combat experience, but also the brutality of the war in Ireland, in which the ill-treatment of civilians and prisoners was commonplace. Moreover, some of these soldiers deserted to Parliament. Troops from Ireland helped the Royalists to slow the Scots' advance into England, and to retain control in the Welsh borders and the south-west for longer than would otherwise have been possible. But such a dispersed and unreliable force was never able to offset the advantage that Leven's Scottish army gave to Parliament.

Marston Moor and Lostwithiel

Leven's army marched into England early in 1644. Over 20,000 strong, it was the largest single body of troops anywhere in the archipelago during the 1640s. A greater proportion of Scottish men, relative to the size of Scotland's population, fought in the wars of the three kingdoms than of any other nation – testament once more to the galvanising power of the Covenant. The entry of the Scots tipped the balance of military power in northern England decisively in Parliament's favour. By April 1644, Leven's army had overrun most of Northumberland and County Durham, pushing the Marquess of Newcastle's Royalist forces back into Yorkshire. While Newcastle's attention was turned northwards to the Scots, the Yorkshire cavalry commander Sir Thomas Fairfax had slipped into Cheshire in January and joined Sir William Brereton in defeating a Royalist army at the battle of Nantwich. He had then moved back across the Pennines and in April routed the Cavaliers at Selby in south Yorkshire. This defeat obliged Newcastle to fall back rapidly on York, with Leven's army hot on his heels.

Newcastle's inability to contain the Fairfaxes, as he had in 1643, was due not only to the Scots' drive southwards, but also to the northward advance through Lincolnshire of the newly raised Eastern Association army under the Earl of Manchester and his hard-fighting lieutenant-general of horse, Oliver Cromwell. A brilliant victory by Prince Rupert at Newark in March 1644 had wiped out some of Manchester's gains of the previous autumn, but he quickly succeeded in retaking all of Lincolnshire, and by June had joined the Fairfaxes and the Scots at the siege of York. Alarmed by the imminent loss of the north, the king agreed to let Rupert leave Oxford in May to relieve York. Rupert advanced north-wards through the Welsh marches, and after leisurely terrorising the Parliamentarians of Cheshire and Lancashire, crossed the Pennines with a large body of horse and foot. He descended on York late in June, forced the Parliamentarians to lift their siege, and on 2 July he and Newcastle brought the three Parliamentarian armies of Leven, Manchester and the Fairfaxes to battle at Marston Moor. The Royalists made up for their numerical inferiority – 20,000 to the Parliamentarians' 28,000 – by sweeping a large part of their opponents' horse and foot from the field. However, by nightfall the Royalist cavalry was scattered across a wide area, leaving the Parliamentarian horse, under Oliver Cromwell, Sir Thomas Fairfax, and the Scottish commander David Leslie, to destroy the unpro-tected Royalist infantry. It was the biggest battle of the English Civil War, and the bloodiest. The Parliamentarians lost about 2000 men, the Royalists twice that number. Even so, with Manchester's army recalled to the Eastern Association soon after the battle, the Royalists still had enough troops to pose serious problems for the remaining Parliamentarian forces. But in the immediate aftermath of defeat the situation seemed hopeless. Newcastle and Rupert hurriedly departed the region (Newcastle taking ship for the Continent), and by the end of November the entire north of England, saving a few Royalist strongholds, had fallen to the Scots and the Fairfaxes.

In the south of England, the first honours of the new campaigning season also went to Parliament. Sir William Waller, commanding the forces of Parliament's newly formed Southern Association, defeated Sir Ralph Hopton's Royalist army at Cheriton, near Winchester, late in March, and by mid-May, when Essex's army left its winter quarters, the king's situation looked desperate. He was without Rupert's cavalry brigade, which had gone north to relieve York, and was apparently unwilling to divert his western army under Prince Maurice from its siege of the strategically unimportant fishing port of Lyme Regis, in Dorset. With only 13,000 troops at his disposal, the king was powerless to prevent Essex and Waller, with their combined strength of 20,000 men, from virtually encircling Oxford. He responded in true Rupertian fashion, however, making a feint to the south and then slipping westwards between the two Parliamentarian armies to Worcester.

With the campaign in the south poised in Parliament's favour, the political and personal rivalries that had convulsed Westminster over the winter intruded upon its management of the war, with predictably disastrous results. Essex still resented having to share military resources and honours with Waller, and he now had to watch while the Saye–St John group diverted yet more of Parliament's funds to the Scots. To make matters worse, he was obliged to take orders from the Committee of Both Kingdoms, which was dominated by his enemies. When the king's retreat northwards (which lifted the threat to London) presented him with the chance to re-assert his authority, therefore, he seized it with both hands. On the advice of the Westerners on his staff, he ordered Waller to pursue the king, and resolved to march his own army towards Devon. The plan was simple – Waller would be tied up chasing the king about the Midlands, leaving Essex free to invade his rival's military sphere in the West Country. Moreover, the recovery of the west would greatly enhance Essex's prestige, and perhaps allow him to broker a compromise peace with minimum reference to the wishes of the Scots and their friends. There was even the prospect of sending a large seaborne expedition to assist the Protestants in southern Ireland.

Dismayed at this division of their forces and the consequent relaxing of military pressure on the king, the Committee of Both Kingdoms supported Waller as best it could, and attempted to recall Parliament's errant lord general. But Essex was deaf to all commands, and by mid-June was advancing determinedly through Dorset towards Devon. In the meantime, Charles led Waller a merry dance through the south Midlands, and then defeated him late in June at Cropredy Bridge in Oxfordshire. News of Marston Moor made it pointless for the king to head northwards, and so with Waller neutralised he decided to follow Essex into the west. Essex demanded that the Committee of Both Kingdoms send Waller to impede the king's progress, but Waller's army was disintegrating through lack of pay, and the Commons radicals frustrated efforts to despatch him westwards. Essex made his final miscalculation late in July by advancing into Cornwall – the most Royalist county in England – where his troops were quickly cut off by the king's army and harassed by the local people. The whole fiasco ended on 2 September with the surrender of the Parliamentarian foot at Lostwithiel – Essex himself having already fled Cornwall by boat. It was a humiliating defeat for the lord general, and would have major repercussions at Westminster. For their part, the Royalists drew heart from this victory, but in strategic terms it failed to make up for the loss of northern England.

The Cessation and Covenant in Protestant Ireland

The cessation and the Covenant worked upon Ireland's Protestant community in much the same way they did upon the English Parliamentarians – exacerbating divisions and strengthening Scottish and pro-Scottish interests. Ormond's negotiations with the Confederates during 1643 had rendered him suspect in the eyes of the New Scots, and the signing of the cessation in September destroyed the uneasy alliance between them. Similarly, the Covenant – which Irish Royalists saw as merely a pretext for rebellion – heightened Ormond's distrust of the New Scots. Hostility between the two camps would have mattered little if Monro's army had been withdrawn for service in England, as the architects of the Anglo-Scottish alliance had initially envisaged; but the cessation persuaded the Parliamentarians and Covenanters of the need to keep the New Scots in Ulster. With most British commanders in Ireland willing to observe the cessation (initially at least), the New Scots were the only force in that kingdom committed to keeping the military pressure on the Confederates. In November 1643, therefore, the Parliamentarians signed a treaty with the Covenanters agreeing to help maintain Monro's army, and making him commander, under Leven, of all the British forces in Ireland.

The cessation and Covenant also strained relations between the New Scots and their British allies in Ulster. Rather than declare against the king, which was what taking the Covenant amounted to, British commanders hoped that by negotiating with Charles they could safeguard Protestant interests in the event of a peace settlement in Ireland. Their resentment that overall command of the British forces in Ireland had been given to Monro and not to someone of English extraction made them doubly reluctant to help the New Scots destroy the cessation. Yet the cessation quickly rendered their situation desperate. It forbade them to plunder the Irish, and yet the money and supplies that the Irish were obligated to provide in return were not forthcoming. Material hardship, coupled with the strength of anti-Catholic feeling among grass-roots Protestants, made observance of the cessation by the British commanders difficult to sustain. Most of the rank-and-file British soldiers were opposed to any kind of truce with papists, and were willing to defy their commanders and take the Covenant – if only to continue what little succour they received from Edinburgh and London. By acquiescing in the cessation, therefore, British commanders ran the threefold risk of alienating their men, being attacked by Monro's army, and jeopardising their supply-lines.

Inchiquin faced a similar predicament in Munster. He had signed the cessation in the hope that it would provide some respite for his beleaguered garrisons, regarding it as a temporary expedient until the king could re-assert the Protestant ascendancy in Ireland. But like the British in Ulster he quickly found that his troops were worse off as a result of the cessation. His disenchantment with royal policies increased in February 1644, when the king, anxious not to offend the Confederates, appointed a young courtier as lord president of Munster. Inchiquin had long coveted this office, and having gone to Oxford in anticipation that it would finally be granted him, returned to Munster 'as full of anger as his buttons will endure'.[4] Without the authority conferred by the presidency it became even harder for him to hold together his forces. From the winter of 1643–4, therefore, pressure mounted on Protestant commanders in the north and south of Ireland to resume the war against the Confederates. Only in Leinster under Ormond did the Protestant commitment to the cessation hold firm.

The king's willingness to entertain Confederate demands did much to undermine any lingering support for the cessation among the majority of

Irish Protestants. In March 1644 a Confederate delegation arrived at Oxford to put their case directly to the king – presenting him with the ideal opportunity to conclude a treaty with Kilkenny. The Confederates' terms were relatively moderate compared with some of their subsequent demands, yet Charles was doubtless aware that conceding any ground to the Irish would raise a storm of protest even in his own court. He there-fore passed the poisoned chalice back to Ormond, issuing him with a new commission to negotiate with the Confederates in Ireland – away from reproachful English eyes. Nevertheless, the mere fact that Charles was willing to receive the Confederates was enough to make many Protestants doubt his commitment to defending their interests. Determined not to allow the Confederates a free run at Oxford, the Protestants of Connacht and west Ulster (who had more or less renounced the cessation by this stage) sent over their own delegation, urging Charles to make peace in England in order to pursue total victory against the rebels in Ireland.

The summer of 1644 saw many Protestant commanders fall away from Ormond and the king, among them Inchiquin. In July he wrote to the king arguing that there could be no peace with the Irish 'which will not bring unto your Majestie and the English in generall, a farre greater prej-udice then the shew of a peace here will bring us an advantage'.[5] In his view, the Irish were the king's worst enemies, and if they were to be crushed then Charles must reach a settlement with Parliament. The promise of 'large supplies' from Parliament, and the opportunity to resume raiding expeditions against the Irish, also weighed heavily with him. He calculated that the tide of military events – the Parliamentarian victory at Marston Moor, and Essex's seemingly imminent conquest of the West Country – would leave Parliament and the Covenanters better placed to fund the Protestant war-effort than Ormond and the king.

The overall effect of the cessation and Covenant was to widen the rift that the English Civil War had opened among Ireland's Protestants. On the one side stood the Irish Royalists – Ormond's supporters in and around the Pale, who accepted the need for peace with the Confederates in order to advance a Royalist victory in England. And on the other stood what might be termed the Irish covenanting interest, which desired peace in England in order to advance a Protestant victory in Ireland. In favouring a negotiated settlement in England and all-out war in Ireland, the grandees of the covenanting interest were on the same wavelength as a strong body of opinion at Westminster, and by the summer of 1644 had come to accept that only by aligning with Parliament and the New Scots would they receive sufficient supplies to resist the Confederates. Their

hand had been forced to some extent, however, by the strength of
support for the Covenant among the Protestant community generally,
and, in the case of the British commanders in Ulster, by Monro's seizure
of Belfast and other garrisons from pro-Ormond regiments in the spring
of 1644. Monro consolidated his command of the British forces in the
north by mounting a successful summer campaign against the
Confederates in Ulster.

Confederate Campaigns, 1644

The majority of Confederates supported the cessation, and in the short
run it worked to their advantage – dividing their enemies and allowing
the withdrawal of Protestant troops to England. In the long term it may
have proved their undoing, however, for instead of conquering all or most
of Ireland when opportunity presented (as it apparently did by late 1643)
they became bogged down in complicated and largely fruitless talks with
Ormond and the king. As a result, the cessation also served to deepen
political divisions among the Confederates. While the leaders of the
Confederate peace faction (who dominated the Irish side of the negotiations) developed a cosy relationship with Ormond, the king's failure to
follow up the cessation with significant concessions to Irish Catholics led
to growing dissatisfaction in Confederate ranks, particularly among the
clergy. As the king's fortunes waned in England from 1644, a faction
would emerge at Kilkenny that questioned the wisdom of putting negotiations with the Royalists before a policy of all-out conquest of Ireland.

Political and personal rivalries frustrated the Confederate war-effort
in 1644, much as they did the English Parliament's Oxford campaign. The
cessation freed the Confederates to deploy their armies against Monro –
the question was, who should command this campaign? The best candi-
date on purely military grounds was the Confederate general in Ulster,
Owen Roe O'Neill. However, Thomas Preston – O'Neill's rival – would not
place himself or his Leinster regiments under O'Neill's command.
Consequently, the Association decided to raise additional troops under
a compromise commander, the Earl of Castlehaven, with O'Neill's and
Preston's armies in a supporting role. The problems with this arrange-
ment were numerous. Both Preston and O'Neill were offended.
Castlehaven lacked military experience and could see little merit in the
campaign. And as a leading Ormondist he was distrusted by O'Neill and
his Ulstermen.

Mistrust and jealousy between the three Confederate generals prevented them from concentrating their forces effectively against Monro. Their advance into Ulster in July was tentative and poorly coordinated, prompting a vigorous Protestant counter-attack. Castlehaven withdrew to Charlemont in mid-Ulster, where the opposing armies remained entrenched until the autumn, when the Confederates retreated. By failing to bring Monro to battle the Confederates had squandered an excellent opportunity to exploit their superiority in men and resources. Had they won a major victory against the New Scots it would have shifted the military balance in Ireland in their own and, ultimately perhaps, the king's favour. But not for the last time, political tensions within the Association had frustrated its military ambitions.

The one redeeming feature of the Confederates' 1644 campaign season was the despatch of a MacDonnell–MacDonald expeditionary force to assist the Covenanters' enemies in Scotland. This scheme, like its predecessors, originated in the fertile mind of the Earl of Antrim. In October 1643, Antrim had escaped from the Covenanters' custody and had made his way, via Kilkenny, to Oxford. With a Covenanter invasion looming, Charles was interested in Antrim's plan – which included shipping 10,000 Confederate soldiers to England – but doubted its author could make good his promises. He therefore incorporated Antrim's proposals into a wider scheme for a series of coordinated anti-Covenanter risings in the Highlands, and an invasion of south-west Scotland by English and Scottish Royalists under Montrose. His hope was that Antrim and Montrose could kindle such a fire in Scotland as would consume both Leven's and Monro's armies, thereby lifting the threat of a Covenanter invasion of England, and freeing the Confederates to send over troops to fight the Parliamentarians.

Back at Kilkenny, Antrim failed to persuade the Confederates to raise troops for service in England. These men would be needed for the campaign against Monro, and the Confederates were reluctant to intervene in the English Civil War before securing major concessions from the king. But they did agree to supply Antrim's Scottish expedition, seeing it as a way of drawing Monro's regiments back to Scotland in defence of their homeland, while Castlehaven's army applied pressure from the Ulster end.

After many delays due to lack of money and ships, Antrim's expedition embarked from southern Ireland in June 1644. It consisted of about 2000 men, mostly battle-hardened Ulster and Scottish Gaels, under the command of Antrim's kinsman Alasdair MacColla. On landing in

Scotland, MacColla's men marched to join Montrose, ravaging the lands of the Campbells as they went. The victories obtained by Montrose and MacColla over the next twelve months not only weakened the Anglo-Scottish alliance; they very nearly destroyed the Covenanter regime itself.

Montrose's Year of Victories

Scotland alone of the three kingdoms was still free of war in late 1643. In the short term certainly, the Covenant and cessation did not have the same divisive impact there that they had in Ireland. Argyll's party used the Covenant as a test to weed out opposition, while fears of an Irish invasion in the wake of the cessation pushed many waverers into the Covenanters' camp. Hamilton's departure to Oxford in November 1643, after he and several of his aristocratic allies had been declared enemies to religion for refusing to take the Covenant, was a great fillip to Argyll's party. The king completed Hamilton's downfall by having him imprisoned in December 1643 on trumped up charges of treason brought by Montrose and the Scottish Royalists at court. Charles felt that Hamilton had betrayed him by failing to prevent a Covenanter invasion. The king's unjust treatment of Hamilton persuaded his brother the Earl of Lanark, and many other moderate Royalists in Scotland, to cooperate with the radical mainstream in sending help to the English Parliamentarians.

In military terms, however, the cessation and the Covenant left the regime at Edinburgh in a vulnerable position. The cessation allowed the Irish Confederates to equip Antrim's expedition; while the Covenant committed the Scots to stripping their own country of resources in order to assist the English Parliamentarians. It was anticipated at Edinburgh that Leven would quickly win the English Civil War for Parliament and then return home to secure Scotland. In the event, however, Leven's army remained in England for three years, and in its absence the Covenanters often had to rely on raw, Lowland levies who proved no match for MacColla's Gaelic warriors.

It was no coincidence that the first major anti-Covenanter rising in Scotland occurred within a few weeks of Leven's army entering England. Encouraged by letters from the king and hopes of support from Montrose, the Royalists of north-eastern Scotland, led by the Marquess of Huntly, seized Aberdeen in March. A month later Montrose and a small party of Scottish horse crossed into Scotland from Cumberland. Their plan was to raise south-west Scotland for the king and then to link up with

Antrim's men from Ireland and Huntly's in the north-east. But Antrim's force was not yet ready to sail, and Montrose met with such a poor response in Scotland that he was soon forced to withdraw. This left the Covenanters free to concentrate on crushing Huntly's rising, which they did early in May. It seemed that the king's strategy for bringing Leven's army to battle on Scottish rather than English soil had failed miserably.

The Covenanters still had to contend with MacColla's force, however, which Montrose took charge of in the southern Highlands in August 1644. Montrose's presence lent the expedition a degree of respectability. He was a Scottish nobleman, a Protestant, and possessed a royal commission. But MacColla's men were so loathed by most Scottish Protestants, who associated them with Catholic atrocities in Ireland, that Montrose was never able to tap more than a fraction of Royalist support in Scotland. All he had to work with, therefore, were a few thousand men, which hardly seemed enough to take on the entire Covenanter regime. The Covenanters were initially unperturbed at what they took to be another MacDonald raid on the western Highlands, and left the Campbells to deal with the problem. But on this occasion they had seriously underestimated their opponents. Montrose proved a skilful commander when it came to the mobile, guerrilla warfare that the highland terrain demanded, while MacColla's prowess in battle was an inspiration to his men, most of whom were experienced fighters with a burning hatred of all Campbells, Lowlanders, and Covenanters (in that order). With these men, intermittently augmented by the clan allies of the MacDonalds and other Highland Royalists, Montrose won six major battles in a row. In the last of these victories, at Kilsyth near Glasgow, on 15 August 1645, his forces wiped out the only remaining Covenanter army in Scotland.

At the height of its success, however, Montrose's army fell apart. Montrose's priority was to defeat the Covenanters in Scotland and then march his army to the king's assistance in England. Many of his best fighters, on the other hand, were inspired less by loyalty to the king than by thoughts of restoring the power of Clan Donald. Next to revenging themselves on the Campbells, the fate of the king paled into insignificance. They failed to appreciate that a MacDonald victory in the Highlands was impossible without a Royalist victory in England. After Kilsyth, therefore, MacColla and many of the Highlanders returned to their favourite pastime of pillaging the lands of the Campbells. Having failed to win many recruits in southern Scotland – partly because of his association with the hated Irish and Highlanders – Montrose was left with less than 2000 men. On 13 September 1645, this small force was annihilated at Philiphaugh by Lieutenant-General David Leslie and 6000 veterans from the Scottish army in England. The battle destroyed the core of the expeditionary force that had landed from Ireland the previous year. Montrose fled to the Highlands, and in 1646 left Scotland for exile on the Continent.

The Impact of Montrose's Campaign

Although Montrose never achieved the breakthrough into England he had sought, the effects of his campaign were by no means confined to Scotland. His victories forced the Covenanters to divert men and resources from their army in England just when their political ambitions at Westminster demanded they maintain as large a military presence on English soil as possible. And with Montrose running amok in the Highlands the Covenanters were reluctant to let Leven's army venture too far, or for too long, from the Borders in case it should be needed in Scotland. That the presence of a large Scottish army in the north alone was vital in clinching a Parliamentarian victory was not appreciated by their English allies. At a time when success in arms translated directly into political power, the Covenanters' long failure to defeat Montrose, and the operational limitations this imposed on Leven's army, had a disastrous impact on their position in England. With their influence at Westminster waning by late 1645, the Covenanters would look to the king to make good on Parliament's promises, and by so doing set in train a sequence of events that led ultimately to their own and the king's destruction.

Montrose's victories also had important ramifications in Ireland. From the Confederates' perspective, the Antrim–Montrose expedition failed to meet their expectations. It led to the withdrawal of only about 2500 New Scots, and stretched Confederate resources to the limit. Yet while Montrose went unchecked in the Highlands, the New Scots could not venture too far into the Irish interior lest they were needed in Scotland. Hence they were prevented from mounting an offensive in 1645 as they had done the previous year. On the other hand, the mere fact that Monro's army remained in Ireland, even if it kept largely to its own quarters, was enough to dissuade the Confederates from despatching reinforcements to Montrose. It also restricted their ability to send troops to assist the king in England. In effect, therefore, the two expeditionary forces – Montrose's and Monro's – cancelled each other out. Montrose's campaigns ensured that Monro would not pose a serious threat to the Confederates; Monro's presence in Ulster prevented the Confederates from mounting a major offensive against the Covenanters in Britain.

It was Montrose who was primarily responsible for bringing civil war to Scotland. Without his leadership, Antrim's expedition would probably have degenerated into a large-scale raid against the Campbells. Yet the civil dimension to the conflict – the struggle between Covenanter and Scottish Royalist – was largely subsumed by the war of Clan Donald against Campbell; Gael against *Gall*; and Catholic against Presbyterian. These clan, ethnic, and religious conflicts had straddled the North Channel for many years, but it took the arrival of MacColla's force from Ireland to bring out their full bitterness in Scotland.

Besides exacting a terrible cost in lives and property, Montrose's campaign had major political repercussions in Scotland. By using the hated 'Irish', Montrose aroused such fear among Scotland's Protestants that he deterred moderate Covenanters and Royalists from sticking their necks out for the king, as they would do under more propitious circumstances in 1647–8. Nevertheless, the Covenanter leadership was worried about moderate Royalists joining Montrose, and to forestall such an alliance felt obliged to give the Earl of Lanark and other Hamiltonians a larger role in parliamentary affairs. Even after Montrose's defeat the radicals never fully regained the political initiative they had enjoyed in the early 1640s. In the third of Montrose's victories, at Inverlochy on 2 February 1645, the fighting men of the clan Campbell had been massacred, and for the next twenty months MacColla and his allies ravaged the Campbell heartlands in Argyllshire. It was not until June 1647 that the Covenanters finally succeeded in driving MacColla out of the western Highlands and back to Ireland, and by then the Marquess of Argyll's reputation and military power had been seriously damaged. The resurgence of Hamilton's party during the winter of 1646–7 was almost certainly linked to the collapse of Campbell power in the Highlands after Inverlochy.

English Force of Arms

The Covenanters' prominent role in English politics was already under threat by the time Montrose's victories exposed their inability to prevail in England, Ulster, and the Highlands simultaneously. From the late summer of 1644 there was a rapid deterioration in relations between the Covenanters and their main allies at Westminster, the Saye–St John group. The Saye–St John grandees had harboured misgivings about the Scots' desire for a covenanted uniformity between the two kingdoms, but accepted the need to bring the English church more into line with that of Scotland as the price of securing the Covenanters' assistance.

But as we have already seen, Scottish confederalism did not stop at the introduction of a Presbyterian uniformity; it also aspired to the creation of a 'joint interest' in governing all three kingdoms.

The full scope of the Covenanters' confederalist desires was revealed in the peace proposals that they drew up in the spring of 1644 in the Committee of Both Kingdoms. A settlement along these lines would have seen the abolition of episcopacy, a covenanted uniformity between the kingdoms, and a permanent role for the Scots in the government of England and Ireland. The Saye–St John group acquiesced in the drafting of these proposals only because it was certain that the king would reject them, and that if it did likewise it would jeopardise further Scottish military support. It was willing to stomach the Covenanters' desires so long as their army seemed capable of striking a major blow against the king. Yet vital though Scottish intervention may have been to securing ultimate victory for Parliament, by the summer of 1644 the Scots had seemingly failed to make the decisive military breakthrough that they and their English allies had anticipated. Their contribution at Marston Moor was played down in English accounts of the battle, which attributed the victory largely to Cromwell and Sir Thomas Fairfax. Once Newcastle's army had been defeated, therefore, the Scottish forces increasingly came to be seen by the Saye–St John group and northern Parliamentarians such as the Fairfaxes (who had to compete with the Scots for military resources) as a liability.

The Scots' military shortcomings were seized upon by all those in England who felt let down or threatened by Scottish intervention. Among the Saye–St John grandees, this sense of disenchantment was rooted in a barely-concealed conviction of England's 'ancient superiority' over Scotland, and a consequent inclination to regard any attempt by the Scots to meddle with English institutions as an affront to national honour. But it was on the narrower issue of church government in England that their quarrel with the Scots mainly turned. The Saye–St John group could not accept the Kirk's claim to a governing, or coercive, power over the laity in matters of religion. No matter that the Scots insisted that it was not their intention to duplicate the Kirk in England, nor that Scottish Presbyterianism permitted more freedom of religious expression (for example, informal 'private meetings' for worship were tacitly allowed) and greater lay control than its English opponents realised or cared to admit. For their part, the Scots were unwilling to give the English the benefit of the doubt on the question of toleration. The Saye–St John group favoured toleration for those Puritans, known as Independents, who wanted to opt out of the parochial church system and form their own congregations of 'visible saints'. The Scots thought congregational Independency a recipe for anarchy; whereas for Saye and his circle it was the Scots' straitjacketing of godly consciences that was socially disruptive.

The fear of spiritual bondage under Scottish-style Presbyterianism was the driving force behind the Independents' emergence in 1644 as a vocal lobby in the Westminster Assembly and among the London godly. But it was the perceived valour of the Independents as soldiers that guaranteed their ministers and apologists such an influential voice. Cromwell and his Ironsides, many of whom were Independents, were widely admired for their martial zeal. Their successes on the battlefield helped persuade the Saye–St John grandees to shift their hopes for absolute victory from Scottish to English force of arms, which suited well with their Anglocentrism.

In gaining Cromwell to their party, however, the Saye–St John grandees lost his commanding officer, the Earl of Manchester. After witnessing the carnage at Marston Moor, and detecting little sign that this or any other Parliamentarian victory would end the war, he concluded that the only way to resolve the conflict was by a swift, negotiated settlement. The spread of radical ideas in his army also alarmed him, and he began to fear that victory by the sword, far from advancing the cause of orthodox Puritanism as he had hoped, would lead to religious anarchy. After Marston Moor, therefore, he resisted further efforts to deploy the Eastern Association army against the king – much to Cromwell's frustration. Manchester's defection to the peace camp reinforced the widespread apprehension in London that if Essex and his adherents continued to command Parliament's armies then capitulation to the king was inevitable.

The Presbyterian Alliance

Although fearful of Essex's power, the Saye–St John grandees finally had him in their sights by September 1644. The lord general's defeat at Lostwithiel, and subsequent revelations that he had shown favour to Catholics and Royalist collaborators, provided his enemies with the political momentum to begin 'new-modelling' the Parliamentarian armies. The New Model Army began life, as John Adamson has recently revealed, in a series of military reforms that the Saye–St John grandees launched from their power-base in the Committee of Both Kingdoms during September and October.[6] The aim of new-modelling was to combine the main Parliamentarian armies – Essex's, Manchester's, and Waller's – into a single and more effective fighting force under officers who would obey the orders of the Committee of Both Kingdoms. It thus made sound strategic sense and attracted a good deal of non-partisan support at Westminster. But new-modelling would also have profound political consequences. The intention of the Saye–St John grandees was to remove Essex from supreme command, and to vest the conduct of the war in men who would fight until the king's party was utterly defeated. Moreover, by providing the necessary political and financial backing for the new force and officering it with men sympathetic to their views, the Saye–St John grandees would effectively make it *their* army. This meant that so long as it prevailed on the battlefield the New Model would provide them with the political muscle to manage the war and the ensuing peace on their own terms, without regard for the Scots or Essex.

In September the Saye–St John grandees began to withdraw their patronage of the Scots, backing moves at Westminster to introduce toleration for a wide range of religious radicals – a proposition anathema to the Scots. Abandoned by their supposed friends, the Scots were forced to seek new allies, and from about October began to court their former enemies in Essex's faction. At a series of high-powered meetings initiated by the Scots and brokered by the French ambassador, the two sides set about trying to patch over their differences. The willingness of the Scots commissioners to relax their position on the royal prerogative was crucial in bringing about a rapprochement. They remained committed to the notion of a covenanted king, but were willing to meet Essex's party half-way on the question of preserving Charles in some of his executive powers, at least in England. This shift in policy by the Scots became vital in the wake of their breach with the Saye–St John group. Military victory and a dictated peace would favour the pro-Independent interest at Westminster. A negotiated settlement, however, that established Presbyterianism in some form and put the king and Parliament on a more equal footing, might leave the Scots holding the balance of power in England.

In many respects, however, the so-called 'Presbyterian alliance' between the Scots and Essex's faction was as much a marriage of convenience as the alliance between the Scots and the Saye–St John group had been.[7] Most leading members of Essex's faction were erastians and moderate Episcopalians. They supported 'rigid' Presbyterianism, first as a bulwark against the rising tide of religious radicalism – 'better a tyrannie then no government' at all, as Essex's chaplain put it;[8] and secondly as the 'purchase-price of Scottish cooperation in the business of negotiation with the king'.[9]

New-Modelling

The Presbyterian alliance encouraged the Saye–St John grandees to press ahead with their plans for military reform, for by the winter of 1644 all three main forces at Parliament's disposal – Essex's army, Manchester's Eastern Association army, and now the Scots army – were in the hands of their opponents. Support at Westminster for new-modelling also increased in November after the king's small army held off the combined forces of Essex, Manchester, and Waller at the second battle of Newbury, and then a few days later retrieved its artillery from nearby Donnington Castle unopposed and in full view of the Parliamentarian armies. 'This was the greatest affront that ever we received,' bemoaned the London Parliamentarian Thomas Juxon: 'Thus has all this year been shamefully lost ... by the neglect and treachery of our great officers.'[10]

With the end of the campaign season, the quarrelling among Parliament's generals shifted to Westminster. Late in November Cromwell presented charges against Manchester in the Commons, accusing his commander of deliberately frustrating the war-effort in order to promote a soft peace with the king. Manchester struck back in the Lords, alleging, among other things, that Cromwell had shown contempt for the Scots and their Presbyterian church. In the middle of this in-fighting, Zouch Tate, an MP closely associated with the Saye–St John party, proposed in the Commons on 9 December that all members of either House who had been appointed to military or civil office since the outbreak of war should resign their places. The resolution for self-denial, which eventually became the 'self-denying ordinance', was generally welcomed among Parliamentarians as a way of resolving the squabbles that were crippling the conduct of the war. At a stroke it would remove from command all the main antagonists – Manchester and Cromwell, Essex and Waller – and allay fears among the more pacific members that the militants were spinning out the war for their own profit. But if some onlookers were inclined to see self-denial as a device to promote unity they were deceiving themselves. The Saye–St John grandees had simply hijacked a back-bench initiative against placemen and jobbery, and used it as cover for ousting Essex from command. Certainly Essex's supporters smelled a rat almost immediately, and quickly persuaded a sizeable minority of MPs and a majority of the peers that the lord general should be exempted from the ordinance.

By mid-January the Lords, or at least the peers backing Essex, had made plain their opposition to self-denying. Desperate to be rid of Essex, the Saye–St John grandees now introduced in the Commons the plans they had been hatching in the Committee of Both Kingdoms since the previous autumn, for new-modelling the armies. By conscription, and by amalgamating Manchester's, Essex's, and Waller's tattered armies, a new, national force of 22,000 horse and foot would be created under the command of the hero of Nantwich and Marston Moor, Sir Thomas Fairfax. The choice of Fairfax was seemingly uncontroversial. He was a general of proven ability and had no political or personal axes to grind. Nevertheless, it is likely that his name was first proposed by one of the Saye–St John grandees – possibly the Earl of Northumberland, who played a leading role in new-modelling and was a long-time friend of the Fairfax family. Moreover, the very fact of Fairfax's appointment spelled the end of Essex's military career. The lord general's supporters in the Commons and Lords did their best to hinder the passage of the legislation for the new army, particularly those parts relating to the appointment of Fairfax and his officers; but a majority in the Commons recognised the necessity of new-modelling, and, by allowing the old armies to disintegrate for lack of pay, forced Essex's party to accept the New Model or be left with no army at all.

Swordsmen and Courtiers

The 1644 campaign season had exposed the need for reform in the Royalist as well as the Parliamentarian war machine. The king's and Parliament's main field armies had proved about equal in striking power and range, which meant that neither was able to deliver a knock-out blow. After the second battle of Newbury, therefore, the Royalists new-modelled their largest and oldest army – the Oxford army – and made Rupert commander-in-chief of all the king's forces. However, instead of providing him with a unified command equivalent in size to the New Model, the Royalists decided to split the Oxford army in two. Between a third and half of it, that is about 4500 men, including 3000 (or half) of the elite 'old horse', was given to George Lord Goring, and was stationed in the West Country. The rest, under Rupert, was garrisoned at Oxford.

Although Goring was an ally of Rupert, and his appointment was intended partly to placate the temperamental new commander-in-chief, it looks very much as if Goring's army was conceived by Digby and his allies as a counterweight to that of Rupert. This, at any rate, was how Rupert came to see it. While the Parliamentarians were reforming and consolidating their armies, therefore, the Royalists were further dividing theirs, and for reasons that apparently had more to do with manoeuvrings at court than with military necessity. The king's failure to stamp out the factionalism and petty rivalries that riddled his high command would have serious repercussions for the Royalist war-effort in 1645.

Independents and Presbyterians

At Westminster, meanwhile, the heat generated by new-modelling had accelerated the process of factional distillation, and over the course of 1645, Essex's faction and the Saye–St John group gradually acquired new names – the 'Presbyterians' and the 'Independents'. These labels originated from the division within the Westminster Assembly between the advocates of Scottish-style Presbyterianism and those of congregational Independency, and their application to the political factions in Parliament has caused some confusion. In fact, the parliamentary or 'political' Independents contained only a handful of men who worshipped in separated congregations. Likewise, the 'political' Presbyterians included few individuals who were eager to replicate the Scottish Kirk in England. Most members of both factions were erastians, who were willing to accept a national Presbyterian church so long as it was regulated by Parliament. The principal religious issue dividing the two factions was the degree of toleration to be allowed under such a system. The political Independents were opposed to any coercive power over godly consciences, and championed the cause of limited toleration for their 'religious' brethren. The political Presbyterians, responding to the spread of heterodox ideas and a seeming breakdown in order (England had recently suffered a wave of Puritan iconoclasm by Parliamentarian soldiers and godly zealots), tended to support the Scots in pressing for a more hierarchical, inclusive church.

The quarrel between the two factions, however, went deeper than differences over church government. The crucial division was over the kind of settlement to be sought with the king. Essex and other leading Presbyterians wanted a peace that re-invested Charles with most of his former powers; in particular, control over the militia and the right to select his councillors. Naturally, they expected to occupy the principal courtly offices once the king had been restored, but they relied on his gratitude, not coercion, to secure them power. Rather than have a dictated peace therefore, they urged that Charles be allowed to return to London to conclude a personal treaty. Lacking an army of their own, the Presbyterians relied upon the Scottish forces to underwrite their terms for settlement; and this meant indulging the Scots' demands for a covenanted uniformity and a junior partnership in the government of England and Ireland.

The Independent grandees, by contrast, favoured a stricter settlement whereby most of the king's personal powers would be invested in a reconstituted privy council, which they would dominate. Less trusting than the Presbyterians of the king's willingness to compromise his power, they sought to reduce him to 'a necessity of granting'. Charles was to be battered into submission, and the New Model was their weapon of choice (attitudes towards the New Model thus became a touchstone of political allegiance at Westminster in the period 1645–8). The Independents were also keener than their rivals to keep England's and Scotland's government 'distinct, without intermixture', and to subordinate Ireland completely to English rule, regardless of the Scots' foothold in Ulster. Peace – or war for that matter – was to be (in Cromwell's words) 'with the English Interest in the head of it'.[11]

Despite acquiring new names, the two main factions altered little in composition. Certainly the core of each faction remained largely as it had been since the winter of 1643–4 and the realignments resulting from the Scottish alliance and the Irish cessation. There was, however, a second, smaller wave of defections among the grandees as a result of the Scots switching factions. Sir William Waller, for example, who had always been zealously pro-Scots, moved over to Essex's party in 1645; while two leading opponents of the Scottish alliance, William Pierrepont and Sir John Evelyn, became front-rank Independents during the winter of 1644–5. Like their predecessors, the Presbyterian and the Independent factions were loose, bicameral coalitions. The majority of Parliament-men remained uncommitted to either group.

The one historian to have challenged this picture of party strife is Mark Kishlansky. In a bold reinterpretation of parliamentary politics, he argued that the emergence of coherent parties did not occur until 1646–7, when the stresses and strains of finding a workable settlement, and the intervention of outside pressure groups, notably the Scots and the City, shattered the traditional, consensual pattern of parliamentary debate and decision-making.[12] It was only at this point that 'adversary politics' – the struggle between organised parties on national issues – was born, not before. The problem with this interpretation is that it seems to fly in the face of what many contemporaries wrote about events in Parliament during the war years. Thomas Juxon, one of Kishlansky's main sources, evidently saw the struggle between the Presbyterian alliance and the Independents as the dominant theme at Westminster by the spring of 1645 at the latest. Kishlansky is more persuasive in debunking the traditional perception of the fledgling New Model as a self-consciously radical force. Even so, it is clear that right from its creation the army was closely identified with the Independents, and quickly came to share their desire to end England's humiliating reliance upon the Scots. This animosity was heartily reciprocated by the Scots, who moved closer to the Presbyterians in common opposition to the New Model. Likewise the Presbyterians, having lost Essex's and Manchester's armies to new-modelling, were now dependent upon Covenanter military power, and thus obliged to defend what many English people came to regard as the indefensible – a Scottish army encamped across northern England.

The Uxbridge Treaty

While the dispute over new-modelling dragged on at Westminster, Parliament opened negotiations with the king at Uxbridge, west of London. Much of the impetus for the Uxbridge treaty on the Royalist side came from the moderates and disgruntled courtiers, who were able to use the second, and as it proved, final, session of the Oxford Parliament to put pressure on the king for a negotiated settlement. On Parliament's side, it was the Scots who made most of the running. Their commissioners attended the talks (which began late in January 1645), and it was the peace terms that they had drawn up in the Committee of Both Kingdoms that were presented to the king. These were so extreme in nature, requiring as they did that Charles renounce his religion and his friends, that only the Scots seem to have taken the negotiations at all seriously. The Independent grandees effectively washed their hands of the whole proceedings, sure in the knowledge that no amount of negotiating would make the king accept a covenanted uniformity. And the Presbyterian grandees and a few ambitious courtiers attempted to subvert the talks entirely by trying to persuade Charles that if he returned to London then opposition to a moderate peace deal would crumble.

The king's negotiating team at Uxbridge was dominated by members of the Hertford–Hyde group, and though desperate to reach an accommodation, even they found Parliament's terms unacceptable. The king himself agreed with Henrietta Maria that the 'rebels' would have to lower their demands drastically before he would consider disbanding his armies. Besides which, he was beginning to receive news of Montrose's successes in Scotland, and the prospect of toppling the Covenanters by force was more agreeable to him than meeting them half-way at the negotiating table. The talks ended in deadlock after just three weeks.

The breakdown of the Uxbridge treaty was a blow to both the Royalist and Parliamentarian peace factions. In the absence of a settlement, the vigorous prosecution of the war became the only option. At Westminster, Essex and his allies in the Lords were bludgeoned into accepting not only the New Model Army but also Fairfax's list of officers, which included a number of religious radicals. On 2 April, Essex and Manchester resigned their commissions. Over 300 Scottish officers who had been serving in Parliament's armies also lost their places, further reducing the Scots' and Presbyterians' role in the war. The one consolation for Essex's party was that a revised self-denying ordinance had been passed that allowed peers and MPs to seek re-appointment to office. Thus a door had been left ajar for Essex's return to command should Fairfax stumble.

With another summer of fighting ahead, the king was more desperate than ever for military reinforcements from Ireland. Aware that Ormond might have problems making the necessary concessions to secure Irish troops, Charles sent a Catholic peer, the Earl of Glamorgan, to Kilkenny with a secret mandate to negotiate a military treaty with the Confederates. He realised too that some of his councillors in England would disapprove of soliciting Irish help, particularly by means of Glamorgan. Consequently, he (or, more probably, Digby) revived a plan hatched the previous spring for removing leading moderates from court. Thus in March 1645, Hyde, Culpeper and other opponents of enlisting foreign military support were packed off to Bristol as a council to help the Prince of Wales shore up the Royalist cause in the West Country. The prevailing philosophy at both Oxford and Westminster was that peace could only be bought with more expense of blood.

Ormond and the Confederates

The king's declining fortunes in England had a significant bearing upon the tortuous negotiations between Ormond and the Confederates for a peace treaty – or, as Charles doubtless preferred to see it, a military alliance to help him win the English Civil War. There were several major obstacles in the way of an agreement, but the most formidable was the increasing political assertiveness of those Confederates determined upon the full restoration of the Catholic Church in Ireland.

The talks were dominated on the Confederate side by the Ormondists. As the king's situation in England grew ever more desperate, the Ormondists became increasingly willing to settle for limited toleration and minimal constitutional reforms (such as would allow Catholics to serve in high office, for example) so long as their political and landed interests were safeguarded. The Royalist defeat at Marston Moor in July 1644 increased their sense of urgency, for Confederate intervention in England would only be rewarded if Charles won the war. The Ormondists' ascendancy began to be challenged in 1644, however, by a group of reformers from outside the ruling clique. The return empty-handed of the Confederate delegation sent to Oxford in the spring of 1644 had raised doubts about the wisdom of allowing a largely unaccountable and Ormondist-dominated Supreme Council to make all the running in the negotiations. And these rumblings of discontent were soon taken up by Ireland's Catholic bishops.

In forbearing to press for complete freedom of worship for Catholics, the Ormondists were dangerously misrepresenting the views of the clergy and many rank-and-file members of the Association. In fact, the clergy demanded not merely the repeal of all penal laws against the exercise of Catholicism, but the right of Catholic bishops to govern their flocks independently of any authority but the papacy. In addition, they insisted upon retaining the ecclesiastical property that the Confederates had seized from the Protestant church establishment since 1641. Few Confederate leaders expected Ormond or the king to grant the clergy's desires regarding jurisdiction and church property, and their response was simply to avoid these issues.

If church leaders were content to take a back seat in the negotiations with Ormond it was because they preferred a more insular strategy. Rather than settle with Charles as a prelude to allying with the Royalists, they wanted the Association to make itself master of all Ireland so that it could assist the king or defy Parliament from a position of maximum strength. In order to pursue this policy the Association needed cash to maintain its armies, and with Ireland depleted of military resources the only option was to go cap in hand to the Catholic powers on the Continent. While they waited for assistance from abroad, the clergy were willing to let the Ormondists make the running in the treaty negotiations.

Unfortunately for the Confederates, the Catholic states were generally too busy fighting among themselves to spare much thought or money for Ireland.

The clergy's belief that foreign aid would be more forthcoming if the Association could be portrayed as a movement for Catholic emancipation was probably one reason for the increasing intrusion of religious issues into the treaty negotiations from mid-1644. Another was their growing suspicion that the Ormondists were intent on a sell-out peace. This impression was reinforced by the fiasco of the 1644 Ulster campaign, and the half-hearted manner in which the Supreme Council prosecuted the war in Munster during 1645. Sir Charles Coote's capture of Sligo and other Confederate strongholds in Connacht during 1645 added to the clergy's sense of frustration. It is likely too that developments in England encouraged the clergy to press their case more vigorously. Despite the obstacles to regular communications between England and Ireland, few at Kilkenny can have been unaware by early 1645 that the king was losing the English Civil War. His desperate need for Irish troops was bound to make him more flexible, and the clergy and those Confederates who were dissatisfied with what was on the negotiating table more strident in their demands.

But there were some issues on which Charles would never compromise. He regarded his royal supremacy as so vital a part of his kingly office and power that he would never concede the right of either Catholics or Protestants to establish a church jurisdiction independent of the crown. His personal interest and scruples aside, the king had sound strategic reasons for refusing to grant major concessions to the Confederates. If he yielded to their demands for an autonomous Catholic church and Irish Parliament, he risked alienating his Protestant supporters in all three kingdoms; but his need for Irish troops was so great by early 1645 that he ordered Ormond to offer the repeal of the penal laws, or in other words toleration for the 'quiet' exercise of Catholicism.

Ignoring the growing discontent among rank-and-file Confederates, the Supreme Council had made some headway with Ormond by the spring of 1645, although only through a willingness to compromise on fundamental constitutional and religious issues. Ormond, on the other hand, despite repeatedly being urged to make swift and increasingly full concessions by Charles, Digby, and Clanricarde, had conceded ground cautiously, even grudgingly, leading some Confederates (and not a few historians) to accuse him of acting in bad faith. In fact, Ormond was in an impossible situation. A loyal king's man and trenchant Protestant, he was committed to defending royal authority in Ireland's church and civil government, and hence it was inevitable that he would find the demands being put forward by the clerical party completely unacceptable. Furthermore, any peace that seriously disadvantaged Ireland's Protestants would have met stiff opposition from the royal council and army in Dublin on which Ormond's own authority, and power to implement a settlement, rested.

Ormond's inability to square the circle that Charles had put him in strengthened the clerical party's hand. In the General Assembly that convened in May 1645, the bishops, with the support of a large section of assemblymen, rejected Ormond's meagre religious concessions. Instead, they insisted that there could be no treaty unless it allowed for the retention of the church property seized by Catholics since 1641. On this issue, as on others involving church jurisdiction, neither Charles nor Ormond would budge. The peace party leaders managed to persuade the bishops not to press their demands, and the negotiations stumbled on over the summer; but there was no longer any prospect of concluding a treaty in time to send reinforcements to Charles before his showdown with the New Model Army.

Naseby

The protracted debates over new-modelling meant that Fairfax's army was still mustering at the start of the 1645 campaign season, and so Parliament requested Leven to march his forces southwards to fill the breach. But Scottish army leaders were too worried by Montrose's exploits in the Highlands to contemplate moving very far from the border. Leven's failure to march south was deeply resented by the Independents; and their resentment turned to anger late in May after the king's army moved, unchecked, into the Midlands and sacked Leicester. Cromwell's friends responded by using the loophole in the self-denying ordinance to get him appointed commander of Fairfax's cavalry. The Presbyterians, meanwhile, tried to pin the blame for Leicester on those responsible for replacing Essex and his army with the untried New Model. Early in June they and the Scots commissioners revealed evidence that the Independent grandees had been plotting with a group of discontented Royalists for the surrender of Oxford, and had deployed the New Model to besiege the town, thereby exposing Leicester to attack. The Presbyterians hoped to discredit the Independents and their army and so have Essex re-installed as commander-in-chief. But for this tactic to work they needed a further military setback – nothing less than the defeat of the New Model. With Essex at the helm again, and the Independents disgraced, a soft peace with the king would be well within reach. As the Royalist double-agent Lord Savile informed Digby, 'iff yow can but beatt or disgrace Fairfaxe his Independent armie, Essex and the Scots will be greater than ever, which I assure yow they look for certainlie; and…will not only revive but improve the former designe, and doe the King's bussines the safest, speediest and noblest way'.[13]

Buoyed by such reports, and convinced that the 'New Noddle' was no match for experienced Royalist troops, Digby pressed the king to do battle with Fairfax's army at the earliest possible opportunity. Rupert, on the other hand, advised striking into Yorkshire and picking up recruits among the northern Royalists. Digby himself was not completely blinded by optimism, and tried to have Goring march his 10,000-strong army from the West Country to join the king. However, the prince's council at Bristol would not countenance such a diminution of its authority, and argued that if Goring marched into the Midlands then all the west would be lost. The consequences of dividing the Oxford army and sending the moderates to Bristol – both largely the result of court intrigue – were now combining to ruin the Royalist cause. But defeat was by no means inevitable even at this stage. If Charles had overridden the prince's council, and had heeded Rupert's advice to wait for reinforcements arriving from Wales, then he would have had a formidable force at his disposal. Instead, he listened to Digby and decided to engage the New Model when his army was still barely half the size of Fairfax's.

The battle that would ultimately decide the fate of all three kingdoms was fought at Naseby, in Northamptonshire, on 13 June. For all their numerical superiority – about 17,000 to 9000 – the Parliamentarians made heavy weather of beating the king's army. It did not help that many of Fairfax's infantry were raw recruits, or that his cavalry on the left wing was commanded by the relatively inexperienced Henry Ireton, whose troopers were quickly put to flight by Rupert. But as at Marston Moor, Rupert failed to regroup swiftly enough to support the outnumbered Royalist foot. Once Fairfax's infantry reserves had halted the Royalist advance in the centre, therefore, and Cromwell had seen off his opponents on the right and then joined Fairfax in rallying Ireton's men on the left, a Parliamentarian victory was inevitable. Casualties were relatively light. It was the capture of 4000 veteran Royalist foot that made the victory decisive. The king had lost the core of his only substantial field army outside the West Country. Almost as damaging was the seizure after the battle of his correspondence with his leading advisers. These letters, most of which Parliament later published, revealed the king's plans for using Irish and foreign troops in England. They seemed to vindicate the Independents' distrust of Charles and their insistence that there was 'noe hopes of peace but by the sword'.[14]

After Naseby the New Model marched into the West Country, and on 10 July, at Langport in Somerset, destroyed Goring's army. This second victory, and the subsequent storming of Bristol, left the outcome of the war in little doubt. Although the mopping-up operation against Royalist resistance in the West Country, Wales, and at Oxford and Newark, would take almost another year, the New Model's triumphs during the summer and autumn of 1645 sealed victory for Parliament in the English Civil War. Almost as important, they confirmed the Independents and their army as the most powerful force in British politics.

The Price of Victory

It needs emphasising that victory in the English Civil War went not so much to Parliament, as to a faction within it – the Independents. It was effectively their army that won the war – a victory rooted in their political dominance at Westminster. The success of the army's campaign in the West Country, for example, depended in part upon Fairfax's careful handling of the clubmen – regional defence groups that had sprung up to resist plundering by either side and to agitate for peace. Fairfax's ability to subdue, and in some cases harness, the considerable military strength of the clubmen was testament to the exceptional discipline of the New Model; and this in turn owed much to the fact that it was regularly and adequately paid. The legislation creating the New Model had also made provision for a new national assessment that would bring in a massive £53,000 a month. Greater powers were given to Parliament's local governing bodies, the county committees, to collect the tax or distrain for non-payment. And, most important of all (as Adamson has highlighted), a new executive body was created – the Army Committee – with a centralised treasury and disbursement office under experienced financiers to oversee the New Model's pay and recruitment. The committee's membership was 'outrageously partisan' – a roll-call of the Independent leadership in both Houses – and it was chaired by a client of the grandest of the grandees, the Earl of Northumberland.[15] In fact, by late 1645 the Independents dominated virtually all of Parliament's 'money-Committees' – which the Presbyterian polemicist Clement Walker rightly perceived as a design to 'draw a generall dependency after them, for he that commands the money, commands the men'.[16]

The New Model's military supremacy, and thus the outcome of the Civil War itself, was underpinned by the political supremacy of its patrons. So long as the factional struggle for control of Parliament's armies, finances, and executive organs had lain in the balance, then a compromise peace was perhaps the likeliest outcome of the war. It was the political ascendancy achieved by the Independents during 1644–5 that had put outright victory within Parliament's grasp. The Committee of Both Kingdoms, self-denial, new-modelling, and the Army Committee – in other words, the creation of a unified military command, and the administrative machinery and revenue to sustain it – were all largely the work of the Independent grandees. Without these developments, neither Parliament's superiority in resources nor its fiscal innovations could have been exploited to decisive effect.

The Independents' triumph was a major turning point in the wars of the three kingdoms. With England in the grip of an Anti-Scottish junto, the inevitable resurgence of English power after the Civil War threatened not just the Irish Confederates but also the Scottish Covenanters. Victory for the Presbyterians, or indeed for the king, would probably have spared Scotland, and possibly Ireland too, from English invasion. But the Independents' determination to usurp the king's prerogative, and to establish Westminster as the seat of power throughout the archipelago, made war with the Scots very likely, and the brutal re-assertion of English rule in Ireland all but inevitable. Of all the possible outcomes of the English Civil War, victory for the Independents was the most likely to prolong the wars of the three kingdoms.

Chapter 4: Anglia Rediviva: September 1645–January 1647

Armies and Settlement

In 1647, an army chaplain, Joshua Sprigge, published a book praising the exploits of Fairfax and his men. He called it *Anglia Rediviva* – England's recovery. Sprigge drew heart from the New Model's victories, seeing in them a re-affirmation of English valour and the national interest. But few of the public shared his optimism (or bought his book), and with good reason, for the Civil War had created more problems than it had solved. Church government had broken down entirely in most places, allowing godly enthusiasts to set up separated congregations – much to the alarm of orthodox Puritans as well as the majority that still clung to the now outlawed Book of Common Prayer. Local government under the Royalists had degenerated into military rule. Under Parliament it was exercised largely by county committees, some of which were dominated by radicals and social upstarts, who were prepared to put loyalty to Westminster before the interests of their communities. To keep their armies in the field, both the king and Parliament had introduced a sales tax – the excise – and weekly or monthly assessments, and it was a case of either paying up or answering to the troops. It has been calculated that Parliament was raising the equivalent of one pre-war parliamentary subsidy every fortnight in taxation – most of which went to pay the army and navy.[1]

With an end to the fighting in sight by early 1646, the public clamour for disbanding the kingdom's armed forces and lowering taxes grew deafening, and yet both were incompatible with the public's other main demand – a political settlement. Charles would not compromise until he was denied all hope of military support; and in a multiple monarchy in which sovereign authority had fragmented into numerous competing politico-military interests this was all but impossible. Power based upon armed force was the only way of even bringing him to the negotiating table, let alone of then imposing terms upon a divided realm. Certainly the grandees in England could not hope to secure a settlement without the means to overawe the king and their enemies – which required money and lots of it. The dominant factions in Scotland and Ireland faced the same difficulty. In all three kingdoms, armies and the oppressive measures needed to sustain them had become an essential part of the quest for settlement.

The politics of the period covered by this chapter were dominated by three parallel sets of negotiations – those between Charles (through Ormond) and the Confederates; between Charles and the Independents; and between Charles and the Anglo-Scottish covenanting interest. All three blueprints for settlement were mutually incompatible, and therefore all three required armies to underwrite them. If the common people were moved to resist the consequent high taxation and plundering then they generally found that the soldiers, and the officials and politicians who maintained them, served their own interests first and the immediate welfare of the community a distant second. Professional standing armies bolstered oligarchic authority and limited the people's capacity to shape political movements that they had helped to create.

The Wars of the Five Kingdoms?

With England rent by war or the search for a durable settlement, the Irish Confederates and Scottish Covenanters were able to achieve a greater measure of independence from the English state. England's troubles encouraged attempts to reconceptualise the nature of the relationship between the three kingdoms. Scottish confederalism represented one such attempt; others will be discussed below.

Yet though English power was temporarily in abeyance, England's size and wealth relative to Scotland and Ireland, and its habit of throwing its weight around as the perennial 'awkward neighbour', made it difficult for the other two kingdoms to ignore. And because the vast majority of Charles's subjects continued to recognise him as their rightful sovereign, national independence outside the Stuart composite monarchy was never really an option. Hence the ultimate goal of many leading Covenanters and Confederates in striving for ascendancy in their own kingdoms was that of intervening in the English Civil War and turning it to their own advantage. National interest meant fettering or upholding the king's authority in England – 'the Seat and Center of his Empire'.[2]

It is revealing that although the collapse of English power freed the Scots and the Irish to pursue independent foreign policies, they did so with the aim of consolidating their position within the Stuart realm. Even when the Covenanters began to share something of the Confederates' hostility towards Westminster, as they did from 1645, they spurned the opportunity to forge separate alliances with Sweden and other Protestant powers, insisting that the English Parliament be party to any treaty.

The 'dialectical processes' (to use John Morrill's phrase) between the Stuart kingdoms and peoples during the 1640s clearly did not apply to France, Spain, or any of the Continental states that kept a weather-eye on British and Irish developments. It is therefore misleading to refer to the 'wars of the five kingdoms' as some historians have done. No European state was sufficiently concerned at events in the archipelago to commit troops there. Indeed, when they did intervene it was usually to *obtain* troops to fight their own wars. The Spanish were desperate for Irish soldiers; the Swedes for Scottish soldiers; and the French showed a fine insensitivity to the proprieties of British warfare by recruiting English Royalists, Scottish Covenanters, and Irish Confederates.

None the less, it was fortunate for the English Parliament that the French crown was too busy during the 1640s fighting the Spanish or its own rebellious subjects to give any military assistance to the king. Not that the French were keen on an outright Royalist victory such as would allow Charles to rebuild his navy and vie for control of the Channel (although even this was preferable in their eyes to England under a warlike Independent junto). Ideally, they wanted to keep the crown weak, with power diffused among their own friends in the three kingdoms – the queen and her Francophile Royalist clique, the Westminster Presbyterians, the Scottish Covenanters, and the Irish Ormondists. This chapter will highlight the role of French diplomats in trying to forge a Royalist–Presbyterian alliance to restore the king.

'Infinite Oppressions': Ditching the Scottish Alliance

The Anglo-Scottish covenanting interest and its French backers faced formidable opposition in the shape of the English Independents. After Naseby and Langport, the Independent grandees made their first concerted attempt to forge their own settlement with the king – an undertaking in which the eradication of Scottish influence from English and Irish affairs was both means and end. To further their respective political programmes, both parties needed to win over the non-aligned majority in the Commons and to sway public opinion, especially in London. During the course of 1645, therefore, a propaganda war broke out between the Scots and their English opponents. While Presbyterian polemicists played upon the threat to order from sectaries and soldiers, pro-army writers appealed to the widespread English prejudice against the 'beggarly' Scots and their clericalist church.

What should have been the Scots' trump card in English politics, their army, had become their biggest liability. The Independents' control of Parliament's finances, coupled with a general reluctance among the English to fund the Scottish forces, meant that Leven's army was starved of pay and forced to live off free quarter and plundering. This of course made it extremely unpopular with its reluctant hosts in the northern counties. The reputation of the Scottish forces would have improved if they had been able to move south after 1644 and steal some of the New Model's glory. But as we have seen, they could not venture too far from the border in case Montrose broke into the Scottish Lowlands. The result was a series of propaganda disasters for the Scots, beginning with their refusal to march south in the spring of 1645. In September, after Montrose's victory at Kilsyth forced Leven's army to abandon its siege of Hereford (which was the furthest south the Scottish forces ever got) and march back into the exhausted northern counties, the parliamentary committees in the north began a long series of letters to Parliament bemoaning the 'infinite oppressions and extortions' of the Scottish army, and pleading that it be removed from the region.[3] So loud was the chorus of northern complaints, and so successfully exploited by the Independents, that it led to the first calls at Westminster for the ditching of the Scottish alliance altogether. The Scots commissioners warned Edinburgh of a 'designe to be rid of our army and to have it returned home to Scotland, thereby to weaken our interest that they [the Independents] may the more easily obtaine their owne desires in matters of religion and of peace or warre'.[4]

'A King of Presbitery'?

Montrose's defeat at Philiphaugh in September did little to reverse the decline in Scottish influence at Westminster. The Scots commissioners in

London tried their best to move the Scottish forces southwards and to tighten discipline in the ranks, but with little success. Their efforts to reform Leven's army were frustrated in some cases by Royalist sympathisers in the officer corps. Alarmed by the growing power of the Independents, elements within the Scottish army had opened secret talks with the English Royalists by March 1645 about a military alliance to restore the king. A leading actor in these furtive transactions was the senior Scottish commander, the Earl of Callander, who was a long-time enemy of Argyll, and (in Hamilton's absence) had emerged as an influential figure among the pragmatic Covenanters. On the English side, the running was made by Cavalier hard-liners, who were willing to make concessions towards the establishment of Presbyterianism as the purchase price of Scottish military support. Their eagerness in courting the Scots increased after Naseby and Langport, which left Leven's army the only force in Britain capable of taking on the New Model.

The cause of negotiating a 'Scotch treaty' was not helped by a further fracturing of the Royalist leadership after Naseby. A summer of military disasters had convinced Rupert and the swordsmen that the king had no option but to make peace with the English Parliament. Like most professional soldiers, Rupert saw no virtue in fighting a lost cause. His great rival Digby, on the other hand, was confident that he could procure an army from the Scots or from supposedly friendly princes on the Continent, and was determined to head off any peace initiative. He convinced Charles that Rupert's surrender of Bristol in September 1645 had been an act of treachery rather than military necessity, whereupon the king ordered Rupert to leave the country. But Rupert was determined to vindicate himself, and defied orders barring him from the king's presence. Anxious to avoid a confrontation, Digby took charge of a cavalry expedition to link up with Montrose, only to have his command scattered by the Covenanters near Carlisle. He escaped to the Isle of Man before sailing on to join Ormond in Dublin. By the autumn of 1645, therefore, the king was bereft of his principal adviser (Digby) and military leader (Rupert).

The divided state of Covenanter and Royalist counsels was a further obstacle to an alliance between their parties. Most of the key figures within the Covenanter diplomatic and military corps, including Leven and the Scots commissioners in London, were adherents not of Callander but of Argyll. Argyll's party was in favour of reaching a political settlement with the king, but not on the minimal terms of the Callander group, and certainly not without the full backing of the Westminster Presbyterians. Equally, there were powerful figures in the king's own camp who were suspicious of any rapprochement with the Scots. Scottish demands for closer union, particularly in religion, flew in the face of the Hertford–Hyde group's belief that episcopacy was 'an entire part of the frame and constitution of the Kingdom'.[5] They abhorred the pragmatic line of Digby, Jermyn, and other less constitutionally minded Royalists, who told Charles that he could either be 'a King of Presbitery, or no King' at all.[6] As much as Digby and Jermyn might dislike the Scots, they favoured the Covenanters and their English allies over the Independents as the lesser of two evils. But to Royalists of Hertford's mind the reverse was the case. They consistently urged the king to negotiate a moderate settlement, and before the end of the year had made at least two attempts to bring Charles and Parliament to terms, using the Independent grandees and the Prince of Wales as peace brokers. The king, however, although he would not accept Presbyterianism or take the Covenant, had not given up hopes of winning over Scottish leaders. Likewise, he continued to seek military support from the Irish Confederates – a policy entirely at odds with trying to build bridges to the Scots.

The king's main hope, however, lay in fomenting the growing divisions between the Covenanters and the English Parliament. If the Independents were sceptical of the continuing benefits of the Anglo-Scottish alliance, then there was frustration in Edinburgh at Westminster's lack of progress towards closer religious and political union. By the autumn of 1645, Argyll's party had evidently decided to join with their English allies in making their own secret approach to the king – a move that reflected the growing conviction among leading Covenanters that if they could not get closer union through alliance with Parliament, then it was logical to seek it in alliance with a defeated and, they hoped, chastened king. By mid-September the Scots commissioners, led by one of Argyll's closest allies, Lord Balmerino, and the English Presbyterians, represented by the Earl of Holland, had agreed on peace terms. If the king consented to the introduction of Presbyterianism then the Scots and their English allies would be willing to relax their demands relating to Ireland and control of the militia. These proposals were forwarded to the king via the French agent in London, Jean de Montereul, and the queen (who was by now in exile in Paris). If Charles approved of the Scots' terms, Cardinal Mazarin – who ruled France in the young Louis XIV's name – offered to support the Covenanters and their English allies in 'obliging' Parliament and the Independents to accept them. The queen, at Mazarin's prompting, agreed to endorse the Scots' terms. As a Catholic, it mattered little to her what kind of Protestant church was established. But Charles remained stubbornly opposed to Presbyterian church government. Moreover, he was being courted by the Independent grandees, who offered to restore episcopacy if he would grant toleration for tender consciences.

The Newcastle Propositions

Against this backdrop of intrigue and secret negotiations, the Commons initiated a new drive for settlement. After Naseby, the Scots commissioners had requested that Parliament resume negotiations with Charles, and to their surprise found their calls for peace taken up by leading Independents. But while the Scots remained wedded to the Uxbridge propositions as the basis of a new treaty, the Independents had something rather different in mind: this time instead of letting the Scots make the running, Parliament's peace proposals would be drawn up by the Commons. And rather than allow Charles to haggle over the terms, as at Uxbridge, the Independents intended simply to demand his assent to pre-determined propositions (which were presented to him at Newcastle the following year, hence the 'Newcastle Propositions').

The first draft of the Newcastle Propositions, which was laid before the Commons in December 1645, completely repudiated the confederalist approach to settlement enshrined in the Uxbridge proposals. The Scots' novel and (in terms of reaching a settlement with the king) complicating demands for a say in the disposal of England's militia and in the management of the war in Ireland were swept aside, and the sovereignty of the English crown, as exercised by Parliament, was strongly re-asserted. A settlement along these lines would have left the Scots as powerless in the face of English aggression as they had been in the 1630s. The other conspicuous loser by the new propositions would be the king, who was to forfeit forever his control over the militia of the three kingdoms. This prospect further alarmed the Scots, for whom the limited military union outlined in the Uxbridge proposals was as vital for their future security as uniformity in religion. The Scots regarded the king's executive power over the militias, exercised with the joint consent of the English and Scottish Parliaments, as a bulwark not only against an unscrupulous monarch, but also, by implication, against an English Parliament dominated by their enemies.

The Newcastle Propositions were so severe that it is difficult to see them as a genuine attempt to reach a settlement. In fact, the Scots were probably correct in thinking that they had little to do with peace at all, and were instead an Independent ploy to reverse the confederalist trend in British politics and to re-assert English sovereignty over Ireland. The propositions may also have been conceived as a reminder to Charles of just what kind of settlement he could expect if he rejected the Independents' secret, and more palatable, terms.

Lisle's Lieutenancy

The propositions' repudiation of a joint Anglo-Scottish approach to the reconquest of Ireland cleared the way at Westminster for the appointment of a new lord lieutenant. In January 1646 the Commons conferred Ormond's office upon Philip Sidney, Viscount Lisle, who was to spearhead what was envisaged as an exclusively English campaign to suppress the Confederates. Lisle was a nephew of the Independent grandee the Earl of Northumberland, and the son of Ormond's predecessor and rival, the Earl of Leicester. Lisle and his New English faction were advocates of plantation and the complete subjugation of Ireland to English rule. Absolute victory in Ireland was to be followed by the confiscation of all Catholic land and its parcelling out among the Adventurers and other Protestant settlers (although in such a way as to marginalise Scottish influence in Ireland). It is interesting to note that Lisle, or at least some of his Independent allies, came very close to ascribing the 'barbarism' of the Irish not to a want of nurture but to racial inferiority. It is only here perhaps, at the fringes of English politics, that one can detect the 'dark forces of ethnic hatred'.

The Independent grandees backed Lisle's New English circle partly for reasons relating to their domestic power-struggle with the Scots and the Presbyterians. But as John Adamson has revealed in his case-study of Lisle's lieutenancy and its geopolitical repercussions, their policy towards Ireland also reflected an 'imperial design'.[7] Independent–New English propaganda on Ireland echoed the views of the Elizabethan writers Edmund Spenser and Lisle's forebear Sir Philip Sidney, that Ireland should be subsumed in a unitary state under English institutions, religion, and law. Indeed, the Independent grandees can arguably be seen as the political heirs of Sidney, whose vision for England has been summed up as 'reform at home, leadership for Protestant Europe, hegemony in the region, and, *sotto voce*, empire across the ocean'.[8]

The Presbyterian grandees, for their part, showed no enthusiasm for bringing Ireland under direct English rule. Their programme for settlement apparently envisioned a state of pragmatic cooperation between the Protestant leaders of each kingdom. Thus they were ready to allow the Scots a hand in reconquering Ireland. In addition, they were apparently willing to consider some kind of pan-Protestant alliance with Ormond and the Irish Royalist interest – possibly even with leading Catholic Royalists such as Essex's half-brother the Earl of Clanricarde. Ormond certainly had many well-wishers among high-ranking English Presbyterians, and if they were serious about reaching an understanding with him then at the very least they would have to limit the amount of land confiscation suffered by his relations and sympathisers among the Confederates.

Lisle's lieutenancy sent a clear message to the Scots that they remained in Ulster on sufferance and had no right to a share in the spoils of reconquest. The Independents' quarrel with the Scots did not affect the basic consensus at Westminster in favour of reconquering Ireland, but by pursuing a rival campaign strategy to that agreed under successive Anglo-Scottish treaties, and courting the hard-line, anti-Ormond faction among the Irish Protestants, they raised further obstacles to defeating the Confederates.

Besides stirring up yet more ill-feeling between the English and the Scots, Lisle's lieutenancy heightened divisions among the Protestants in Munster, where the new lord lieutenant was to establish his bridgehead in Ireland. Inchiquin, appointed lord president of Munster by Parliament early in 1645, had remained on close terms with Ormond, and like him had friends among the English Presbyterian grandees. The Independents' propaganda campaign against Ormond (and by implication, against a Presbyterian–Scottish settlement in Ireland) soon extended to include Inchiquin – a reaction encouraged by Lisle's ally and Inchiquin's rival in Munster, Lord Broghill. All in all, the situation seemed ripe for exploitation by the Confederates. But their unity, like that of the Covenanters, was crumbling, and over the same fundamental issue – how to counter the threat of a resurgent England.

Rinuccini

The Earl of Glamorgan arrived at Kilkenny in August 1645 with secret instructions from Charles to make him the best deal possible in obtaining Irish troops. Within a few weeks he had signed an agreement with the Confederates conceding most of their demands – including full recognition of the Catholic religion – in return for which they promised to send the king 10,000 troops. It was further agreed that this treaty was to remain secret until it had been confirmed by the king, and an agreement had been reached with Ormond regarding the Confederates' secular grievances. Ormond almost certainly knew about Glamorgan's treaty, at least in outline, and doubtless found it repugnant. Nevertheless, with the major religious issues off the agenda, he was able to reach an agreement with the Confederates in November that satisfied the peace party leaders. But it is a measure of Ormond's unease at Glamorgan's treaty that while he was finalising terms with the Confederates he put out feelers to the Westminster Presbyterians and to the British forces in Ulster.

In the event, the quarrel between the Independents and Scots at Westminster undermined Ormond's overtures to the Ulster Protestants. The Committee of Both Kingdoms had sent commissioners to Ulster with the aim of strengthening the English and parliamentary interest in the region as a check upon the New Scots. The commissioners quickly succeeded in alienating the New Scots, and without Monro's army a pan-Protestant alliance against the Confederates became unrealistic. If Ormond was to undermine the Glamorgan treaty, therefore, his best remaining option was to play upon the growing divisions within the Association; and here he found a powerful, if unwitting, ally in the figure of the papal nuncio, Giovanni Battista Rinuccini.

In 1643 the Confederates had asked the Vatican to send them a nuncio (papal envoy) in the hope that his presence would strengthen their authority and quicken the supply of money from the Catholic powers. The Confederates' request had been seized upon by the newly elected pope, Innocent X, as an opportunity to advance the cause of Catholicism, and the influence of the papacy, throughout the Stuart dominions. Early in 1645 he had appointed Rinuccini, a proud and energetic Italian archbishop, as nuncio, with instructions to establish in Ireland 'an unalterable right to the public exercise of the Catholic religion'.[9]

Rinuccini, who landed in Ireland in October 1645, has traditionally been seen as the prime mover behind clerical demands for a settlement that allowed freedom of worship for Ireland's Catholics and the restoration of papal jurisdiction. But as Tadhg Ó hAnnracháin has shown, Rinuccini simply gave leadership and direction to a party already committed to these goals.[10] Rinuccini exacerbated the factional struggle between the clerical party and the Ormondists, he did not instigate it.

As much as the Ormondists might have liked to ignore the nuncio, in practice this was impossible. The Association derived much of its legitimacy in the eyes of ordinary Confederates from its endorsement by the Catholic Church, and as the Holy See's leading representative in Ireland,

Rinuccini wielded immense influence over both the clergy and the Confederate rank-and-file. Moreover, his primary objective, which he was very resolute in pursuing, was directly at odds with that of the Ormondists. Whereas the latter were intent on a settlement with the king, which meant playing down the religious issue, the nuncio's mission was all about raising the profile of the Catholic Church in Ireland. Rinuccini's hand was strengthened by the ready money he brought with him from the Vatican and France. This was a larger sum than the Confederates could immediately lay their hands on, and Rinuccini implied that there was more to come. With cash to pay the Association's armies, Rinuccini could even dictate its military operations.

Like Ormond, Rinuccini disapproved of the Glamorgan treaty. But while Ormond thought it conceded too much to the Confederates, Rinuccini was adamant that it conceded too little. Within a few weeks of arriving at Kilkenny he had persuaded Glamorgan to write in even more concessions to Irish Catholicism. He also objected to the idea of a twin-track settlement in which the Ormondists got what they wanted by way of a public treaty while the clerical party's demands were addressed in secret. Then suddenly, late in December, Glamorgan's entire mission collapsed when Ormond had him arrested. Ormond had been obliged to take this step by the capture of Confederate correspondence containing a copy of the Glamorgan treaty, which Parliament's Ulster commissioners promptly relayed to Westminster. By arresting Glamorgan, Ormond hoped to distance both himself and the king from the earl's proceedings when the news reached England. Rinuccini exploited Glamorgan's arrest to delay the peace process, and then obtained a further postponement while details were sent to Ireland of a new and more favourable treaty concluded at Rome between the pope and Sir Kenelm Digby, an agent of the queen.

Whether Rinuccini was ever committed to any of these treaties seems doubtful. His preferred solution to the English problem was the same as that of the clerical party – to conquer all of Ireland and then either defy Parliament or drive a hard bargain with the king as the fortunes of war in England dictated. In light of Charles's tottering fortunes in England, this strategy made a whole lot more sense than that of the peace party, which continued to favour military intervention in support of a cause that had no armies left in Britain and of a king who was in no position to honour even the smallest of Confederate demands. The Royalists' defeat in the English Civil War lent the nuncio's strategy a compelling logic, and it was probably his appeal to reason as well as conscience that gave him such extraordinary influence among the Confederates. Indeed, by April 1646 even the Ormondists had recognised that Charles had been utterly defeated, and hence that 'the clearing of one of his dominions [i.e. Ireland] will be of greater consequency to his M[ajesty]s' service than an offer to assist him in England'.[11] Moreover, from a purely military perspective, their preferred method of 'clearing' Ireland of the king's enemies – namely, by joining forces with Ormond's Irish Royalists – was arguably more practical than Rinuccini's solution of a unilateral Confederate conquest. But Ormond's insistence (in accordance with the king's wishes) that a peace treaty must involve sending troops to England prevented his Confederate allies developing a more insular military strategy that might have formed the basis for compromise with the clerical party. Similarly, Rinuccini's high-profile support for the free and public exercise of Catholicism, and his objection to the Association returning the reins of government to a Protestant viceroy (Ormond) on conclusion of a treaty, raised barriers not only to an agreement with Ormond but also to one between the contending Confederate parties. Rinuccini's intervention and the king's determination, even in defeat, to solicit military support from Ireland were pulling the Association apart.

The King Surrenders

The Royalist war-machine in England was falling apart by the end of 1645. Oxford, Chester and a few other major garrisons still held out for the king, but the only sizeable blocks of territory that remained in Royalist hands were Devon, Cornwall, and central and north Wales, and these regions were now exhausted. On every front, Parliament's armies were relentlessly rolling back the king's shattered forces. The Royalist position in Scotland was no better. Although Huntly was still defying the Covenanters in the north-east, and it would be many months before MacColla was driven out of the western Highlands, the king's cause north of the border had effectively been crushed with Montrose's army at Philiphaugh.

As the net began to close around Charles at Oxford, so his isolation, both physical and political, increased. Most of his leading advisers were desperate for him to come to terms with Parliament while he still had a few bargaining counters left. The king, although attracted by the Independent grandees' secret offers to restore episcopacy, rightly feared that they intended to appropriate his prerogative powers and make him a puppet monarch. The Scots and Presbyterians were more respectful of royal sovereignty, but their great drawback in his eyes was their commitment to Presbyterianism. 'The nature of Presbyterian government', he informed the queen, 'is to steal or force the crown from the king's head. For their chief maxim is... that all kings must submit to Christ's kingdom, of which they are the sole governors.'[12]

As the prospect of a Royalist military revival receded, Charles's only viable option was to surrender himself to the Independents or the Scots in the hope of starting a bidding war between them for his favour. The problem for Charles, however, was that the Independents were reluctant to make a bid. They took the news of Glamorgan's treaty with the Irish, and of the Scots' intrigues with the queen and the French, particularly badly; and like everyone except the Scots and the most 'rigid' Presbyterians, thought that if the king was allowed to come to London to negotiate in person, as he repeatedly requested, his presence would spark a Royalist uprising in the capital. At the same time, Charles was coming under increasing pressure from the queen in Paris to conclude a French-sponsored treaty with the Covenanters. She and the Scots commissioners in London delegated the French agent, Montereul, to confer with Charles at Oxford in an attempt to overcome his religious scruples and his refusal to disavow Montrose. But Charles would not compromise, and by late March 1646 Montereul was so anxious to prevent him selling out to the Independents that he proceeded to make terms on his own initiative (the Scots commissioners being too worried on the same score to protest). After a hurried exchange of fudged promises and vague assertions, Charles was left believing that he would be honourably received by the Scottish army at Newark, and that the Scots and the French crown would use their influence, and if necessary their armies, to procure a settlement that would restore his 'just rights'. For his part, he agreed to receive instruction from Presbyterian divines, and to satisfy the Scots on religion so far as his conscience would allow. The issue of Montrose and the king's other friends was left unresolved. Communication difficulties between Newark, Oxford, London, and Paris added to the general misunderstanding; as did the divisions among and between the Committee of Estates in Edinburgh and their commissioners in London and Newark. Scottish commanders at Newark, for example, were deeply unhappy about the easy terms Charles had apparently been offered, and were unwilling to honour them.

In the end, the king and the Scots did not so much come together as were pushed. The surrender of Chester early in February robbed Charles of his last major port of entry for Irish troops, and in March his last significant body of infantry was defeated at Stow-on-the-Wold. As for the Scots, their cherished notion of a covenanted uniformity was taking a battering at Westminster. The Independents pushed through measures for reducing the size of Leven's army (on which the Scots relied to underwrite their terms for settlement); had the Scots' complaints about the Newcastle Propositions publicly burnt; and, following disclosure of further details of Glamorgan's treaty, succeeded in giving Lisle command of all Protestant forces in Ireland – an overt snub to both Monro and Ormond. In March, Parliament passed an ordinance that established Presbyterian church government but made it subordinate to parliamentary commissioners – creating, as Baillie caustically put it, 'a lame Erastian Presbyterie'.[13]

The one bright spot for the Scots was their growing support in the House of Lords and in the City. Since his resignation as commander-in-chief in April 1645, the Earl of Essex had worked hard to build a pro-Scots party in the Lords; and as frustration mounted during 1646 that military victory was not being translated into a political settlement, his support among the peers increased. The lack of a settlement, particularly of church government, also aggrieved the Scots' friends in the City – the London Presbyterian clergy and the 'Covenant-engaged citizens'. Working closely with Essex's party at Westminster, the covenanting citizens and ministers organised petitions to Parliament in November 1645 and again the following March in support of Scottish-style Presbyterianism. This call for a fully-fledged Presbyterian church reflected not just a desire to stem the growth of socially disruptive religious ideas, but also a sincere attachment to the Covenant 'in the Scots sense'.[14] The Presbyterian polemicist Thomas Edwards, for example, argued for a 'nearer union and communion' between the kingdoms, declaring his readiness to 'fal and perish … with the Kingdom of Scot[l]and, and the Presbyt[erian] party in England, standing for the Covenant'.[15]

Historians have undoubtedly underestimated the strength of English support for the Covenanters' programme. Certainly in London there was a powerful body of 'Scottified' opinion that favoured some form of British settlement. Faced with the breakdown of authority in England, and of English authority abroad, the Presbyterians drew inspiration from Scottish confederalist ideas much as some Independents apparently did from Spenserian imperialism. And perhaps if the Covenanters' campaign against Montrose and MacColla had begun in earnest in 1644 under a capable general, freeing Leven's army to make a decisive military breakthrough in England, a closer union informed by British values might actually have emerged.

The Scots, although heartened by their growing support in London, remained eager to have Charles join their army. Once he was safely in their grasp it would put him beyond the clutches of the Independents and their sympathisers among the royal councillors at Oxford. More importantly, it would give them a priceless opportunity to persuade him to accept their own terms for settlement, for they had little doubt that the king's attachment to episcopacy was based purely on ignorance. Regardless, therefore, of what had been offered Charles by Montereul, the Scots' leaders at Newark expected the king to assent to Presbyterianism and abandon Montrose. Charles damned the Scots as 'abominable relapsed rogues' and resolved to 'eschew all kind of captivity'.[16] But when his final efforts to obtain favourable terms from Parliament were rebuffed, and Montereul informed him that the Scots were still eager to receive him, he decided to delay no longer. Disguised as a servant and attended only by John Ashburnham (one of his courtiers) and a royal chaplain, he rode quietly out of Oxford on 27 April and slipped through the besieging Parliamentarian forces. After lingering to the west of London in the forlorn hope of receiving some last minute offer from Parliament or the City, he moved secretly and circuitously northwards and on 5 May arrived at Montereul's lodgings near Newark. Right to the last, he and the Scots had been striving to obtain assurances from the other without giving away anything substantial in return – Charles to preserve his conscience, friends, and freedom; the Scots to lure him to their army. But there was no disguising the fact that from 5 May Charles was the Scots' prisoner. His despairing flight to the Scottish army, more than the surrender of Oxford and his other remaining garrisons in the ensuing months, marked the end of the English Civil War.

Benburb and the Ormond Peace

Charles's hopeless condition by the spring of 1646 stretched to breaking point the credibility of the Ormondists' case for an easy-to-swallow (for the king) settlement and intervention in England. Although the news that Chester had surrendered made them question the wisdom of rushing troops to England, they remained eager to conclude an alliance with Ormond. On 28 March 1646, therefore, the Supreme Council and Ormond signed the treaty on civil issues that had been worked out the previous November. Rinuccini was not informed, and both sides agreed to delay publication of the treaty until Confederate troops had landed in England – whenever that might be. The Ormondists used this delay in an effort to obtain concessions from Ormond on religious issues, including his consent to the publication of Glamorgan's secret treaty alongside their own. But Ormond threatened to disown the Confederates if they insisted on Glamorgan's terms.

Each further straitening of the king's circumstances in England ratcheted up the quarrel in Ireland – heightening Ormond's pressure on the Supreme Council to send troops to Charles, and doubtless the nuncio's conviction of the folly of such an enterprise. Faced with the king's surrender to the Scots, the peace party lowered its demands still further, and dropped the idea of publishing Glamorgan's treaty altogether. Rinuccini was appalled – the more so when he realised soon afterwards that he had been duped over the signing of the treaty of 28 March. He concluded that the only way of preventing the Ormondists selling out the Association was to overthrow the Supreme Council.

Rinuccini's capacity to mount a coup was strengthened by a series of Confederate military successes during the summer, beginning with Owen Roe O'Neill's spectacular victory over the New Scots at Benburb, in Ulster, on 5 June. Much of the credit for this victory must go to Rinuccini himself, who had channelled a large slice of his funds to O'Neill. With this extra cash, O'Neill had been able to recruit more troops and to go onto the offensive. Monro's army, weakened by the loss of regiments to shore up the Covenanters' campaigns in England and Scotland, was outgeneralled and out-fought and lost almost half its complement of 5000 men. Lack of supplies and siege equipment prevented O'Neill from following up his victory; although in fact he was more interested in quartering his army in the rich pastures of Leinster than in fighting on in war-torn Ulster. Then in August he received a call from the nuncio to move his army south to help crush the Ormond treaty. Rinuccini's money had also enabled Preston to roll back the British forces in Connacht, but this campaign too had stalled by August through lack of supplies, and pleas from both the Ormondists and the nuncio to put his army at their disposal.

O'Neill's victory at Benburb, by shifting military power within the Association to the Ulster militants, caused consternation among the Ormondists, and persuaded them that the Ormond treaty should be published without delay. Their mandate to begin proceedings for returning Ireland to royal authority was strengthened in July, when Digby returned to Dublin from France with news that the king and queen approved of the Ormond treaty. At the same time, the chief French agent in Ireland announced that his government would broker the treaty and provide military assistance against the English Parliament. The French were concerned at the threat the Westminster Independents posed to Charles and to their fellow Catholics in Ireland. But not the least of their motives in backing the Ormond peace was to undermine the influence of those Confederates, such as O'Neill, who were cordially disposed to France's great rival, Spain. Encouraged by these assurances from the French and Digby, Ormond published the treaty on 30 July. The Supreme Council followed suit on 3 August and began preparations to relinquish power to Ormond. Although the published treaty articles contained nothing about Catholic church property, the Ormondists had probably received promises that substantial religious concessions would be made once they had honoured their pledges to help the king.

Rinuccini and his supporters responded swiftly to the treaty's publication. A clerical assembly that the nuncio had convened at Waterford declared that the terms of the treaty violated the oath of association by failing to make provision for the public exercise of Catholicism. Confident in the support of O'Neill, who was already moving his army southwards, Rinuccini and the clerical party pressed for more substantial concessions on religious and constitutional issues. Although the peace party promised to return to the negotiating table, they continued preparations to hand over the reins of Confederate government to Ormond. To facilitate this transfer of power and to overawe the opponents of the treaty, the peace party invited Ormond to Kilkenny. When news reached Waterford that Ormond and a body of Royalist troops were *en route* to Kilkenny, Rinuccini, with the full support of the clergy, published a declaration on 1 September excommunicating all those who acknowledged the treaty.

By invoking the ultimate religious sanction of excommunication, Rinuccini had taken a big gamble. But he had judged the mood among the Confederate rank-and-file well. Preston had been wavering in his support for Rinuccini, but doubting that his men would obey him in defiance of the excommunication order he had little choice but to affirm his allegiance to the nuncio. Likewise, several key members of the peace faction defected to Rinuccini's camp in September. With the authority of the peace party shattered, and O'Neill's and Preston's armies committed to the nuncio, Ormond was forced to scuttle back to Dublin, narrowly avoiding capture in the process. On 15 September the clerical party imprisoned the authors of the peace treaty, and eleven days later established a new Supreme Council headed by Rinuccini.

The nuncio's success in September 1646 is largely attributable to his great spiritual authority and his having the wherewithal to pay the Association's armies. The majority of Confederates evidently desired a treaty with Ormond, but not on terms that were unacceptable to the clergy. It was, in the words of Ó hAnnracháin, 'the incompatibility of these two objectives which defined their unhappy dilemma'.[17] But what also worked in Rinuccini's favour was the state of affairs in England. He was probably not alone in thinking that the king's defeat there had rendered obsolete the notion of a treaty that was conditional on rushing troops to England. Those who backed the nuncio may well have shared his conviction that it was vital to strengthen the Association's position on their side of the Irish Sea in light of the king's evident weakness on his.

The Dublin Offensive

His opponents in disarray and the Confederates' armies at his command, Rinuccini set about pursuing his objective of outright military victory, and began to organise an attack on Dublin. Possession of the city would give the Confederates a massive strategic and propaganda boost. Moreover, Rinuccini was convinced that its capture would persuade the Vatican to send more money to Ireland, without which it would be impossible for the Confederates to retain the military initiative. These considerations were not without merit. However, it is arguable that the nuncio would have been wiser to exploit his ascendancy by systematically destroying the Ormondists' power-base, particularly in military affairs, before committing the Association to a venture that many Confederates considered extreme and that in the event of failure would undermine his own and the clerical party's authority.

From the outset, the campaign against Dublin was a fiasco. The new Supreme Council's desire not to alienate either Preston or O'Neill obliged it to employ both their armies. Inevitably, the burden of maintaining a dual command of over 15,000 men in the winter months was just too great for the Confederates to sustain, with predictable results in terms of military discipline. It was not long before Preston had grown so alarmed at the foraging activities of O'Neill's Ulstermen (an 'unlimited multitude of licentious caterpillars', as he called them) that he made secret offers of military support to Ormond in return for assurances on religious issues.[18]

The final blow to the Confederate campaign against Dublin was administered, indirectly, by Ormond. Angered by what he saw as the

Confederates' treachery in reneging on the treaty, and with Dublin under threat of siege, he sent commissioners to Westminster with an offer to surrender Dublin to Parliament in return for military support and assurances of favourable treatment of Irish Royalists. Once again, however, his overtures to Parliament foundered on the rock of factional rivalry in England. The Independents, keen to promote Lisle as lord lieutenant of Ireland, had managed to wrest control of Irish affairs from the Presbyterians, and their subsequent failure (which was possibly deliberate) to follow up Ormond's offers led to the collapse of the negotiations late in November. Once the prospect of gaining Dublin had receded, the Independents renewed their preparations for Lisle's expedition, Broghill taking three English regiments over to Munster in December. But there was one positive result of the talks as far as Ormond was concerned and that was the arrival of a parliamentary fleet in Dublin Bay, which persuaded the Confederates of the futility of continuing their siege of the city. O'Neill promptly withdrew his forces, while Preston redoubled his efforts to forge a royalist alliance with Ormond based upon the March treaty. Under pressure from Clanricarde and Digby, Ormond opened a dialogue with Preston, but effectively scuppered any chances of an agreement by refusing to budge on the issue of church lands. Without supplies for his army and under threat of excommunication, Preston broke off talks and dispersed his troops into winter quarters.

The failure of the attack on Dublin was a major blow to the Association as well as to Rinuccini personally. An understandably angry and frightened Ormond was now busily exploring the option of surrendering the city to Parliament, which was clearly not in the Confederates' best interests. Moreover, the campaign had made a mockery of the nuncio's strategy of total conquest. The military momentum needed for total conquest could only be sustained through sizeable injections of cash and munitions from the Continent. But the Vatican had more immediate calls on its resources, while what little money the French and Spanish invested in the Association was with a view to recruiting Irish troops.

Isolated and demoralised by late 1646, Rinuccini and the clerical party allowed a group of moderates, headed by Nicholas Plunkett and the bishop of Ferns, Nicholas French, to pursue a policy of compromise and accommodation. Although both Plunkett and French were of Old English extraction, they were trusted by the nuncio as 'good Catholics', and were able to construct a middle ground in Confederate politics that bridged the factional divide. They worked particularly hard over the winter of 1646–7 to reconcile the defeated peace party, persuading Preston to re-affirm his loyalty to the Association, and the Supreme Council to release the Ormondist leaders imprisoned in September.

But these were essentially short-term measures; they did not address the Confederates' fundamental predicament – how to contend with Protestant England. Both Confederate solutions to the English problem – rushing assistance to Charles in the hope that the king's gratitude would win substantial concessions; or making Ireland impregnable to attack and renegotiating its relationship with England from a position of maximum strength – had been exposed as unviable. The first had foundered in the face of the king's defeat in the English Civil War and the impossibility of reconciling the royal supremacy in religion and Catholic demands for an independent church. The second had failed through lack of resources, and the ruinous impact of political divisions upon military strategy and operations. Fortunately for the Confederates, England's recovery at the end of the Civil War was attended by numerous complications. Until the conflicting interests of king, Independents, and Covenanters had some-how been squared, there was little prospect of English hostility towards Ireland's Catholics being translated into concerted military action.

'False Juggling': the King in Captivity

Possession of the king was central to the calculations of all the main play-ers in British politics. Without his consent no final settlement was deemed possible. The Scots therefore, though they had anticipated Charles's arrival, could scarcely believe their good fortune when he finally turned up at Newark. For all the New Model's victories, the Scots and the Presbyterians now had the winning hand and could seemingly play it at will. They had little doubt that they could persuade the king to accept the Covenant, and they could thereby gain a strong enough party to impose their own terms upon Parliament and the Independents. Their only major worry was that Fairfax and his men would resist a covenanted settlement; and, as Adamson has shown, the Earl of Essex had already addressed this problem. Essex had conceived a scheme to combine the City militia, Parliament's armies in the West Country and south Wales under two of his closest allies, Edward Massie and Roland Laugharne, and the Scottish forces as a counterweight to the New Model. But if this imaginary puissance was actually to materialise it required the king's acceptance of Presbyterianism, for without it the Scots were not prepared to commit their army on his behalf.

The news of the king's flight to the Scots left some Independents angry, others 'drouping sorrowfull', but all 'generallie in a grit fricht'.[19] They expected, as the Presbyterians did, that Charles would cave in to his captors' demands. In a desperate bid to regain the initiative, the Independent grandees procured a Commons' order that the disposal of the king was a matter for the English Parliament, and sent a powerful force of New Model cavalry to seize Charles at Newark. By this time, however, Essex and his party had secured a narrow majority in the Lords, which countermanded all orders for removing the king from Leven's army. Nevertheless, the Scots were anxious to avoid any risk of confrontation with the New Model until Charles had taken the Covenant, and therefore, after persuading him to order the surrender of Newark, they hurriedly decamped with their prize to Newcastle. But once they began talking in earnest with the king they soon discovered that he had no intention of making any serious concessions. He refused to take the Covenant or to countenance the establishment of Presbyterianism in England. His determination not to compromise was reinforced by a feeling that the Scots had betrayed him. He complained bitterly to the queen of their 'false juggling' and of their 'barbarous usage' of him.[20] The only concession that the Scots were able to extract from him was a final admission of military defeat. On 19 May, Charles issued orders to all the forces that were acting in his name to lay down their arms. In Scotland, Huntly complied immediately, and Montrose left for the Continent. Antrim and MacColla, on the other hand, continued to defy the Campbells, but without the legitimacy of fighting in the king's name many of their Highland allies deserted them and made peace with Edinburgh.

But while the Covenanters' possession of the king helped to strengthen their position in Scotland, it left them perilously exposed in Ulster and England. When Ormond learnt of the king's (misplaced) confidence that the Covenanters would join with Montrose to fight for him, he naturally assumed that the New Scots would be similarly disposed to join with his Irish Royalists against Parliament. But Monro was anxious not to jeopardise his alliance with the increasingly powerful pro-Parliament interest in Ulster, nor his supply lines from England, and relayed to London a copy of a letter that the king had sent Ormond in April – and which Ormond had optimistically forwarded to Monro – outlining Charles's hopes of a military alliance with the Covenanters. In vain the Scots commissioners in London denounced this letter as 'a most damnable untruth'.[21] Indeed, such was the distrust of the Scots at Westminster that Monro himself was suspected of treachery.

English suspicion of the New Scots turned to disdain after their defeat at Benburb in June. Benburb altered the balance of power in Ulster, giving the British forces a clear numerical superiority over the New Scots. It thus weakened the Covenanters' pretensions to a 'joint interest' in Ireland, and made their enemies even more determined that they should have no part in managing the war. After Benburb the Independents redoubled their efforts to undermine Monro's authority as commander-in-chief.

The longer the Scots detained the king without striking a deal with him, the more vulnerable their position in England became. The Independents were quick to exploit patriotic resentment at the Scots' refusal to hand over Charles, and at the Scottish forces' continued plundering in the northern counties, and on 19 May secured a Commons vote that England had no further use for the Scottish army. Although Essex's party in the Lords rejected this vote, it again exposed the weakness of the Presbyterians while they remained dependent upon the Scots.

Unable to secure a majority in the Commons, the Earl of Essex turned to his allies in the City to pressure MPs into accepting the Presbyterian alliance's terms for settlement. At the instigation of Essex's party, and with the help of London's Presbyterian ministry, the Common Council drew up a remonstrance, which was presented to both Houses on 26 May, demanding 'the neerest conjunction and uniformity in Religion' with Scotland, and the immediate despatch of peace propositions to the king.[22] The pro-Scots majority in the Lords gave the remonstrance an enthusiastic reception, and promised to root out sectaries and to preserve the union with Scotland; but in the Commons the Independents were strong enough to ensure that the remonstrance was effectively ignored. Nevertheless, on the back of this successful mobilisation of metropolitan power, Essex's party managed to tone down some of the more offensive (from a covenanting perspective) clauses in the Newcastle Propositions. This was small comfort to the Scots when set against their losses at Benburb and the growing possibility of war with England if they failed to reach agreement with the king. Relations between the Scots and their English enemies had now become so strained that the 'weightiest heads' in the Commons believed that 'the civill warr of the civill war' was imminent.[23]

The Great Combustion

The king's flight to the Scots distressed some Royalists almost as much as it did the Independents. It was reported that many of the king's party in

Newark regretted that they had ever engaged in his service, and one Royalist gentleman was so disgusted by the king's actions that he allowed himself to become a propaganda tool of the Independents, declaring before the Commons that Charles's surrender to the Scots was not only 'infinitely prejuditiall to himselfe and this Kingdome, but dishonorable to the English nation'.[24] His sentiments were shared by Sir Edward Hyde. Better that the king had been captured at Oxford by the New Model Army, thought Hyde, than to have thrown himself upon the mercy of the Scots. 'I thought it an unkingly thing', he declared, 'to ask relief of those who had done all the mischief.'[25]

Hyde was a central figure in the 'great combustion' that broke out among the Prince of Wales's advisers in June: a quarrel that both encapsulated and hardened the differences among the Royalist elite. The New Model's conquest of the West Country over the winter of 1645–6 had forced the prince and his council to take ship for Jersey. By June 1646 the council had received orders from the queen that the prince should join her in Paris, for rumours abounded that if Parliament got its hands on him the Independent grandees would set him up as king in place of his father. The debate over how to respond to these orders split the prince's entourage down the middle. Lord Digby (who had sailed to Jersey from Ireland) and Lord Jermyn headed a group that urged the prince's immediate removal to France, arguing that their greatest hope of restoring the king lay with the French, 'not only for the assistance they were to receave from them in men or money, but for what the Scotts should doe for the Kinge; and that…without the Prince's goinge into France, they would doe nothinge'.[26] Hyde and his supporters responded that the king's best policy lay in fomenting the divisions between Independents and Presbyterians, and remaining true to his principles in the hope of a 'resurrection of the English affection and loyalty'.[27] They argued that placing the prince in the custody of a foreign power, whose interest was antithetical to that of England, would reconcile the parties at Westminster, undermine the prospect of a negotiated settlement, and alienate the affections of the English people.

Underlying these two contrasting positions were conflicting notions of what constituted an acceptable settlement. Digby and Jermyn were willing to employ Scottish or French troops to restore the king so long as it gave him the opportunity somewhere along the line to recoup, and ideally extend, his lost sovereignty. Hyde and his friends, on the other hand, were anxious to restore not just the monarchy but the whole panoply of English law and government – or 'the Patria' as Hyde put it[28] – without which, they argued, the honour and power of the crown and the nation would be seriously impaired. Restoring the king by foreign conquest obviously ran entirely counter to such sentiments. This desire to demarcate and preserve an English frame of government, belief in the superiority of England's laws and institutions, and distrust of the Covenanters and French, had strong echoes in the thinking of the Independent grandees. In fact, there are grounds for arguing that the fundamental division in British politics by late 1646 was no longer that of Royalist versus Parliamentarian and Covenanter, but between Hyde's Royalist 'patriots' and leading Independents on the one hand, and the covenanting interest and pro-Scots Royalists on the other. Certainly the debates on Jersey ended extremely rancorously, with a 'visible strangenesse' growing between royalist patriots and politiques.[29] When the prince left for France, eager to sample the delights of Paris, Hyde and those councillors who shared his convictions remained on Jersey.

The Return of Hamilton

It was just as well for Hyde and his friends that they were not privy to the king's thoughts during his Scottish captivity at Newcastle. For besides urging the queen to bring the prince to Paris by force if necessary, he continued to wheedle for military support from the Scots, the French, and his other foreign sympathisers. He secretly urged Ormond to continue treating with the Confederates for an army; he even contemplated soliciting help from the pope. But in the short term his best hope lay in building a party for himself among the Covenanter leaders – many of whom had come to Newcastle to kiss his hand – and in this he was helped considerably by the re-emergence of the Duke of Hamilton as a force in Scottish politics. Imprisoned on the king's orders late in 1643, Hamilton had not been freed until April 1646, when the New Model had captured the fortress in Cornwall where he was being held. At first he was understandably reluctant to serve the king again, but his brother, the Earl of Lanark, persuaded him that the distressed state of Scotland demanded it. In the changed circumstances since his imprisonment, Hamilton recognised that the Scottish Parliament and army would not join wholeheartedly in prosecuting the king's cause in England unless Charles took the Covenant. He also appreciated that the rise of the Independent party at Westminster made closer religious and political union with England vital for Scotland's future security.

Hamilton's rehabilitation increased the divisions within the Covenanter leadership. The king distinguished four main factions among the Scots by June – Montrose's hard-line Royalists (who were not represented at Newcastle), the 'neutrals' under the Earl of Callander, Hamilton's party, and Argyll's party. Both the neutrals and Hamilton's party favoured a moderate settlement, but personal rivalry between their leaders precluded an alliance. The king shrewdly observed that although the majority of the Scottish nobles were now aligned with Hamilton, most of the ministry and the parliamentary gentry and burgesses still adhered to Argyll. So now, in addition to the hostility and scorn that the Scots' retention of the king and defeat at Benburb had aroused among the English, Covenanter unity itself was beginning to crumble. By mid-June it was becoming clear to the Scots that the king would not accept their terms for settlement, and therefore that his presence among them was more a liability than an advantage.

The king's intransigence, and Hamilton's reappearance, threatened the Covenanter cause in general and Argyll's pre-eminence in particular. Hence it was Argyll who took the lead in trying to repair the breach with Westminster before the quarrel between the two kingdoms turned into open war. This meant accepting Parliament's terms for settlement – a pill made easier to swallow for the Scots by the success of their English allies in moderating the Newcastle Propositions. The covenanting grandees still found the propositions distasteful, but were desperate to reach a settlement while they still had possession of the king. On 25 June, Argyll addressed the two Houses in the name of his countrymen and accepted a slightly modified version of the propositions that the Scots had denounced just a few months earlier as an affront to the Covenant.

The Newcastle Propositions were presented to Charles late in July. There was little optimism that he would accept them, containing as they did a demand that he take the Covenant and agree to settle Presbyterianism. Yet it was precisely because they paid at least lip-service to the idea of a covenanted uniformity that the Scots pressed them upon him. Likewise, the queen, the pro-Scots Royalists, and the French pleaded with him to be flexible. But Charles remained adamant that Presbyterianism was 'destructive to monarchy' and repugnant to his 'conscience, crown, and honour'.[30] Nor could he submit to the propositions relating to Ireland without fatally undermining Ormond's long-awaited (although as it proved, abortive) treaty with the Irish Confederates.

Shifting Strategies: Argyll and Hamilton

The king's refusal to accept either the Scots' own terms or the Newcastle Propositions helped bring about a major shift in Argyll's thinking during 1646. For the previous six years or more he had publicly championed the cause of Scottish intervention in England and Ireland. Now, however, he began to throw his weight behind a policy of abandoning the king to the English Parliament and withdrawing Scottish forces from England and Ulster. MacColla and the MacDonalds still occupied most of his lands in the western Highlands, and looked set to do so for months to come. Argyll needed Leven's and Monro's veterans to drive them out and thereby recoup the military and political influence he had lost after Inverlochy. The return to power of his great rival, Hamilton, made it all the more necessary for Argyll to look to his domestic power-base. Yet scaling down Scotland's archipelagic commitments would risk leaving the Covenanters powerless to curb English aggression – a problem made all the more acute by the rise of the Independents and their imperialist designs upon Ireland, which threatened Scotland with military encirclement. Argyll's solution to this problem was bold to say the least. According to Clement Walker, he secretly abandoned the Westminster Presbyterians late in 1645 and joined counsels with 'the Independent Junto'; his ultimate aim being to transform Scotland 'into a free state like the Estates of Holland'.[31] Although this is undoubtedly an exaggeration, it is clear that the policy of Scottish withdrawal that Argyll had been pushing (particularly in Ulster) from late 1645 was very much in tune with the Independents' desire to reverse the confederalist trend in English and Irish affairs. Moreover, by consolidating his power and reputation in Scotland, and not over-extending Covenanter resources on fruitless (not to say counter-productive) intervention in the other two kingdoms, Argyll could pursue a policy of talking softly to the English while carrying a big stick. A united Covenanter Scotland, perhaps in alliance with Sweden or France, was not a force to be trifled with, and would give Argyll considerable leverage at Westminster. In some ways, therefore, Argyll's strategy for dealing with England paralleled that of Rinuccini in Ireland.

Argyll's shift away from an interventionist approach was mirrored by Hamilton's abandonment of his neutralist stance of 1642–3 in favour of a forward policy in England. Like Argyll, Hamilton had powerful friends at Westminster. But he had no clan power-base to fall back on, as Argyll did. In fact much of his influence in Scotland before 1637 had derived from his intimacy with Charles, and the court offices that went with it.

Argyll's policy of rapprochement with the Independents was never an option for him. His political survival depended upon a settlement in which monarchy would serve as a buttress not only for Scotland's autonomy but also for his own influence. This meant restoring to Charles his prerogative powers in all three kingdoms, and establishing a strong and permanent Scottish presence at court. More immediately, it required that Leven's and Monro's armies be maintained as deterrents against the Independents seizing the king and using his powers to dominate both England and Ireland. In essence, Hamilton now favoured a watered-down confederalism, and as the Scots became increasingly alarmed at the spread of radical ideas in England, and fearful of the Independents' intentions towards the king, he was able to attract a powerful following among moderate Covenanters.

The King between the Two Kingdoms

The king's persistent refusal to accept the Newcastle Propositions or take the Covenant made it impossible for the Hamiltonians to make an effective case for holding him or for maintaining a Scottish military presence in England. Neither Hamilton nor indeed Argyll would risk war with the 'Sectarian army' for an uncovenanted king. Nor did they relish the prospect of taking Charles back to Scotland, where he would doubtless try to resurrect Montrose's party and stir up new quarrels between the two kingdoms. The Covenanters' position in England had become untenable, and by late summer even their English allies were keen that they hand over the king and return home.

For many months the Independents had been able to exploit the stream of northern complaints about Leven's army to sustain their majority in the Commons and to depict the Scots' friends at Westminster as traitors to the national interest. Moreover, despite the fact that the Civil War was now over, the majority of MPs were unwilling to disband the New Model while the Scots continued to occupy English territory. The Presbyterian grandees began to realise that the withdrawal of the Scots would weaken their enemies much more than it would them. At a stroke it would undermine the Independents' ascendancy in the Commons and their argument for maintaining the New Model. And with the Scots gone, the Presbyterians could seek less stringent terms from the king – even drop the requirement that he take the Covenant, which had proved the greatest stumbling block to a settlement.

In mid-August the Scots agreed to quit England upon payment of the arrears they claimed Parliament owed their army. The Presbyterians worked hard to secure the best deal they could for them, and after heated debate at Westminster the sum of £400,000 was fixed upon – half to be paid before the army withdrew. The Presbyterians' readiness to end their reliance on the Scottish army was a sign of their growing confidence. Indeed, by early September the Earl of Essex was marshalling his support in the Lords and his military following in the City and West Country to make himself 'generalissimo' of the New Model and to force the Commons 'to concur towards the king'.[32] But the design collapsed on 14 September when Essex died of an 'apoplex' after catching cold out hunting. His untimely death was a major blow to both the Presbyterians and the Scots. Only Essex had the power and popularity to overawe the Independents and impose a moderate settlement.

The death of Essex made Hamilton and his supporters even more agitated at the thought of surrendering Charles to a hostile English regime. They begged Charles to consider how desperate his condition would be in England once the Scottish army had returned home, which must inevitably follow if he refused to accept a Presbyterian settlement, for this was the minimum price at which most Scots would engage for him. The king, however, was determined to hold out for easier terms, feeling sure that the Scots' nerve would crack at the thought of their native sovereign in the clutches of the Independents.

The king's intransigence and the threatening noises coming from Westminster and the New Model left the Scots little choice but to begin preparations for handing him over to the English. Nevertheless, they were anxious for the English Parliament to respect his regal powers, particularly in relation to Scotland. They asked that he be received in London 'with safety, freedome, and honour', and that no settlement be forced on him to the detriment of Scottish interests.[33] These were perfectly reasonable demands, but they were rightly construed by the Independent grandees as an attempt by the Scots and their English allies to set the agenda for the king's restoration in England. And as usual when the Scots threatened their plans for settlement, the grandees tried to rouse Parliament and the people in defence of English honour. On 26 October, one of their 'northern beagles' – the Yorkshire MP Thomas Chaloner – delivered a speech in the Commons arguing that the Scots had no legitimate interest in the king while he remained in England.[34] Parliament was the supreme authority in the kingdom, Chaloner insisted, 'accountable to none but God Almighty', and as such could dispose of both the king's person and office as it saw fit. He did not need to add that by appropriating the royal prerogative, Parliament could claim regal power over all the king's dominions. In pressing for the complete subordination of regal authority to the English Parliament, Chaloner's speech evinced a deeply Anglocentric view of the relationship between the three kingdoms. Although Chaloner had been speaking for the grandees, his arguments struck a chord with more radical Independents, in particular Henry Marten, who virtually demanded the king's execution. Like the trauma of civil war, or the logic of the Puritan impulse, the challenge to English identity inherent in Scottish confederalism was fuelling a radical reappraisal of England's government and constitution.

It was no accident that Chaloner's speech was subsequently published – flouting parliamentary etiquette governing the confidentiality of its debates – nor that he delivered it on the very day of a formal meeting between leading Parliament-men and the Scots commissioners to discuss the disposal of the king. The Independent grandees were strongly represented at this meeting, and they made the same point as Chaloner, only more forcefully. The Earl of Northumberland told the commissioners that 'the kings auncestors came into this kingdom by conquest and nowe he being conquered they might dispose of the kingdome and affaires as they pleased'.[35] Sir John Evelyn was blunter still, invoking the grisly fate of Mary Queen of Scots (Charles's grandmother) to remind the commissioners of the power the English could wield over a Scottish royal 'prisoner'. The Scots, understandably, were outraged, and riposted that 'if the Kinge of England were conquered yet they [the Independents] had nether conquered the kinge of Scottland nor the Kinge of Ireland. And that he [had] lost but England wch he might reconquer.' The grandees' views on disposing of the king sounded to the Scots more like 'a deposeinge of the Kinge', and they were threatening to declare war before they would allow that to happen. 'Yow thinke yow walke in a mist,' they told the grandees, 'but we p[er]ceave yow well ynoughe ... we have reason to beleeve yow intend when opportunity is given to fall uppon us, but we neyther feare yow nor care for yow.' Fighting talk.

The Departure of the Scots

The chauvinistic rhetoric emanating from London bolstered Hamilton's support in the Scottish Parliament, which re-assembled at Edinburgh on 3 November. He and his party were convinced that the Independents intended to abolish monarchy and 'governe like the Turk – through their army', and by December a sizeable number of the parliamentary gentry and burgesses apparently shared their fears.[36] In the main executive committee of the Scottish Parliament, the Committee for Common Burdens, the Hamiltonians could muster almost as much support as Argyll's party, and on 15 December the committee resolved to issue a declaration in support of Charles's title to the English crown and demanding that he be allowed to travel freely to London. The next day, however, Argyll and the Kirk rallied their supporters and after a debate of 'much violence and bitternes' the committee agreed that if the king did not consent to the Newcastle Propositions then the Scottish people would settle the government of Scotland without him, and offer him no guarantee of support even if the English deposed him.[37]

Right to the last the Hamiltonians pressed Charles to take the Covenant. But he was more than ever convinced that to abolish episcopacy in favour of Presbyterianism was a 'great sin'.[38] In the hope that he would see sense, the Hamiltonians tried to keep Leven's army up to strength – 'it is a sad thing that so manie Gallant men most [sic] be disbanded befor government ather in Church or State be settled in England or Irland'.[39] But most Scots blanched at the idea of risking war with England by keeping their army there in the name of an uncovenanted king; and besides, the burden of maintaining such a large force was too great for a nation exhausted by years of war and racked by plague epidemics. In January 1647, Argyll's party pushed through legislation for reducing the army to 7000 men. Royalist sympathisers were purged and effective command was given to Argyll's ally, Lieutenant-General David Leslie. The Scottish Parliament finally lost patience with Charles on 16 January 1647, when it resolved to take a vote on whether he should be left at Newcastle. Hamilton and his supporters attempted to have the wording changed to 'Whither or not his Majestie who wes our Native King...should be delivered up to the Sectaries avowed enemies to his liffe and Government.'[40] But this new motion was rejected and, by the narrowest of margins, the Scottish Parliament voted to leave Charles in England. On 30 January, Leven's army abandoned Newcastle and its royal prisoner to the English. By 3 February the Scots had received the first half of their £400,000, and within a few days all their forces had withdrawn into Scotland.

Although the Scots recognised the danger in continuing to harbour an unregenerate Charles, surrendering him to an English Parliament dominated by the Independents seemed almost as threatening, particularly to

Hamilton and his faction. If the English radicals gained custody of the king and imposed their own settlement, then as the duke informed one of his correspondents, 'some of us shall not onely want power, but wish to be out of the world'.[41] But for all their foreboding over the fate of monarchy and their kingdom, the Scots actually had reason to feel optimistic. Granted, their relinquishing of Charles was a public relations disaster: the Earl of Lauderdale had a point when he said that delivering up the king 'would make them to be hissed at by all nations; yea the doggs in the streets would pisse uppon them'.[42] Yet by withdrawing from England, the Scots would hand the political advantage at Westminster to their allies, who should then, with careful management, be able to quash Lisle's lieutenancy, disband the New Model, and secure a moderate settlement that satisfied at least some of the Scots' concerns for their kingdom's security. With the war over and the Scots off the scene, it was the Presbyterians who seemed the most likely to profit from England's recovery.

Chapter 5: The Rise of the New Model Army: February–December 1647

Settlement Deferred

The structural tensions inherent in the Stuart multiple monarchy – a contributory factor in the outbreak of the wars – posed a major obstacle to the attainment of a well-grounded peace. Although Charles could and did appeal to his duty to defend the interests of all his peoples, in practice this was impossible given their incompatible political and religious objectives. After his defeat in the English Civil War, he effectively required the backing of two of his kingdoms in order to mend his fractured realm – or of one, if that kingdom was England. The summer of 1646, when he was presented with the Newcastle Propositions, was his best chance of making peace with his British kingdoms; the summer of 1647 would be his best opportunity to reach a settlement in England. In both instances he preferred to sow division among his subjects and hold out for better terms.

The three kingdoms responded in different ways to the deferral of settlement. Ireland's position within the Stuart multiple monarchy was never more isolated than in the 18 months following the collapse of the Ormond peace. Ormond himself showed little inclination to reopen a meaningful dialogue with the Confederates, and the dominant party at Kilkenny was not prepared to make the necessary concessions to regain his trust. Lesser parties on both sides remained committed to a Royalist–Confederate alliance, but their actions merely served to undermine the Confederates' only feasible alternative, which was to conquer all of Ireland and solicit help from the Continent.

In England, the resentment that Charles provoked in trying to play the New Model's supporters off against the Scots hastened the emergence of radical pressure-groups in London and among the soldiery. The conservative reaction that gripped all three kingdoms in 1647–8 can be traced directly to the growing pressure within English politics for a radical new dispensation in church and state, involving greatly reduced roles for the monarchy, the Lords, and an established church.

Why England alone of the three kingdoms should have witnessed such a systematic questioning of the fundamentals of government and society is an intriguing question. Part of the answer lies in the differences between the kingdoms' social and economic structures. Scotland and Ireland contained some of the poorest, most sparsely populated, and least agriculturally developed regions in the Stuart realm; conditions that were not conducive to the emergence of a prosperous, economically independent, and literate middling sort of the kind that had appeared in some parts of England. Above all, perhaps, neither kingdom possessed a social and intellectual milieu to rival London in size, wealth, or demand for news and ideas. Londoners represented the biggest market for the amazing – and in European terms, unrivalled – variety of printed works that poured from England's unregulated press during the 1640s. The few printers in Scotland were closely monitored by the authorities, while in Ireland there were probably no more than half a dozen printing presses in the entire kingdom.

Differences in national political culture also shaped the kingdoms' varying responses to the deferral of settlement. The reverence in which the English held their common law, the richness and intricacy of this legal legacy, and the interest that anyone could claim in it as the 'birthright' of 'freeborn Englishmen', were potentially destabilising factors when the legitimacy of the institutions that framed and enforced the law was in doubt – as was the case in England by mid-1647. At one level, the concept of fundamental law was a 'profoundly integrative' creed that exerted appeal across virtually the entire political spectrum.[1] For some contemporaries, however, particularly those exposed to the egalitarian ethos within sectarian Puritanism, it could assume a highly individualistic strain that abandoned faith in the letter of the law for an assertion of the universal principles of equity and justice.

The failure of the covenanting revolution to generate a doctrine of the natural rights of man may well have been linked to the more qualified authority of Scots law compared with English common law. Furthermore, the Covenant, which had always held greater appeal north of the border than south, imposed strict corporate limits upon individual political expression. It tied the subscriber to collective action in defence of 'His Majesty's just power and greatness' as well as the 'true religion and liberties of the kingdoms'.[2] The Covenant prescribed a set of divinely ordained objectives that depended for their fulfilment upon preserving the institutions of Kirk, Parliament, and crown, thereby restricting the scope for individual reinterpretation. Thus the 'legalism and theological finality' of the National Covenant and its 1643 successor may have discouraged any tendency in Scotland towards the fissiparous political and religious environment that troubled post-Civil War England.[3]

To the list of propitious conditions in England for sustaining a debate over constitutional first principles must be added the fact that it was the only one of the three kingdoms to experience a full-scale *civil* war. The Covenanters and Confederates had each arrived at more or less consensual internal settlements in the period 1638–42. Their wars were mostly against irreconcilable religious or 'national' enemies, not members of the same political community. When they did squabble among themselves it was largely over how best to secure their respective settlements within the Stuart realm, rather than over the frame of government and the locus of authority within the national polity. But it was essentially these issues that the war in England had been fought to decide, and that, as a result of the king's intransigence, were still provoking controversy and division in 1647.

The Presbyterian Ascendancy

The withdrawal of Leven's army strengthened calls in England for disbanding Parliament's forces and restoring the traditional peace-time order. Many parts of the country, particularly the north and the west Midlands, had endured years of warfare and plundering, and the epidemics and economic dislocation that spread in their wake. To add to the general misery the 1646 harvest had failed, driving up the price of basic foodstuffs and forcing tenants to default on their rents. Even those regions that had escaped the fighting had been taxed at unprecedented levels. By 1647 there was widespread longing for a return to the rule of law, which the majority of English people equated with a restoration of the king.

The Presbyterians, as the enemies of the army and the sects, were well placed to capitalise on this desire for a return to 'known ways'. Moreover,

with the Scots gone, the stream of reports about their plundering in the
northern counties dried up, depriving the Independents of their most
effective means of sustaining a Commons majority. No longer could they
play upon wounded English pride or fears of a peace dictated by the
Scots to blacken the reputations of the Presbyterians. The Scots' withdrawal also removed any justification for maintaining another of the
Independents' political props, the New Model Army – unless it was for
deployment against the Irish rebels. The non-aligned majority in the
Commons now swung behind the Presbyterians' programme of disbanding the army, settling church government, and lowering taxes. To make
matters worse for the Independents, the impact of the 'recruiter' elections (the elections from late 1645 for filling the seats at Westminster
vacated by Royalist MPs) began to tell in favour of the Presbyterians by
late 1646. Whereas most of the recruiters for the northern counties were
opponents of further Scottish intervention and therefore aligned with
the Independents, the Welsh and West Country constituencies had
elected a large number of Presbyterians and crypto-Royalists. By mid-
January 1647 it was clear even to observers abroad that the Presbyterians
were 'much the more powerfull in the Citty of London & in the houses'.[4]

By the time the king arrived at his designated place of residence,
Holdenby House, Northamptonshire, in mid-February, a group of
Presbyterian peers led by the earls of Warwick and Manchester had
opened secret negotiations with him on the softest of terms – namely,
that he consent to the establishment of Presbyterianism for three years,
and to parliamentary control of the militia for ten. The requirement that
he take the Covenant, which had doomed previous attempts to negotiate
with him, was dropped. Despite some initial blustering from the king,
there seemed a strong likelihood that he would accept this package. But
although Charles might be amenable, the Presbyterians still faced the
problem that had bedevilled them since new-modelling – a lack of sufficient military power to impose a settlement upon their enemies. To reap
the rewards of peace, the Presbyterians must replace Fairfax's army with
a new, streamlined force under commanders they trusted. Charles was to
be kept 'on ice' until they had restructured the kingdom's armed forces.

The Presbyterians' plans for new-modelling were introduced in the
Commons in mid-February. The regiments of several Presbyterian
colonels of horse would be amalgamated to form a cavalry brigade of
5400 troopers; pay for existing infantry units, except garrison forces, was
to cease. This left the problem of how to dispose of in excess of 14,000
New Model foot. The preferred solution was to disband the more radical

of these troops and send the conformable remainder to Ireland. This Irish expeditionary force would constitute Parliament's main field army, and could be brought back to England to crush domestic opposition as occasion required.

The Presbyterians' military plans appeared distinctly more workable in light of a timely offer from their beleaguered ally in Dublin, the Marquess of Ormond. Although Ormond's previous approach to Parliament had broken down just a few months earlier, the fact that the king was now in parliamentary custody convinced him that a rapprochement with Westminster was essential. He certainly needed to do something, and quickly, for conditions in Dublin had become so desperate that the citizens would no longer support even those few troops that remained to defend the city. The collapse of the July 1646 treaty and the subsequent dominance of the clerical party at Kilkenny ruled out any possibility in Ormond's mind of doing a deal with the Confederates. And while handing over Dublin to the Parliamentarians ran counter to his desire for a free Ireland under the crown, he was at least fortunate in that it was no longer the Independents but his Presbyterian allies who were now in control at Westminster. On 5 February, Ormond's council resolved to renew negotiations with Parliament, but this time on less stringent terms. Ormond was now willing to hand over Dublin and his office of lord lieutenant to Parliament without the king's prior consent. This offer was communicated to the Commons on 20 February – two day after Parliament's (or rather, the Independents') lord lieutenant, Viscount Lisle, had finally set sail for Munster. The Presbyterians now saw the chance to kill two birds with one stone. With Dublin under parliamentary control they would have a secure bridgehead in Ireland from which to deploy a downsized New Model against the Confederates. And with Ormond's office effectively in their gift they could scrap Lisle's commission as lord lieutenant.

As the momentum for disposing of the New Model increased, so too did the confidence of its enemies. Spurred on by the Covenant-engaged faction in the City, the Presbyterians in both Houses introduced a series of measures in March for dismembering the army and weeding out pro-Independent officers such as Cromwell. Indeed, the City and the dominant clique in the Lords (which included crypto-Royalists) wanted to go even further and to order the army's immediate disbandment without pay. The Presbyterian leaders in the Commons – Sir Philip Stapilton and Denzil Holles – apparently tried to temper this headstrong reaction against the New Model, but they lacked the finesse that the Independent grandees had displayed during their own ascendancy.

Soldiers and Levellers

The seemingly imminent triumph of the Presbyterians galvanised their more militant opponents in the capital. In March the *Petition of Many Thousands*, known as the 'Large Petition', was presented to the Commons – 'the supreme authority of this nation' – requesting the abolition of the king's and the Lords' negative voice, and an end to 'all oppressions over soul or body'.[5] This petition was the work of a group of London radicals who were later known by their enemies as 'Levellers'.

In new research on the Levellers, Phil Baker has questioned whether they had emerged as an organised movement with a coherent political programme before the autumn of 1647.[6] Nevertheless, there can be no doubt that the men who would come to be recognised as their leaders – John Lilburne, Richard Overton, and William Walwyn – were well known to each other and had collaborated in writing and publishing radical pamphlets since 1645. Overton, Walwyn, and Henry Marten, for example, had been responsible for the July 1646 petition *A remonstrance of many thousand citizens*, which denounced kingship in general and Charles in particular.

But it was not just royal tyranny that the Levellers opposed – it was all forms of arbitrary government. At the core of their programme was a commitment to freedom of conscience, inalienable civil rights, and the principle that all government derived its legitimacy from, and must therefore be accountable to, the people. Many of their ideas were rooted in the experience and beliefs of the separatist congregations in London. These Puritan sects emphasised the primacy of the individual believer's experience of God, which potentially gave their thinking a strongly egalitarian edge – although not even the Levellers believed that this God-ordained equality extended to political rights for women.

The Large Petition made no reference to the army; and indeed, in so far as the soldiers relied upon an unaccountable 'state junto' to maintain them in pay they were implicitly part of the problem rather than the solution. During the course of 1647, however, the nascent Leveller movement came to see the soldiers as fellow sufferers under, and therefore allies against, the growing tyranny of parliamentary rule. This reaction against Parliament among its erstwhile supporters, though exacerbated by the Presbyterian ascendancy at Westminster, was rooted in a pre-existing critique of the parliamentary grandees and their apparatus of power – particularly their centralised executive committees. The rise of the dedicated politician was indeed no less subversive of the people's legal 'birthright' than the emergence of professional armies. However, it was precisely because of the symbiotic relationship between the army and its grandee patrons that the Levellers' campaign against a powerful executive made relatively little headway in the ranks.

The massive literature the Levellers have generated bears little relation to their actual contribution to events. Even in London they were a tiny minority, with an uncertain following in the army and just a handful of friends in the Commons. Yet to most people, wedded as they were to notions of hierarchy and *inequality*, and alarmed by the cracks the war had opened in the foundations of society, the Levellers represented a frightening new phase in the kingdom's apparent slide towards anarchy. It was in the fear that they aroused – which spread to Scotland and probably Ireland too – rather than through anything they actually did, that the Levellers made their greatest impact.

'Enemies to the State': the Army and Parliament

The London radicals were still an isolated group in the spring of 1647 and could easily be ignored by the Westminster Presbyterians. A much greater threat was posed by the petitions that began to circulate among the soldiers during March demanding indemnity (from subsequent prosecution for acts committed under military orders), payment of arrears, and clarification on who would be their commanders in Ireland.

The army by this stage contained men of all persuasions – from ex-Royalist troops who had joined their vanquishers simply for love of soldiering and the lure of regular pay, to Puritan lay preachers. There was even a sizeable contingent of Presbyterians among the officer corps. It was politicised to the extent that it was generally anti-Scots, and favoured a settlement that preserved English liberties and restored the king to his 'Honour, Crowne, & Dignity'.[7] On one issue, however, there was virtual unanimity, and that was the manifest injustice of being disbanded without indemnity and full arrears of pay. The Westminster Presbyterians' folly in even suggesting such a course was compounded by the fact that the soldiers revered Parliament, and with tactful handling would almost certainly have disbanded or served in Ireland without demur.

Oblivious to the rumblings of discontent in the army, Parliament sent a commission to Fairfax's headquarters at Saffron Walden, Essex, in mid-March to confer with senior officers on which regiments would make up the 12,600-strong force that the two Houses had determined should serve in Ireland. When the commissioners met the officers, however, they were bombarded with the questions that the soldiery had been asking all month: who would command them in Ireland? What was to be done about indemnity? Would arrears of pay be honoured in full? Some of the officers refused to endorse all these questions, but it was agreed that a petition be drawn up encapsulating the army's material grievances. Any anxieties among the rank-and-file on political or religious grounds were laid aside as 'beyond the proper concernments of soldiers'.[8]

Despite the petition's respectful tone and modest requests, the Presbyterians were outraged that Parliament's own army should seem to question its orders. The Commons ordered Fairfax to suppress the petition, and summoned its supposed organisers to Westminster for interrogation. The Presbyterians' calculated insensitivity to the soldiers' grievances reached its height on the evening of 29 March, when the Commons passed a motion, hastily penned by Holles, declaring that if the army petitioners persisted in their mutinous ways they would be 'looked upon and proceeded against as enemies to the State and disturbers of the public peace'.[9] This was tantamount to a declaration of war against the army, and was taken as such. To be branded enemies of the state after loyally serving Parliament; to be denied the basic right to petition – these were insufferable affronts to the soldiers' sense of honour and justice. Holles's 'declaration of dislike' instantly joined the army's list of grievances, and was to push the soldiers down the same path as the London radicals towards questioning the nature and legitimacy of parliamentary authority.

Ormond, Lisle, and Inchiquin

If gratuitously offending the army was a major blunder, the Presbyterians could at least congratulate themselves by the spring that they had complete charge of Irish affairs at Westminster. Early in April they seized control of the Committee for Irish Affairs at Derby House – the body set up to handle Ormond's overtures to Parliament the previous autumn. As the issues of Ireland and the disposal of the army had come to take centre stage at Westminster over the winter of 1646–7, so the Committee for Irish Affairs at Derby House had replaced the Committee of Both Kingdoms as Parliament's main executive organ.

Having treated Ormond with kid gloves, the Presbyterians showed no such respect to Parliament's own lord lieutenant, Viscount Lisle. Lisle was apparently convinced that regiments of the New Model would follow him out to Ireland so that he could begin his campaign of reconquest. In fact, Ormond's offer to surrender Dublin, and the Presbyterians' mishandling of the army's grievances, effectively destroyed Lisle's Irish crusade before it began. But this was not immediately apparent to his enemies in Ireland, who included not just the Confederates but also significant sections of the Protestant community. Lisle was surrounded by a New English coterie that despised anyone formerly associated with Ormond and the Irish Royalist interest. High on their list of suspect Protestants was Inchiquin, the Parliamentarian lord president of Munster. Lisle and his men quickly set about undermining the authority of Inchiquin and his following – partly, as Inchiquin conceived it, for 'our not adhering to the Independent party'.[10] During March he vigorously lobbied his Presbyterian friends in London against Lisle's lieutenancy, complaining that it bore 'the semblance rather of a conquest than of relief'.[11]

Even if Lisle had not tried to undermine Inchiquin's power it is unlikely that his lieutenancy would have survived the Presbyterian ascendancy at Westminster. His commission as lord lieutenant was subject to renewal by Parliament on an annual basis, and by April 1647 his first year in office was almost up. On 1 April the Presbyterian grandees in both Houses used their majorities to block the renewal of his commission and to vest the government of Ireland in two lords justices. At a stroke, Inchiquin was restored to full authority in Munster; Ormond was conciliated in as much as no one would succeed him as lord lieutenant; and the way was cleared for the Presbyterians to choose their own commanders for Ireland. The next day the Commons appointed Philip Skippon and Edward Massie as field marshal and lieutenant-general respectively of the forces designated for Ireland. Skippon was generally accounted friendly to Ormond, while Massie was virtually a crypto-Royalist by this stage. Significantly, they were given no authority in Munster, where Inchiquin was to be supreme commander. The dismantling of the Independents' Irish policy continued on 8 April, when Lisle's brother, Algernon Sidney, was replaced as governor-designate of Dublin by Colonel Michael Jones – a career soldier from an Anglo-Irish family.

The junking of Lisle's commission allowed Inchiquin to oust his opponents from command and to restore his own men. Lisle returned to England in mid-April a defeated and humiliated figure. But Inchiquin's position in Munster was still far from secure. In appealing over Lisle's head to Parliament he had tied his fortunes even more closely to the English Presbyterians, and his hold on power would only be secure so long as they remained in the driving seat at Westminster. Even at the height of the Presbyterian ascendancy in the spring of 1647, he and his friends continued to come under fire from the Lisle–Broghill circle. Inchiquin saw that the only way to answer his critics and retain the confidence of the two Houses was to score victories against the Confederates – something that Lisle had conspicuously failed to do. By May, Inchiquin's army, enlarged by the regiments brought over by Lisle and Broghill, was in the field and capturing Confederate strongholds.

The Protestant position in Leinster also improved with the arrival at Dublin early in June of the parliamentary commissioners to negotiate the city's surrender, accompanied by Colonel Jones and 2000 troops. Ormond and the commissioners quickly agreed terms, and on 18 June signed treaty articles. Ormond was to hand over his garrisons and lieutenancy, in return for which his estates would be secured and the Protestant Royalist interest protected. In July, Ormond surrendered his sword of office and shortly afterwards retired to England. By reconciling Ormond and destroying Lisle's partisan and divisive lieutenancy, the Presbyterians had enabled a modest Protestant counter-offensive in Ireland. But there were still not enough money and troops coming from England to make total reconquest feasible. Jones's force, and the scourings of the parliamentary finance committees, did little more than plug the gaps. The Protestants' best hope was still the disunity among the Confederates, and as on many previous occasions, they would not be disappointed.

The Confederates at War

After a hectic six months in which the Irish Confederates had come close to civil war, some of the Association's leaders were desperate to contain the bitter rivalry between the peace and clerical parties. The more conciliatory tone of Confederate politics by early 1647 is generally ascribed to the influence of Nicholas Plunkett and Bishop French. However, there is disagreement among Irish historians as to whether the two men headed a distinct middle group at Kilkenny or merely represented the more moderate wing of the clerical party.[12] What is clear is that the Plunkett–French policy of reconciliation and compromise was supported by Rinuccini – in part because he had run out of other options. The failure of his campaign against Dublin, the lack of further funds from the Vatican, and the general war-weariness of the people combined to make the immediate renewal of large-scale military operations impossible.

In an effort to restore legitimacy to Confederate government after the clerical coup of September, elections were held in December for a new General Assembly. The clerical party seems to have done better in these elections than the Ormondists, although when the assembly convened at Kilkenny on 10 January the majority of members were apparently non-aligned, with the political initiative in the hands of Plunkett, French, and those anxious to restore some measure of harmony to the Association's proceedings. The initial debates were dominated by arguments over what to do about the Ormond treaty. The clerical faction insisted that it was unsatisfactory and should be annulled, while the Ormondists, though conceding that it was weak in terms of religious guarantees, argued that further concessions were still possible. But despite their strong desire for an accommodation with the king, the assemblymen recognised that the peace party's conviction that Ormond would yield more ground on religion, or that Charles was in a fit position to honour such terms, was pie in the sky. On 2 February the assembly formally rejected both the Ormond treaty and the Glamorgan treaty, by which the Ormondists had hoped to secure Irish Catholicism.

It was no coincidence that three days after the assembly's rejection of the treaties, Ormond and his council decided to make their final – and on this occasion, successful – approach to the English Parliament. Although Ormond continued desultory talks with the Confederates throughout the spring, it was merely to forestall another attack on Dublin. The Confederates were initially uncertain as to his true intentions (as he meant them to be), and it was not until late March that they discovered just how serious he was about surrendering Dublin to Parliament, and by then it was too late. In desperation, they gave serious consideration to the idea of a foreign protector for Ireland, with the pope and the kings of Spain and France all being touted for the role. But in the absence of con-sensus the notion was shelved.

Confederate anger with Ormond may have influenced the outcome of elections in mid-March for a new Supreme Council. The clerical party clearly came out the winner, although again it seems to have allowed Plunkett, French, and their associates to make the running in terms of policy. From 4 April, when the assembly dissolved, it was the moderates on the council who effectively dictated Confederate policy for the rest of the year.

The major problem facing the council was how to prevent the peace party's despair of a Royalist settlement in Ireland – which increased with Ormond's surrender to Parliament – from undermining the entire

Association. The council's task was made considerably more difficult by a flare-up in the Franco-Spanish war on the Continent, and a corresponding increase in the French demand for Irish troops. The French, themselves dismayed by the failure of the Ormond peace, looked for recruits among their disgruntled friends in the peace party. In Munster, for example, it was reported that large numbers of Confederate officers, many of them adherents of the leading Ormondist, Viscount Muskerry, were beginning to desert their posts and enlist with the French. Little wonder that Inchiquin was gaining ground in the province. Indeed, by June he anticipated that the Munster Ormondists would rather submit to him and Parliament than allow Rinuccini and O'Neill to separate Ireland from the English crown. That same month, Muskerry seized command of the Munster Confederate army, claiming that he needed to protect himself from O'Neill – although a likelier motive was his desire to preserve his troops for service with the French. After Ormond's withdrawal to England in July, Muskerry relinquished his command to his ally Viscount Taaffe, who likewise engaged to supply men to the French. Rinuccini, however, believed that Taaffe was saving his army 'as a counter-poise to that of Ulster'.[13]

The cause of Catholic unity fared little better in Leinster. For the Supreme Council to ensure that Leinster Ormondists remained firmly within the Confederate fold it needed to do two things – strike a deal with Ormond, and have O'Neill withdraw his hated Ulstermen from the province. The first of these had clearly become impossible by late spring; and the second was proving difficult in the face of O'Neill's desire to quarter his troops where the pickings were richest, namely Leinster. In fact, it made more sense strategically to *continue* O'Neill's army (the largest the Confederates possessed) in the province, where it could join with Preston's forces against the Association's most formidable enemies – Inchiquin and Jones. But political necessity – the need to keep the Leinster Confederates happy – strengthened the Supreme Council in its mistaken conviction that the Protestants in the north were still a major threat. With the nuncio's approval, therefore, the council allowed O'Neill to withdraw his army to Connacht, which had offered him £9000 to besiege Sligo.

The one success story that the council could point to in the spring of 1647 was the seeming rehabilitation of the Leinster general, Thomas Preston. As part of their policy of reconciliation, the moderates had saved Preston from prosecution by the General Assembly for having conspired with Ormond over the winter. In response to the landing of

Parliamentarian troops from Chester, the council ordered Preston to go onto the offensive in April, and over the next few months he captured several Protestant strongholds around Dublin. Nevertheless, he still had hopes of a Royalist alliance, and to that end he and Muskerry apparently contemplated joining their armies in order to force the council and Rinuccini to accept whatever terms Ormond might offer. But Preston vacillated as usual. Out of loyalty to the council he continued his advance in Leinster, but he proved susceptible to Lord Digby's siren-song, which sustained his dreams of a Royalist alliance or, failing that, of emulating Muskerry and Taaffe in seeking service with the French.

The push–pull effect of Ormond's surrender and the French recruitment drive clearly undermined Confederate unity during the first half of 1647. But the Association still had three armies in the field by the summer, albeit two of them in wavering hands. Moreover, Ormond's departure simplified the issues considerably. The struggle in Ireland was now a straightforward conflict of Parliamentarians versus Confederates, and as such could only be decided on the battlefield. Unfortunately for the Confederates, Preston was better at sieges than at set-piece battles, and on 8 August the Dublin garrison under Jones inflicted a crushing defeat on him at Dungan's Hill in east Leinster. As in most of the major engagements of the Irish wars, it was the superiority of the Protestant cavalry that told. Three thousand of Preston's veteran foot – the core of the Confederates' best trained and equipped army – were put to the sword in or after the battle. This defeat was a major blow to both the Confederate peace party and the moderates on the Supreme Council, and necessitated recalling O'Neill's army to Leinster. The moderates' hope of uniting the Association behind a summer's successful campaigning had been shattered, and worse was soon to follow.

Hamilton's Achievement

If Ormond's departure simplified the issues in Ireland then so too had Benburb. The New Scots army was a spent force after June 1646, and only maintained a foothold in Ulster in the hope of extracting its arrears of pay from the English Parliament. The rout of Monro's army, like the withdrawal of Leven's from England, was a consequence of Scottish over-extension both politically and militarily. The terms offered to Charles in the Uxbridge Treaty had represented the high-water mark of covenanting confederalism. With the treaty's collapse, the withering of the under-funded Covenanter armies had been inevitable. However, the contraction of Scottish military commitments at least enabled the Covenanters to re-assert their power in Scotland. By the end of 1647, Huntly's half-hearted resistance in the north-east had been crushed, and MacColla and the Irish had been forced out of their last strongholds in the western Highlands. For the first time in three and a half years the Covenanters were masters of their own kingdom.

Hamilton's return to the political fray in mid-1646, and the controversy in Scotland over the surrender of the king, injected new momentum into Scottish politics. Hamilton exploited Scottish fears that the Independents were intent on destroying the monarchy and on 'mastering ... the utmost corners of all the three Kingdomes', to forge an alliance of moderate Covenanters and Royalists.[14] At the same time, he attempted to shift the basis of the union between Scotland and England away from the two nations' Parliaments and towards the person and powers of the king. Charles may not have been the surest foundation on which to build a new political order, but he was hardly more dangerous than an Independent junto at Westminster.

Hamilton's achievement during 1647 was to devise a form of settlement that retained enough confederalist elements to allow for Scotland's future security, while acknowledging the fact that the king would never take the Covenant. Moreover, his concern to link the interest of Scottish autonomy with the preservation of the king chimed with the sympathies of a significant section of the Scottish people. The Stuarts were kings of Scotland long before they assumed the English throne, and the Scots' attachment to Charles I was partly a matter of national pride. The Scottish Parliament, on the other hand, had been of little importance in national life until the late 1630s, and commanded less respect than the Westminster Parliament did among the English. The only viable alternative to Hamilton's revised regnal union – Argyll's *de facto* republic, propped up by an alliance with Sweden or France – held virtually no emotional appeal for the Scots.

The Scottish Parliament's vote of 16 January 1647 for surrendering the king created a wave of shame and revulsion among the Scots that soon worked in Hamilton's favour. By mid-March, the Hamiltonians had won sufficient support, particularly among the nobles, to have a new commission despatched to England – headed by one of their supporters, the Earl of Lauderdale – with a fresh set of negotiating instructions. The requirement that Charles take the Covenant was no longer to be insisted upon; instead he was merely to 'give his consent that it may be confirmed as a Law'.[15] This instruction was clearly the work of the Hamiltonians, and was probably drawn up in the knowledge of the secret terms that the English Presbyterians had offered to Charles in January. On 20 March, a week before Parliament was dissolved, a new Committee of Estates was appointed in which a majority of the nobles, and a sizeable minority of the gentry and burgesses, were aligned with Hamilton.

Although the fate of the king continued to excite concern at Edinburgh, the Presbyterian ascendancy at Westminster meant that the Scots had less to fear from the New Model and the sects by March 1647 than at any time since Naseby. The demise of the Independents' Irish policy was another encouraging sign for the Scots. Lisle's lieutenancy has been identified by John Adamson as central to an 'imperial design' for English mastery within the British Isles that threatened Scotland with military encirclement.[16] Nevertheless, it is likely that the Hamiltonian gains of March owed as much to domestic developments, in particular the 16 January vote, as to contemporary events in England or Ireland. In fact, there is mileage in the notion that Edinburgh was forcing the pace of politics at Westminster by March, rather than vice versa. Certainly the gung-ho attitude of the Presbyterian grandees during the spring was inspired in part by the rise in Scotland of a faction willing to intervene in England regardless of whether the king took the Covenant.

Yet in anticipating help from Scotland, the Westminster Presbyterians were deluding themselves. Although Hamilton was convinced that his own supporters on the Committee of Estates outnumbered those of Argyll, in fact the two parties were about evenly matched. The result for many months was deadlock, particularly on the crucial issue of what to do with the restructured Scottish army under Argyll's ally Lieutenant-General David Leslie. As far as Hamilton was concerned, an invasion of England was out of the question while an army loyal to Argyll still dominated Scotland. If the Westminster Presbyterians pushed the New Model too far, therefore, they would do so without the safety net of a Covenanter army.

The Rise of the New Model Army

The Presbyterians' insensitive handling of the New Model was to transform the soldiers into a political force in their own right. Holles's 'declaration of dislike', and Presbyterian allegations that the army was infected with royalism, were seen by the soldiers as slurs upon their honour and loyalty, and as evidence that Parliament itself had become corrupted. The

Presbyterians' mishandling of the Irish expedition was another stimulus to political consciousness in the ranks. The appointment of Skippon and Massie to command in Ireland was impossible to justify on military grounds. It was clearly a political decision based on a desire to remove Fairfax and Cromwell. Likewise, the Presbyterians' offer of a month's pay to those soldiers who volunteered for Ireland was correctly perceived as 'a Designe to ruine and break this Army in pieces'.[17] As it was, a few of the officers, mostly Presbyterians, were willing to engage for Ireland; but the vast majority of their men had turned against the Irish service by the end of April.

Yet still the Westminster Presbyterians continued on their collision course with the army, voting late in April that once the soldiers had disbanded they would receive £70,000 in arrears of pay (they were owed over a million). By this stage the army had been without pay for months, and the Presbyterians evidently assumed that before too long the soldiers would simply desert – just as they had in all previous armies when deprived of maintenance or the chance of plunder. The fact that the New Model held together is an indication that this was no normal army. When it was established in 1645 it may have looked much like its predecessors, but by 1647 the New Model had acquired a rudimentary self-image as a champion of the kingdom's honour and liberties. This was due partly to its unbroken series of victories, and to the plaudits it had received as the instrument of restoring peace; partly also to its close association with the Independents and the cause of resisting the tide of Scottish confederalism. Yet military life, and particularly the experience of battle, set the soldiers apart from the rest of society, and also rendered them open to new and radical ideas. Although it might claim a popular mandate, the army never lived up to its billing as the 'champions and true representants' of the people.[18]

Faced with a new kind of warfare in which petitions, pamphlets, and parliamentary orders were the principal weapons, the soldiers began to organise for political action. Each company or troop elected two soldiers, known as 'adjutators', to represent their views to the high command; contacts were established with friendly civilians and soldiers in regional commands; and teams of writers were assembled to pen pamphlets for an army press.

The soldiers' demands began to broaden in scope during April and May. In its official representations to Parliament, the army focused on the redress of material grievances and on vindicating itself against Presbyterian slurs upon its honour. Individual regiments and units, however, began to voice more general concerns, reflecting the soldiers' sense

of themselves as guardians of the national interest. Calls were heard for
the punishment of the 'tyrants' responsible for the 'declaration of dislike';
for securing the liberty of the subject; and for justice 'according to the old
Law'.[19] Among the first to suffer from the army's increasing politicisation
were its Presbyterian officers, who either resigned their commissions or
were driven out by their men, to be replaced in many cases by militants.

Holles and other leading Presbyterians seem to have realised by
mid-May that the army could not be brow-beaten into submission. But so
confident were they that it was riven with dissension over service in
Ireland and pay issues that instead of trying to appease the soldiery they
began to marshal their own military resources to quell what they imagined was merely a recalcitrant hard-core of Fairfax's men. Measures were
introduced for strengthening the London militia; garrisons and regiments under Presbyterian officers were put on a war footing; and the
pro-Scots commander of the Northern Association army, Major-General
Sednham Poynts, was ordered to mobilise his men.

The violence of the Presbyterians' reaction against the soldiers
stemmed partly from another mistaken belief – that radical Independents
were plotting with the adjutators for a military coup. In fact, the concerns
of John Lilburne and his fellow London radicals for constitutional
reform, liberty of conscience, etc., seem to have generated relatively little
interest among the soldiers before the summer. The most important contacts between the army and the Independents were at the level of the
grandees, not the militants on the fringes. But the Presbyterians were now
convinced that the army was 'one Lilburne throughout'.[20] On 23 May they
sounded out the Earl of Lauderdale and the French ambassador about
the possibility of the Covenanters marching their army back into England,
or of carrying the king to Scotland. Encouraged by what they heard, the
Presbyterians forced a vote through the Commons on 25 May for the
immediate disbandment of Fairfax's infantry with just two months'
arrears of pay. Parliament had called time on the New Model.

The Seizure of the King

The Presbyterians' military preparations, and especially their secret
discussions with the Scots, caused great alarm among the officers and
adjutators. They had already noted worrying signs of collusion between
the king and the Presbyterians. On 12 May, for example, the king had
written to Parliament offering to establish Presbyterianism for a three-
year trial period, and to relinquish the militia for ten. This was ostensibly

a response to the Newcastle Propositions, but in fact was the king's reply to the secret terms that the Presbyterians had offered him in January. The Presbyterians and the Scots commissioners had accepted the king's letter as a basis for settlement, and on 20 May the Lords had voted that Charles should be invited to Oatlands – a royal residence just 15 miles from London. The adjutators feared, with good reason, that the Presbyterians were planning to carry the king off to London and then to invite in the Scots. They decided to get their retaliation in first, therefore, and by 27 May it was reported that Holdenby was 'as it were besiedged by some of the Army'.[21]

A key figure in the army's seizure of Charles was Oliver Cromwell. He was in close contact with the Independent grandees, and like them was alarmed by the Presbyterians' scheming with the Scots and the French. On 31 May he approved a plan to be implemented by Cornet George Joyce and leading adjutators to replace the king's guards at Holdenby (who were commanded by a Presbyterian) with men loyal to the army. Joyce arrived at Holdenby on 1 June with a force of about 1000 horse, and although he encountered no resistance from the troops guarding the king, soon began to fear that the Presbyterians were preparing a counter-strike. On 4 June therefore, he conveyed his royal prisoner to Newmarket, where the army was about to hold a general rendezvous. Although Cromwell later denied that he had sanctioned Joyce's *removal* of the king to army headquarters, there is strong evidence that he and at least one of the Independent grandees – Sir Arthur Hesilrige – had approved of securing Holdenby against the Presbyterians.

The army's seizure of the king sent a thrill of horror through the English Presbyterians and their allies. Lord Inchiquin's London agent told his master to forget about receiving further money from Parliament and to prepare for the downfall of his friends in England. Hamilton was advised by Lauderdale to think seriously about sending an army to rescue the king, and whether Scotland could be secure 'when England is con-quered by the Independents'.[22] At a stroke the army and its Independent backers had turned the tables on their enemies. It was now the Presbyterians and Covenanters who faced ruin, and so long as the king remained under the army's power it was not a case of whether the Scots would invade England again, but when.

The Heads of Proposals

When news of Joyce's arrival at Holdenby reached Westminster the Commons' Presbyterian ardour rapidly cooled. On 3 and 4 June the

House rescinded the declaration of dislike and voted the soldiers their full arrears of pay and a comprehensive indemnity ordinance. But the Presbyterian grandees were determined not to give up without a fight, and once again pressed the Scots commissioners for an army from Scotland – a request that Lauderdale apparently agreed to; even though Hamilton, back in Edinburgh, would not countenance invasion until Leslie's army had been disbanded or remodelled. Nevertheless, the Presbyterian grandees and the Scots commissioners organised a mission into France to persuade the queen to send the Prince of Wales to Scotland that he might command the anticipated invasion force.

The Commons' votes of early June came several months too late to appease the army. The soldiers' demands had now moved beyond merely the redress of their material grievances. At its general rendezvous at Kentford Heath near Newmarket, on 5 June, the army entered into a 'Solemn Engagement' not only to obtain satisfaction on military issues, but also to remove the Presbyterian grandees from power, as enemies of the kingdom. The Engagement also hinted that the army had a larger undertaking in hand – to secure 'an establishment of common and equall right and freedome to the whole'.[23] To see that these engagements were met, a General Council was set up consisting of senior officers and four adjutators – two commissioned and two rankers – from each regiment.

From mid-June the army stepped up the pressure on the City Presbyterians. It issued a series of declarations demanding a purge of both Houses and fixed-term Parliaments; it presented charges to the Commons for the impeachment of eleven leading Presbyterian MPs, including Stapilton and Holles; and on 25 June it moved its headquarters to Uxbridge, just fifteen miles from Westminster. The reluctance of the City to risk war with the army, and the adjutators' success in subverting the troops under Poynts and other regional commanders, left the Presbyterians defenceless, and late in June the eleven members quit the Commons. A few days after their withdrawal the Independent grandees reappeared in force on the Committee for Irish Affairs at Derby House. As a result of these developments, relations between Parliament and the army improved dramatically, and Fairfax withdrew his headquarters to Reading.

The collapse of Presbyterian resistance was partly the result of growing public awareness that not only was Charles being treated with honour and kindness by the soldiers, but he and the army were preparing the ground for a moderate peace settlement. Having been held under tight security at Holdenby, the king was now allowed to receive visitors, to see his children, and even to worship under Anglican ministers. This lenient treatment of Charles reflected the soldiers' conviction that the army rather than a corrupted Parliament was the only proper instrument for restoring the king and brokering an equitable settlement. An army declaration of 23 June maintained that there could be no firm and lasting peace 'without a due consideration of, and provision for the Rights, Quiet, and Immunity of His Majesties Royall Family, and his late partakers [i.e. the Royalist party]'.[24] The soldiers' quarrel with the Presbyterians had broadened into a crusade for national redemption.

The New Model's terms for settlement were drafted by Henry Ireton in consultation with the Independent grandees and the army's closest friends among the London radicals. Known as the Heads of Proposals, they were approved by the General Council in mid-July in readiness for presentation to the king and ratification by Parliament. Inevitably, the Heads reflected the varied agendas of those consulted in their formulation. The concerns of the London radicals and their friends in the army were evident in the provision for biennial Parliaments and a redistribution of parliamentary seats. Likewise, the Independent grandees' interests were served by clauses for creating parliamentary interval committees and a 'Council of State', comprising 'trusty and able persons [i.e. themselves]', to supervise the kingdom's armed forces.[25] At the same time, the Heads were exceptionally generous to the king in that they allowed him control of the militia and nomination of his councillors after ten years, and left room for the establishment of a non-coercive episcopacy. Almost no mention was made of Scotland, which was to be left to it own devices. The war in Ireland was to be carried on exclusively by the English Parliament. Significantly, the Heads also proposed rewarding those Royalists who had repudiated the Presbyterians' design to bring in the Scots.

The Heads represent the fullest expression of the realignment that had occurred in British politics since 1645. The possibility of the army brokering an exclusively English settlement was welcomed by the Marquess of Hertford and other Royalist patriots, and they were joined by a number of hardliners in the king's party who had come to regard the Scots as the 'Scum[m]e of the world', especially for having abandoned Charles at Newcastle.[26] The summer of 1647 was in fact not the first time that officers, Independents, and Royalists had come together to promote a settlement. In the autumn of 1646, leading members of the Hertford–Hyde group had collaborated with Cromwell, Ireton, and the Independent grandees in an effort to persuade Charles to accept peace terms contrary to those of the Scots and their allies. What linked these three interests was not only hostility towards covenanting confederalism, but also an appreciation that there could be no viable church settlement that either ignored the strength of feeling in England for episcopacy and the Prayer Book, or that failed to extend freedom of worship to the godly. Both the 1646 terms and the Heads endorsed this compromise of toleration and a 'moderated' episcopacy. Pro-Scottish alliance Royalists and the Presbyterian grandees had worked hard to turn Charles against the Independents' peace overtures in 1646, as they did again with the Heads. But whereas in 1646 they could count on the queen's support, not so in 1647. Although she generally favoured a treaty with the covenanting interest, the Scots' 'betrayal' of Charles the previous January had temporarily undermined her commitment to a Presbyterian settlement.

Soldiers and Citizens

An agreement between the king and the army was too awful for the Presbyterian grandees to contemplate. The eleven members held 'private meetings ... for to countermine the army', and organised a propaganda campaign for bringing Charles to London to conclude a personal treaty.[27] The Commons responded by re-asserting its control over the London militia – a blow to the City's pride that was the spark for a Presbyterian counter-revolution. On 26 July, a mob of apprentices and reformadoes (disbanded soldiers) stormed the two Houses and, with several of the Presbyterian grandees covertly directing proceedings, forced MPs to do its bidding. When the issue of the City militia was forced back onto the Commons agenda that day, some of the apprentices actually sat in the House and voted with MPs! If the eleven members did not instigate this counter-revolution (which is a moot point), then they certainly used it in a final desperate bid to defeat the army. Encouraged by the Presbyterian grandees, the Covenant-engaged faction raised the City's defences and prepared to defy the army. By the time Parliament re-assembled on 30 July, the speakers of both Houses, 57 MPs, and eight peers had fled London to the protection of the army.

The Presbyterians' seizure of Parliament was quickly followed by another blow to the Independents and the army – this time administered by the king. After allowing the prominent Royalist Sir John Berkeley to make some amendments to the Heads, the army presented them to the king on 28 July. But to the astonishment of Berkeley, Charles responded with 'very tart and bitter Discourses', telling the senior officers 'you cannot be without me; You will fall to ruin if I do not sustain you'.[28] Charles was playing his usual game of holding out for better terms. Lauderdale had been with him, raising false hopes of the Scots' and Presbyterians' willingness to fight for his restoration. The king was also aware of events in London, and secretly encouraged the City 'to stand upon their defence'.[29] His rejection of the Heads cost him what little support he had among the more militant element in the army – a group moving ever closer to the London radicals.

While Charles schemed and prevaricated, the army acted. On 29 July the New Model began to advance on London, determined to finish what it had started in June. The citizens, understandably, were unwilling to stand alone against Fairfax's veterans; indeed, many of them were more scared of the Presbyterians' unruly reformadoes than they were of the army. On 6 August the army entered London unopposed, escorting the speakers and the fugitive members back to Westminster in orderly triumph. The reformadoes 'slunk away', and the last of the eleven members had exited the political stage by mid-August – some going into temporary exile on the Continent. The two Houses gave command of the Tower to Fairfax, who left sufficient forces in the City to prevent unrest while the Independents set about remodelling civic government. Spearheading the assault on the Presbyterian interest was the Lords, which was now solidly Independent – the Presbyterian peers having fled or been imprisoned. In the Commons, however, the Presbyterians retained a majority and blocked all the Lords' initiatives. Pressure was now building from the adjutators for a wholesale purge of the House, but the grandees orchestrated a show of force sufficient to overawe the Presbyterians and to assuage the army radicals, at least temporarily.

Although the army and Independent grandees now controlled the capital, the king's rejection of the Heads left them in a vulnerable position. Such support as they enjoyed among the common people rested largely upon the hopes they had raised of delivering a swift peace. If a settlement was not forthcoming then popular expectation would rapidly turn to resentment. Likewise, the king's blithe intransigence (he was ensconced in relative freedom and comfort at Hampton Court) and willingness to treat with the Scots threatened to widen the fractures within the army and the Independent interest. Some of the adjutators were now demanding a much tougher stance against Charles, indeed a more radical settlement altogether, and were deeply suspicious of Cromwell and Ireton and their continuing efforts to treat with the king on the basis of the Heads. Moreover, with Fairfax's headquarters now at Putney, the army was more open than ever to infiltration by the London radicals and their ideas. In the Commons it was a similar story, with Cromwell and other leading Independents having to intervene to prevent their former collaborators Henry Marten and the radical officer Thomas Rainborowe carrying a vote for making no further overtures to the king. Unfortunately for the grandees, Charles would still not wholeheartedly endorse the Heads. Predictably, he was having difficulty with the fact that they made no provision for episcopacy, and tacitly repudiated his supremacy in religion.

In an effort to bring Charles to terms, and to put their negotiations with him on a firmer legal footing, the Independent and army grandees began proceedings in September to turn the Heads into parliamentary propositions. By early November, despite opposition from radical Independents and Presbyterians in the Commons, the revised Heads, now in the form of fully drafted bills, were ready for despatch to the king. They were less conciliatory to the Royalists than the original Heads, but still breathed enough of their spirit to retain the support of Cromwell and most of the soldiers. But time was running out for the Independent and army grandees. On the one hand, the London radicals and the adjutators were preparing constitutional blueprints of their own that repudiated the idea of a settlement with the king. On the other, the Scots had renewed their offers of military support to Charles. Indeed, if the Independents were desperate to close with the king, then so too were the Scots. Charles was now the only barrier between the Scots and what for many of them was their worst fear – a resurgent and uncovenanted English regime.

Covenant or King

The slowness of the Scots in coming to the aid of their beleaguered king was largely down to Argyll. The chief of the Campbells wanted to maintain the status quo in Scotland, at least until his lands had been cleared of the MacDonalds, and if he desired intervention in England at all it was on condition that Charles take the Covenant – which he probably realised the king would never do. Hamilton, on the other hand, was prepared to invade England on the king's behalf, but reasoned that it would be pointless to do so while Argyll retained control of Scotland's main field army under David Leslie. Intervention 'at the old rate of satisfaction in Religion and the Covenant' would simply alienate the king while embroiling Scotland in a war with the Independents.[30] Hamilton was therefore obliged to downplay the threat from England until he could have Leslie's army disbanded and raise another under his own command. In the interim, he exploited the fact that his party did not enjoy an out-right majority on the Committee of Estates, and that the king had made no specific request for Scottish military assistance. Indeed, Hamilton was far from certain that the king actually wanted to be rescued. Conse-quently, by disguising his policy on Leslie's army as a peace-keeping ini-tiative between the two kingdoms, he was able to keep a channel open to Viscount Saye and Cromwell just in case Charles and the army should strike a deal.

The New Model's seizure of the king in June put pressure on both Hamilton and Argyll to appear more strongly for the king. Once again the message from Edinburgh's pulpits was that Scotland could never enjoy security while England was dominated by the enemies of the Covenant. News in August that the army had extinguished the Scots' last hope for a covenanted settlement in England – the London Presbyterians – galvanised the Committee of Estates. On 17 August the committee appointed two extra commissioners to be sent to England – the Earl of Lanark (Hamilton's brother) and the Earl of Loudoun – with instruc-tions to request the English Parliament to bring Charles to London so that he could again be presented with the Newcastle Propositions. But while Argyll had wanted it made clear that the commissioners' instruc-tions did not commit Scotland to intervening in England, Hamilton insisted that they should in no way prejudice the king's interests – a requirement that could be stretched to cover all manner of under-takings on Charles's behalf. The Hamiltonians also began to push hard for the disbandment of Leslie's army. The issue came to a head at a meet-ing of the Committee of Estates on 15 October, where it was decided by one vote that the army be maintained until the Scottish Parliament assembled in March 1648.

Argyll's victory in retaining the army was merely a consolation prize. As a sop to the Scots commissioners, the English Parliament had made a few minor alterations to the Newcastle Propositions and had then presented them to the king at Hampton Court on 7 September. A week or so later, to the satisfaction of the Independents, the king had declared a preference for the Heads of Proposals over the Hampton Court Propositions, thereby ruling out any possibility of a settlement 'at the old rate'. If the Scots commissioners were to prevent Charles closing with the Independents, they must implement Hamilton's strategy of negotiating a deal with the king on the basis of his letter of 12 May, in which he had committed himself merely to establish Presbyterianism in England for three years. Lanark and Lauderdale were ready to make the necessary concessions; and Loudoun's covenanting scruples were fighting a losing battle with his fears for the king's and Scotland's safety. Even before the commissioners began talks with Charles on 22 October, they had assured him that so long as he satisfied them in point of religion he need not take the Covenant. By early November it was reported that the commissioners 'p[ro]mise lustely, and he [Charles] begins to listen'.[31]

Inchiquin and the Confederates

The army's triumph in August alarmed more than just the Scots. 'I know not what days may be here for us, since the Independents have got all in their hands in England,' wrote one Protestant officer in Munster – a sentiment that his commander, Lord Inchiquin, shared.[32] Having protested vigorously to Parliament and Fairfax that he was the victim of a smear campaign by Lisle's faction, Inchiquin then played right into his enemies' hands by endorsing a remonstrance from his officers in August, declaring their support for king, Covenant, and the 'former Parliament'. Inchiquin and his men had received false reports from England that the army had purged Parliament and that the Presbyterian grandees had fled to Edinburgh. Convinced that the New Model's opponents in Britain were preparing a counter-strike, Inchiquin authorised an approach to leading Scots stating his faithfulness to the Covenant and asking for supplies. But in his hatred of the Independents he had jumped the gun. Neither the Scots nor anyone else was yet in a position to challenge the Independents, and all Inchiquin succeeded in doing was to confirm his enemies' suspicions that he sympathised with the Hamiltonians and the Westminster Presbyterians.

While the Independents remained in power, however, Inchiquin could not afford to break with them. Parliamentary supplies, though meagre, were vital to the Munster war-effort. In order to satisfy a doubting Parliament and to silence his enemies, Inchiquin needed to proceed vigorously against the Confederates. Only by killing Catholics, his friends in London advised, could he hope to regain parliamentary favour and with it precious supplies. During September, therefore, he waged a campaign of terror in Tipperary that was to leave the county devastated for years to come. In one particularly brutal incident, his men drove over 700 Irish – women and priests as well as soldiers – into Cashel cathedral and butchered them, leaving bodies 'five or six deep in many places'.[33] While

Inchiquin's cavalry raided Munster with impunity, the commander of the Confederate army in the province, Viscount Taaffe, had succumbed to the paralysis that had gripped Preston earlier in the year. Lord Digby still dreamed of an Ormondist–Royalist alliance in Ireland, and Taaffe heeded his advice to preserve his army for the king's service, allowing Inchiquin's men to plunder to the outskirts of Kilkenny. The Supreme Council only managed to persuade Taaffe into the field by threatening to send in O'Neill and his Ulstermen.

Inchiquin's victories in Munster could not allay the Independents' suspicion that he was conspiring with the Presbyterians and the Scots. Consequently he remained low on their list of deserving causes, especially with the New Model soldiery clamouring for pay and provisions. With little or no support from England, Inchiquin's army was in a 'miserable' condition by November, 'having no choice but to starve or fight'.[34] The two Munster armies, Inchiquin's and Taaffe's, met at Knocknanuss in County Cork on 13 November. Inchiquin had about 5000 men; Taaffe about 8000, including Alasdair MacColla and the remnant of the force that had fought under Montrose in Scotland. But the bravery of MacColla and his Redshanks could not make up for Taaffe's failings as a general, nor for the superiority of Inchiquin's cavalry, and the result was another Confederate rout. Irish losses were about 3000 and included MacColla and most of his men. By December, Inchiquin had conquered all of Munster save a few Confederate garrisons.

Dungan's Hill and Knocknanuss were blows from which the Confederate Association never recovered. Munster was lost for good, and O'Neill's return to Leinster in the wake of Dungan's Hill left much of Connacht and Ulster contested territory with the Protestants. Yet Rinuccini still believed that with money from Rome, O'Neill's army could win the war for the Association. He apparently failed to appreciate that for most Catholics in Leinster and Munster, conquest by Parliament 'was little or no worse than domination by the Ulster army'.[35] As it transpired, Rome was only good for a few thousand pounds in additional aid. And although the Confederates' defeats left Rinuccini and his 'client-general', O'Neill, in an unchallengeable position militarily, they restored the political initiative to the peace faction. The aggressive strategy of the moderates, that Rinuccini and the clergy had backed, had been thoroughly discredited – in part, because the plundering activities of O'Neill's army had tarnished the nuncio's prestige. In the new General Assembly, which convened on 12 November, the peace faction emerged strong enough to commit the Association to seeking an alliance with the exiled English court in Paris.

The government of Ireland was to be offered to the queen and the Prince of Wales, but only after the pope had approved a religious settlement. To this end Viscount Muskerry, Geoffrey Browne (both prominent Ormondists) and the ineffectual Antrim were sent to Paris; Nicholas Plunkett and Bishop French, to Rome. This was enough of a compromise to satisfy the clerical party, even though an appeal to Rome would effectively by-pass the demands of Rinuccini and the Irish clergy. The Royalist drift in Confederate policy was now unmistakable, and would accelerate as the king's position in Britain improved during the course of 1648.

The Putney Debates

Masters of all England during the summer, the Independent and army grandees faced a major test of their leadership by the autumn. What the king had given them with one hand in acknowledging the superiority of the Heads over the Newcastle Propositions, he had taken away with the other in treating with the Scots commissioners. His perceived wilfulness in holding out for better terms, but especially his renewed flirtation with the hated Scots, had inflamed radical opposition in the army and at Westminster. The grandees' control over the peace process was under threat from three directions by late October – the Hamiltonian Scots; a caucus of discontented adjutators; and an unholy alliance of Presbyterians and radical Independents in the Commons. Potentially the most dangerous of these threats was that posed by the adjutators. If the grandees lost control of the army they would lack the power to overawe Parliament and enforce their terms for settlement.

The first serious challenge to the Heads and their promoters from within the army emerged in October with the publication of *The Case of the Armie Truly Stated*. Recent work on *The Case* by John Morrill and Phil Baker has questioned the long held assumption that it was the work of the 'Leveller' John Wildman and expressed the views of the London radicals and their recently-intruded representatives in the army, the so-called 'new agents'.[36] It now seems that *The Case* was written by and for the soldiers, and articulated the concerns of a group of adjutators whose principal objective was to frustrate a negotiated settlement with the king. *The Case* demanded an immediate purge of Parliament, which was then to pass laws for redressing the army's grievances, widening the franchise, and holding biennial Parliaments. Rather than seek the king's approval for this settlement, its promoters envisaged simply imposing it upon him.

The Case commanded sufficient support in the army to warrant discussion by the General Council. On the back of the adjutators' grievances, however, their friends among the London radicals – those, such as Wildman, who had been consulted over the Heads of Proposals back in the summer – intruded their own constitutional blueprint upon the council, the *Agreement of the People*. This was probably penned by Wildman, and reflected a more civilian and radical agenda than *The Case*. It called for the dissolution of Parliament and the establishment of a new political order based upon a written constitution to be subscribed by all adult males. At its heart was the concept of 'law paramount' – certain inalienable rights inherent in a sovereign people, such as liberty of conscience and equality before the law, that not even Parliament could touch. The discussion of both sets of proposals – the adjutators' and the London radicals' – began at Putney on 28 October.

Although the Putney debates are justly celebrated for the speeches made on the second day in support of manhood suffrage, in fact the franchise issue was not uppermost in the minds of those present. The most divisive argument at Putney, as Morrill and Baker have established, centred around the future role of the king in any settlement. There were some very harsh words spoken against Charles at Putney. Several officers called him 'that Man of Blood' and urged his punishment, possibly even his execution.[37] But it is difficult to identify any majority position with regard to the king, beyond a general unwillingness to continue treating with him. Some officers, notably Ireton, still saw a role for both the king and the House of Lords. At the other end of the spectrum were the likes of Wildman, who leaned strongly towards abolishing monarchy and Lords altogether. The issue of the king and Lords split officers, adjutators, and London radicals alike. A fragile consensus only emerged at Putney after the grandees secured tacit assent to the principle that Parliament should remain the ultimate arbiter of a settlement – not the army, and much less the direct will of the people as interpreted by an unrepresentative civilian clique. In turn, the grandees agreed to a compromise package based upon the proposals made in *The Case*. The idea of a negotiated settlement with Charles was quietly dropped, and Parliament was to be required to pass legislation for redress of the soldiers' grievances and remodelling the constitution. The issue of king and Lords was left unresolved. What little support the *Agreement* had among the soldiers was easily suppressed by the grandees when the army rendezvoused at Corkbush Field, near Hertford, in mid-November. The soldiers had made army unity their law paramount, leaving the London radicals frustrated and isolated.

The Engagement

The Putney debates reveal a significant hardening in Cromwell's attitude towards the king. Cromwell as good as admitted that the only reasons for not proceeding against Charles were the political difficulties involved and the inscrutability of God's will as to when and by what means (Parliament's? the army's?) it would be done. It was doubtless the king's double-dealing, and in particular his treating with the Scots commissioners, that accounted for this shift in Cromwell's position. The final insult to Cromwell's and Ireton's trust in Charles came on 11 November, when the king escaped from Hampton Court contrary to his parole. Charles's own intransigence had driven him to this course. Having given the army and Independent grandees nothing to show for five months of negotiations, he had put them under immense pressure to get tough with him. Anxious to avoid the inevitable backlash, he had decided to leave England – an idea that the Scots commissioners, keen to get him out of the Independents' clutches, had seconded. He had also received reports, almost certainly false, that the Levellers were planning his assassination. He fled with Berkeley and Ashburnham to the south coast, intending to take ship for France, but through indecision and poor planning ended up on the Isle of Wight in the custody of the parliamentary governor, Colonel Robert Hammond. When Berkeley returned to army head-quarters late in November in the hope of reopening talks with the grandees, he got short shrift from Cromwell and Ireton, and hastily withdrew. The talk among the officers now was of trying Charles rather than treating with him.

Soon after his arrival on the Isle of Wight an unrepentant Charles sent a message to Parliament offering a compromise between his own views and the Heads of Proposals. The Independents in the Lords, doubting the sincerity of this offer, drafted four propositions and sent them to the Commons to be converted into bills. These four bills represented what were now the Independents' minimum terms, and included a proposal giving Parliament control over the armed forces, directly or indirectly, in perpetuity. If, but only if, Charles assented to them, a committee of Parliament would treat with him on all other contentious issues. The Independent grandees succeeded in pushing the bills through the Commons, but not without a struggle. They had to contend with the Presbyterians, who favoured more lenient terms, as well as with the radical fringe of their own faction, who were now adamantly opposed to having any further truck with Charles. The king's escape from Hampton Court had been the last straw for Marten, Chaloner, and other radicals. From November they would be consistently 'bloudy minded' against the king.

Although Charles found the four bills unacceptable, he shrewdly calculated that by failing to reject them outright he could put more pressure on the Scots commissioners to lower their terms. The prospect of a settlement on the basis of the bills was indeed worrying for the Scots. The bills made no mention of the Covenant and tacitly repudiated any idea of a joint interest between the two kingdoms. Almost to the last, the commissioners held out for tougher safeguards on religion than the King was prepared to concede. But on 26 December, two days after Charles had been presented with the four bills, they secretly signed a treaty with him – known as 'the Engagement' – by which Scotland would send an army into England 'for defence of His Majesty's person and authority, and restoring him to his government'.[38] In return, Charles made the concession on religion that he had offered on 12 May – a Presbyterian church in England for three years. The Covenant was not to be forced on anyone, but the Scots got the next best thing – the suppression of the sects. The Scots implicitly conceded the king personal executive authority throughout his domains, but sought to restrict his capacity to harm them through the stipulation that he endeavour 'a complete union of the kingdoms'. To kick-start this process, the king was to ensure free trade between England and Scotland; the appointment of 'a considerable and competent number of Scotsmen' to the English Privy Council; and the placing of Scotsmen in his own, the queen's, and the prince's households. In its emphasis on preserving the king's prerogative, and the creation of a 'British' court, this Hamilton-sponsored confederalism has been described by Adamson as a 'new form of royalism' in which the monarchy would serve as a buttress for Scottish autonomy.[39]

A little noticed feature of the Engagement is that it sanctioned not just a Scottish invasion of England, but also an Irish one. The Scots commissioners had held secret talks in October with Ormond, who had promised them that if Scotland invaded England, he would organise a Royalist campaign in Ireland. Lisle's lieutenancy had made it abundantly clear that an Independent regime in England posed just as great a threat to Ireland's autonomy as it did to Scotland's. The Engagement thus reflected the convergence of interest between the Hamiltonian Scots and the Irish Royalists in common opposition to the Independents. Moreover, once the Scots had engaged for the king, the consequent revival of his power in Britain would provide a political and military platform for all those in Ireland who saw Charles as the only bulwark against subjection to Westminster.

For those in Scotland and Ireland apprehensive of English imperialist designs, the New Model's 'conquest' of the king, London, and Parliament in 1647 added a frightening new dimension to England's resurgent power within the archipelago. They were now faced not just with an Anglocentric junto at Westminster, but with an English army seemingly dominated by sectaries and Levellers. The king was well aware of such fears, and it was entirely understandable that he preferred to exploit them in order to effect a conquest of his own, and for the minimum of concessions, rather than compromise his sovereignty by closing with the New Model. Far from being his 'ultimate folly', therefore, the Engagement represented a shrewd political gamble.[40] By harnessing the reaction in his kingdoms against the rise of the New Model Army, Charles acquired the resources to wage a second civil war.

Chapter 6: The Second Civil War and the English Revolution: January 1648–January 1649

The War of the Engagement

The 'Second Civil War' is a term of convenience, used to describe the various uprisings, battles, and naval actions that occurred in and around England and Wales between March and August 1648. The 'war' consisted of several overlapping and interrelated conflicts – a series of local insurrections of varying intensity and character; a bungled Royalist military campaign to reverse the outcome of the First Civil War; and a Scottish invasion to overthrow the 'prevailing party' in England and restore the king.

Although more recent accounts of the war have been sensitive to its British dimension, it is possible to go further, and to see the conflict primarily as a three-kingdoms reaction to the agglomeration of power achieved by the Independent grandees. The Engagement, for example, which laid the foundation for English and Irish Royalist strategy in 1648, was a direct response to the Independents' military conquest of king, London, and Parliament. The Engagers were adamant, as was Inchiquin in Ireland, that they 'quarrelled not with the [English] Parliament, but with the army and their adherents'.[1] 'The Scottish quarrell', remarked Clement Walker, 'is not against the English Nation, but against the trecherous and hypocriticall Grandees.'[2] By mid-1648 even leading Confederates did not regard their principal enemies as the Parliamentarian–Covenanter interest as a whole, but rather that section within it which in their eyes stood most averse to the king's person and restoration. Similarly, the

161

complaints about high taxes, free quarter, county committees, and the spread of sectarianism, that provided much of the impetus behind English provincial unrest in 1648, related not so much to parliamentary rule *per se*, but to the policies of the Independents. After all, if the Presbyterians had had their way in 1647 then most of the New Model soldiers would have been disbanded or sent to Ireland (thus reducing taxes and ending free quarter), the county committees would have been scrapped, and the sects and Levellers suppressed. The most common demand from the provinces in 1648 was that a personal treaty be concluded with the king – which intentionally or not was a swipe at the Independents. They were the faction that had conspicuously resisted the idea of a personal treaty. The Second Civil War should thus be seen as the English and Welsh stages of a wider conflict, the War of the Engagement, which encompassed all three kingdoms and had its origins in the Independents' military and political victories between 1645 and 1647.

The Vote of No Addresses

The king's rejection of the four bills left the Independent grandees in a difficult position. It was an affront that could not be ignored, but in adopting an even tougher stance against the king, as they must, they widened the gap between themselves and the English people, not to mention the dominant factions in the other two kingdoms. The Heads of Proposals had raised the hopes of many in England, including some Royalists, that the army and its allies at Westminster would be happy instruments of the king's restoration and a return to normality. Six months on, however, and the kingdom still groaned under the heavy tax burden needed to maintain the army; the county committees continued to distrain the goods of defaulters; and many parishes remained either destitute of a minister or obliged to worship according to the Presbyterian service book, the Directory, which even some Puritans disliked. Resentment at the oppressiveness of Parliamentarian rule was accentuated by the continuing economic downturn. Even in relatively prosperous counties such as Essex, the run of bad harvests and a slump in the cloth trade had left many of the poorer sort close to starvation.

In an effort to point up the king's intransigence as the main obstacle to a settlement, the Commons voted on 3 January 1648 that no further peace offerings were to be made to Charles or received by him. Known as 'the vote of no addresses', this was primarily an Independent initiative, although many MPs supported it in protest at the king's treating with the Scots behind Parliament's back. The vote was preceded by some very angry speeches from resentful Independents. The aptly named Sir Thomas Wroth desired that the king be impeached, declaring 'from divells and Kings Good Lord deliver me'.[3] He was followed by Ireton and Cromwell, who urged that the kingdom be settled without Charles, and made a particular point of praising the army for its fidelity to the nation's interests. The Independent grandees could not afford to lose the support of the army by continuing to treat publicly with the king. On the other hand, by forbidding further overtures to him, even temporarily, they risked a split within their own ranks. A number of peers, among them the Earl of Northumberland, feared that the vote would lead to an imposed settlement that threatened both the monarchy and the nobility.

Immediately after passing the vote of no addresses, the Commons re-invested the powers of the Committee of Both Kingdoms exclusively in its English members. The resulting new committee was known as the Derby House Committee, and superseded the Committee for Irish Affairs at Derby House as Parliament's main executive body. The Independent grandees dominated the committee, and used it to wrest even more of the initiative from the two Houses; 'all Affaires of moment being hammer'd in the shop at Derby House'.[4]

The Engagement clearly threatened the grandees' power in England, and they responded by attempting to threaten the Hamiltonians' power in Scotland. Their first line of attack was to court Argyll's party, which was known to oppose war with England for an uncovenanted king. At Westminster, the Independents made speeches praising Argyll and his supporters as 'the onely men that upheld the English interest in Scotland'.[5] In addition, they sent parliamentary commissioners to Edinburgh – ostensibly to maintain peace between the two kingdoms, but in fact to bolster Argyll's faction with money and offers of English support. Their second stratagem was to renew their overtures to the king, although they had to proceed in great secrecy so as not to upset the army nor openly flout the vote of no addresses. With Saye as their spokesman, and Ashburnham as an intermediary, they spent much of the period from January to May trying to reach an agreement with the king, probably on the basis of the Heads of Proposals. The plan was to disengage the king from the Hamiltonian Scots; and though they failed in this endeavour, the mere fact that they were continuing to treat with Charles was enough to reassure some of their more nervous colleagues such as Northumberland. The Independents' third ploy was to woo potential English allies of the

Hamiltonians, which they endeavoured to do by pressing for further Presbyterian church reforms, and by conciliating the City (the Hamiltonians were relying on London to rise against the army as it had in 1647).

The Derby House grandees could be guardedly optimistic by early March. They had managed to retain the confidence of the army (or most of it) and to keep the Presbyterians quiet. All now depended on the state of play in Scotland, where a new Parliament was shortly to meet. If the Engagement could be killed off there, then it might deter the Independents' enemies in England and Ireland from rising against them. If not, then the grandees would find themselves caught between their desire for a moderate settlement and their reliance upon an army that renewed bloodshed would render implacable against the king.

'A Pretext of Religion': Selling the Engagement

The signing of the Engagement was publicly announced in Edinburgh on 21 January. Although final ratification of the treaty rested with the forthcoming Scottish Parliament, the Hamiltonians considered this a mere formality and began to prepare for war. The Scots commissioners spent most of January in London making plans with leading Presbyterians and Royalists for a series of uprisings in England to coincide with a Scottish invasion; while in Edinburgh, Hamilton began sounding out Montereul about French military support. In mid-February the Scots commissioners reported in person to the Committee of Estates in Edinburgh; Lauderdale setting the tone by asserting that there were four things that the English could not stomach – 'the Covenant, Presbyterianism, monarchical government, and Scotsmen'.[6] The committee promptly approved the Engagement, signalling that a majority of Scotland's leading men were now aligned with Hamilton.

Argyll's party and the Kirk were appalled once it became clear that the king had made only minimal concessions to Presbyterianism, and they denounced the Engagement as destructive of the Covenant and as a stalking horse for revanchist royalism. Whereas the Kirk had generally approved of invading England in 1647 when Argyll still had the upper hand, a war waged by the Hamiltonians for an uncovenanted king was another matter entirely. Bolstered by money and fair words from the English commissioners, Argyll's party toyed with the idea of staging a coup, New Model Army-style. But the Engagement had divided Leslie's nominally pro-Argyll army just as surely as it had Scotland's politicians, and after three years of MacDonald plundering, the Campbells were a spent force militarily. Sensing the weakness of the radicals, the extreme Royalist wing of the Covenanters, led by Callander, was ready to declare openly for Charles, without the pretence of making war to uphold Presbyterianism; but the Hamiltonians reasoned that without 'a pretext of religion' it would be impossible to engage the moderate Covenanter majority for the king.[7]

The new Scottish Parliament assembled on 2 March, and it quickly became clear that the radicals' accustomed dominance of parliamentary proceedings was a thing of the past. The Engagers had triumphed in the elections, and the majority of members now 'ran in a string after Duke Hamilton's vote'.[8] Not only did Parliament approve the Engagement, but under pressure from Callander's faction the Hamiltonians agreed to commence plans for garrisoning the English border towns of Carlisle and Berwick, which would represent an act of war against England. In protest, Argyll and his supporters quit Parliament, whereupon the Hamiltonians forced them to resume their seats. News of the divisions at Edinburgh had reportedly 'much abaited the affection and action of London and the King's partie' in England, and the Hamiltonians were anxious to avoid further bad press.[9] Their own attempts to use scare-stories about Leveller activity in London (of which there had been relatively little) to bounce the Kirk into supporting the Engagement had failed miserably. The clergy refused to endorse an invasion of England unless it was conducted by true Covenanters with a royal pledge to settle Presbyterianism in all three kingdoms. But there was no chance of a compromise on these terms. It would have alienated Callander's faction, the English Royalists, and Ormond's party in Ireland.

The more the Hamiltonians clung to a policy of trying to reconcile the interests of the king's party with those of the more rigid Presbyters – their 'maxim of union' as Montereul called it – the more they risked losing the support of both. In a last concerted effort to placate the clergy, Parliament explained on 11 April that 'This Kingdom cannot expect securitie from thame who have bene the undermynderis and destroyeris of Religion Libertie and Covenant in England,' and that it would prosecute Scotland's quarrel with 'the prevalent pairtie of Sectaries' until 'uniformity in Religion be setled according to the Covenant'.[10] Despite this emphasis on upholding the Covenant, the Kirk still gave out that the Engagers were using religion merely as a cloak to hide their royalism. From the English Royalists' perspective, on the other hand, it seemed that the Scots were still insisting on their 'Damnable Covenant'. The

queen and her circle in Paris were willing to accept the Hamiltonians' assurances that this emphasis on the Covenant was merely to satisfy the Kirk, and
that their main priority was to restore the king; but Royalist patriots in
England were less inclined to give the Scots the benefit of the doubt. Hyde
would later describe the Engagement as 'scandalous and derogatory to the
honour and interest of the English nation' – a view apparently shared by
many of his friends.[11] Similarly, although the English Presbyterians were not
averse to using the threat of a Scottish invasion to extract concessions from
the Independents, they too were far from united on whether such an invasion should be countenanced, even covertly. Denzil Holles, in exile in
France, held talks with Jermyn and other leading courtiers in April, and like
them was probably pinning his hopes on a Scottish invasion, but many
Presbyterians in England, particularly those genuinely enthusiastic about a
godly church settlement, seem to have heeded the Kirk's warnings that the
Hamiltonians were 'malignants' in disguise.

The Royalist Association

The revival of Royalist military prospects in Britain had a major impact
in Ireland. The resurgence of the king's party rendered the Royalist
middle ground in Irish politics more tenable than it had been since
Naseby. At the same time, it diverted the attention and resources of an
apprehensive Westminster away from the Irish war-effort, thereby (from
a Parliamentarian perspective) frustrating the most promising opportunity to finish off the Confederates in years. The Engagement had created
the ideal conditions for Ormond and his allies in Ireland to raise new
armies for the king.

The Ormondist faction was strongly represented on the new Supreme
Council that assumed the reins of Confederate government late in
December 1647. The council was eager to conclude a truce with
Inchiquin: partly on military grounds – after Knocknanuss, Inchiquin's
forces threatened Kilkenny itself – but also because he was known to sym-
pathise with Ormond's plans for a Royalist alliance in Ireland. Ormond's
agent, Colonel Barry, detected a similar sentiment among Confederate
leaders early in March. Indeed, as Rinuccini suspected, the council's willingness to make peace with Inchiquin was part of a wider strategy to draw
the entire Association into Ormond's projected alliance.

Ormond's overtures to Inchiquin were guaranteed a favourable
reception. Inchiquin knew that he had powerful enemies among

the Independents who controlled Parliament's money and executive committees, and that they were trying to destroy his career and his command. The vote of no addresses put a further obstacle in the way of his safety by seeming to end all prospect of a moderate settlement in England. He was anxious not to repeat his mistake of the previous August, when he had committed his army to what he thought was a Presbyterian offensive against the Independents only to discover that he was on his own. But by early 1648 he could clearly see that the enemies of Independency were on the march in Britain. Indeed, he encouraged his men to desert Parliament by referring to 'the Scotts engagement and the promiseing appeareance for the king in severall partes of England'.[12] What probably clinched it for Inchiquin personally was Ormond's promise that he would return to Ireland to lead the Royalist cause. Inchiquin had great respect for Ormond. Certainly no one else could have persuaded him to enter into an alliance with the Confederates. After strengthening his links with the pro-Engagement factions at Westminster and Edinburgh, and purging his army of Independent sympathisers, Inchiquin announced his defection on 3 April.

Ormond's next move was to scupper the Confederates' peace initiative to the queen in Paris. Late in February he left England for France, sure in the knowledge that Cardinal Mazarin would back him. The last thing Mazarin wanted was Ireland under a papal or Spanish protectorate. Ormond could also count on the support of two of the Confederate commissioners sent to Paris, Viscount Muskerry and Geoffrey Browne, who carried with them private instructions from Preston and Taaffe to seek terms from the Prince of Wales 'as will not only settle this Kingdome, but likewise with some assistance in England regaine his rights and Interest in his other dominions'.[13] To this end they requested that the prince come to Ireland with money and arms. The despatch of the prince to Ireland was likewise central to Ormond's plans. Wherever the prince went, the resources of the royal court were sure to follow, and as ever in Ireland, money and supplies were key. Having declared for the king, the Confederates could expect no further money from Rome, while Inchiquin would be cut off by Parliament without a penny. Money was desperately needed if they were to hold their armies together. Ormond's trump card at Paris was the confidence placed in him by the king and queen. The queen waited the minimum time that propriety demanded to see if the pope would approve the Confederate's terms for a religious settlement, and when that had not arrived by May she declared in favour of Ormond's plans. Muskerry and Browne then returned to Kilkenny to spread the good tidings.

Meanwhile, back in Ireland, Inchiquin's announcement of his defection had encouraged the Supreme Council to hold talks with him about a truce. Rinuccini was vehemently against any rapprochement with the Cashel butcherer, and began to muster support among the bishops. The nuncio regarded the proposed truce as merely an elaborate plot to make a new treaty with Ormond in which the clergy's demands concerning church lands and freedom of worship would again be sidelined. Although the council secured the support of leading Munster and Leinster Confederates for its proceedings, Rinuccini and 14 bishops signed a declaration against the truce.

The threat of clerical censure unnerved the peace party, just as it had in the summer of 1646. But by 1648 Rinuccini's position was too weak for him to isolate the peace party leaders as he had two years earlier. Dungan's Hill and Knocknanuss had discredited his strategy of all-out military conquest, not least because it had left the Catholics of Leinster and Munster almost wholly reliant for their defence upon O'Neill's rapacious Ulstermen. Nor did Rinuccini have the money to revive the Confederate war-effort as he had done in 1646. Moreover, the situation in Britain had changed. The improvement in the king's military prospects by early 1648 lent the peace faction's policy of allying with the Royalists a credibility it had manifestly lacked since 1645. The arguments in favour of such an alliance were even strong enough to persuade a sizeable minority among the clergy, including a number of the bishops, to reject the nuncio's stance.

Believing that his life was in danger at Kilkenny, Rinuccini fled to O'Neill's army in May – a move that reinforced the impression that the nuncio was in thrall to the Ulster Gaels, whom many Confederates suspected of wanting to depose Charles in favour of a foreign prince or even O'Neill. No one was more alarmed by this prospect than O'Neill's fellow Confederate generals Preston and Taaffe, and when the council signed a truce with Inchiquin on 20 May it received the backing of both men. A week later Rinuccini excommunicated all supporters of the truce – which simply deepened the divide in Confederate ranks. So eager were some Confederates for the king's re-establishment, and so fearful of the intentions of the Ulster 'nuncioists', that they would rather join with heretics to fight O'Neill than vice versa. A Confederate civil war had become unavoidable.

The Outbreak of the Second Civil War

The opening shots of the Second Civil War were fired in South Wales with the revolt in March of the disgruntled Parliamentarian officers

Major-General Rowland Laugharne and his colonel, John Poyer. Although the risings in Wales grew out of local and personal rivalries, the royal court at Paris managed to recruit the insurgents, or at least their leaders, in the king's cause. Laugharne's brigade had been one of the military units that the Earl of Essex had hoped to weld into a counterweight to the New Model in 1646, and it is possible that Laugharne had retained links with Essex's former collaborators, the Earl of Holland and the exiled Denzil Holles, who had friends at court. Laugharne was given a general's commission from the Prince of Wales, and sent envoys to Paris to plead for supplies and money. Unfortunately for the Welsh insurgents, the court's main interest in their proceedings seems to have been as a means of putting pressure on the Scots to speed up their invasion preparations. The court spurred on Laugharne with offers of supplies (which never materialised), and assurances that the New Model would soon have its hands full trying to fend off the Scots.

As it turned out, a Scottish invasion was still several months away when Laugharne's 8000-strong army was defeated by Colonel Horton and a contingent of the New Model at St Fagans, near Cardiff, on 8 May. Horton had been outnumbered three to one, but his troops had been better disciplined, better armed, and better paid. St Fagans and the arrival a few days later of Cromwell with more New Model regiments effectively settled the issue in South Wales. That Poyer succeeded in holding out in Pembroke Castle for another two months, tying up Cromwell and 8000 soldiers in the process, would have mattered only if the Scots had invaded during that time. But opposition in Scotland to the Engagement had made that impossible.

Raising the Army of the Engagement

The Hamiltonians had largely dropped their 'maxim of union' by mid-April – something they should probably have done months earlier. On 18 April, Argyll and his supporters again walked out of the Scottish Parliament, and this time the Hamiltonians let them go. Their priority now was to prepare for the invasion of the 'Independents' kingdome', and to this end they used their English Royalist allies to secure strategic bridgeheads south of the border. On 28 April, Sir Marmaduke Langdale and his men seized Berwick, and the next day Sir Philip Musgrave took Carlisle. On 4 May, Parliament gave orders for raising a new army that would incorporate Leslie's force, and a week later Hamilton was appointed commander-in-chief – to the annoyance of Callander, who had coveted the post himself and had to settle for second-in-command. Leven and Leslie, the two most able Scottish generals, were forced to resign and refused to serve respectively.

Given the almost daily warnings the Hamiltonians were receiving from London and Paris that unless they invaded soon then all would be lost, they were relieved finally to be making progress towards honouring their end of the Engagement, and in wildly optimistic mood imagined that the new army would be ready by June. In fact, the levying of men proved slow and difficult work. Argyll and other leading anti-Engagers encouraged opposition to the recruiting, and the Kirk and many local Presbyteries came out strongly against the new levies. Even in the Highlands, where Scottish royalism was strongest, support for the Engagement was far from universal. Some of the clans were split over whether to back the Engagers, and those that did offer to raise men were rebuffed by the Hamiltonians, who feared alienating Lowland opinion further by being seen to accept help from 'godless' Highlanders.

Resistance to the Engagers was greatest in the radical south-west, the heartland of Covenanted Presbyterianism. Discontent in the region erupted in mid-June with an abortive popular rising on Mauchline Moor, south of Glasgow. The insurgents were quickly scattered by Hamilton's cavalry – just as the New Model had crushed whatever resistance it had encountered from the English clubmen. But the episode revealed how passionate opposition to the Engagement had become. As in 1644, the terms of intervention in England were dividing the Scots to the point of civil war; except that in 1648 it was the radical Covenanters rather than the Royalists who were preparing to take on Edinburgh.

The Independent–Presbyterian Alliance

Despite the best efforts of Argyll's party, the Kirk, and the Independent grandees, to destroy the Engagement, it was clear by the end of April that they had failed. The Hamiltonians were raising an army, and the knowledge of that fact was a spur to aggrieved English people across the political spectrum. The freeholders of Essex had adopted a petition late in March demanding a personal treaty and the disbandment of the New Model. London had been awash with unrest for months. A large crowd of apprentices shouting 'Now for King Charles' had effectively seized control of the capital early in April and it had taken 1600 New Model cavalry to restore order. Although many of the City's Presbyterian leaders were distinctly ambivalent about the Engagement, and inclined to believe Argyll's party that it was a Royalist blind, nevertheless their abiding hostility to the New Model and all that went with it – sectarianism, high taxes, etc. – meant that the Derby House junto could not rely on them in a crisis. What the City fathers wanted was for Parliament to conclude a personal treaty with the king that would restore him to his prerogative powers and establish a national Presbyterian church. They settled at the end of April for the removal of New Model units from the City and the appointment of Major-General Skippon – a firm Presbyterian yet trusted by Parliament and the army – as military commander of London. But the grandees would have to acquiesce further to civic demands if they were to make the Common Council fast to Parliament amidst the rising tide of Royalist feeling in London.

The failure of the grandees' secret overtures to Charles left them with a hard decision. In order to appease the City, and to have any chance of frustrating the Hamiltonians' invasion plans, they would have to make a u-turn on the vote of no addresses. On 28 April, therefore, leading Independents in the Commons voted with the Presbyterians for reopening parliamentary negotiations with the king on the basis of the propositions sent to him at Hampton Court the previous September. Parliament reiterated this message on 6 May, this time stressing a readiness to join with Scotland 'for the speedy Settlement of the Peace of both Kingdoms, and Preservation of the Union according to the Covenant and Treaties'.[14] The grandees supported such pronouncements with one eye on the City and the parliamentary Presbyterians, and the other on the Engagers. By highlighting their commitment to a traditional settlement on terms approved by both kingdoms, the grandees gave Argyll and the Kirk further grounds to challenge the Hamiltonians' main argument for invading England – that the Independents were bent on destroying king, monarchy, and religion. Although the Westminster Presbyterians must have suspected the grandees of ulterior motives in supporting negotiations, those who were strongly committed to a godly church settlement or who shared the grandees' distrust of Charles and the Hamiltonians, had little choice but to work with them if an unconditional restoration was to be avoided. In trying to avert a Scottish invasion, the Independent grandees and 'true Presbyterians' found that they needed each other.[15]

David Underdown has referred to the votes of 28 April as 'a great turning-point' – the moment when the 'moderates' and the 'radicals' in the Independent faction finally parted company and the Independent–army alliance collapsed.[16] It is certainly true that the political programmes of the grandees and an increasingly powerful body of militant opinion in the army began to diverge after April. Yet, as we shall see, Cromwell and Fairfax remained on friendly terms with the grandees for months to come, and continued to share their concern to maintain 'the fundamental government'. It is clear also that the 28 April votes did not split the Independent leadership. Even the most radical of the grandees, Sir Henry Vane junior, remained on board. But then this is hardly surprising, for the grandees' support for the votes was largely a public relations exercise. It allowed them to look as if they were backing a moderate settlement (which indeed they wanted, but not on terms that would preserve 'the Union according to the Covenant'), confident that Charles would not agree to the Hampton Court Propositions – a slightly amended version of the Newcastle Propositions.

What the April votes do point to is an increase in the number of radical Independents – the faction that had emerged in opposition to the grandees the previous autumn and that was defined by its bitter opposition to any compromise with Charles or the 'Scottified' interest. It was also the repository for that handful of republicans at Westminster, such as Thomas Chaloner, who were eager to cut not only the king but also the Lords out of the legislative trinity, and to vest sovereign power solely in the people's representatives – that is, the Commons.

In the opposite corner at Westminster were those who wanted peace at almost any price, even a Scottish invasion. Prominent in this category were the half dozen or so crypto-Royalist peers, who had seized the initiative in the Lords by June and were so eager for Charles's restoration that they refused to declare Hamilton and his army enemies to the kingdom. Yet the pro-Engagement party also included a number of firm Presbyterians – men whose hatred of the grandees and the New Model outweighed their misgivings about a settlement by means of the Hamiltonians. The threat of Scottish intervention, therefore, besides deepening the divide between the grandees and the radical Independents, led to a major split within the ranks of the old Essex–Holles group Presbyterians. While some of this group joined the anti-Engager Derby House junto, others aligned with the pro-Engager crypto-Royalists. It is this split within Presbyterian ranks that is the most significant political realignment of 1648, for it allowed the Independent grandees to retain control at Westminster (after some trimming on their part) while helping to undermine resistance to Parliament in the provinces.

Revolt in the Provinces

The Second Civil War in England was preceded by a wave of petitions to Parliament calling for a personal treaty with the king and an end to the various ills associated with maintaining the New Model and the continued failure to reach a settlement. The petition adopted in Essex at the end of March was presented to Parliament by 2000 people on 4 May. It reportedly had 20,000 signatures, and was described by one of Hamilton's correspondents as 'the summe of your desires'.[17] The presentation of a petition from Surrey on 16 May was the occasion of 'great fighting' between the petitioners and the Parliament's guards, in which 10 people were killed and about 100 injured. Petitioning movements also sprang up in Kent, Sussex, Hampshire, and Dorset, while concerned groups in London, from the mayor and Common Council downwards, petitioned Parliament almost daily during the summer. The thinking behind these petitions was principally to take advantage of the times in order to wring concessions from a vulnerable Parliament. Most of the petitioners were not committed Royalists eager to dust off their swords and breast-plates. But this is not how it seemed to alarmed Parliamentarians. In Kent, the parliamentarian ruling faction branded the county's petition seditious and tried to suppress it by force, breeding a resolve among the petitioners 'to act the last Scene of this Trajedy with our Swords in our hands'.[18] Repressive measures had turned the Kent petitioning campaign into armed insurrection.

The Parliamentarians' over-reaction in Kent played right into the Royalists' hands. The Hamiltonians and the royal court had laid plans over the winter for a series of coordinated risings across England designed to link up with the invading Scottish army – which was expected by May at the latest. To what extent, if any, the petitioning campaigns formed part of these plans is not clear, but they certainly proved a Godsend to the Royalists, who were able to play upon the petitioners' craving for a traditional settlement, and resentment at Parliament's heavy-handed response, to rouse many of them to armed resistance in the king's name. Certainly in those areas where petitioning campaigns never got off the ground, unrest tended to remain localised and mostly confined to small groups of hard-line Cavaliers.

Yet the Royalists faced major problems in trying to wage war by populist insurrection. Popular discontent, once roused, tended to have a life of its own, and was hard to channel for specific military purposes. In the case of Kent, the Royalists had planned to wait until the New Model had gone north to deal with the Scots before raising the county. The Kentishmen were then to join with insurgents from Sussex, Surrey, and Hampshire and march on London. Instead, the draconian tactics of the Kent authorities had set the county ablaze by late May, when a Scottish invasion was still months away and the bulk of the New Model still in the south.

On 30 May, Fairfax marched 4000 New Model troops from Surrey into Kent. The Kentish insurgents numbered about 11,000, but they were scattered across the county and no match for Fairfax's veterans. After some fierce fighting, mainly in and around Maidstone, Fairfax succeeded in pacifying the county, although he was unable to prevent a force of about 1500 insurgents crossing the Thames into Essex. The rising in Kent had given the Royalists time to raise several thousand men from among Essex's petitioners and militia, and these, with the Kentish insurgents and Royalist volunteers from London and elsewhere, made a formidable force. But Essex was not called Parliament's 'beloved' county for nothing. Shadowing the insurgents as they moved north towards Colchester was a large force of Essexmen as well as New Model troops, and they were soon joined by Fairfax and his men, who had crossed the Thames from Kent on 11 June. After a fierce battle in which he sustained 500 casualties, Fairfax bottled up the Royalists in Colchester and settled down for a long siege.

Most of the serious fighting in the Second Civil War – until the Scots invaded, that is – was confined to Wales, Kent, and Essex. But there were numerous 'brushfires' to be stamped out in East Anglia, the Midlands, and the West Country; and overall, the New Model and local Parliamentarian forces were kept busy with siege-work (Colchester and Pembroke) and counter-insurgency operations for most of the spring and summer. The pattern of unrest was shaped by three main factors – the Royalists' focus on the Home Counties in the hope of stirring up rebellion in London; popular discontent occasioned by the quartering of New Model troops in the south-east; and the local influence of the anti-Independent interest. It was not entirely a coincidence that the parliamentary seats and landed estates of the Independents' leading enemies, particularly those who had been associated with the Earl of Essex's network, tended to be concentrated in East Anglia, Wales, and the West Country.

Conversely, the region in which anti-Scottish feeling was strongest – northern England – did not rise in any considerable numbers for the king. The people there were still recovering from three years of military occupation by the Scots and could muster little enthusiasm for a war predicated on another Scottish invasion. And while the common people generally loathed the Scots, the Presbyterian gentry of Yorkshire and Lancashire felt the same way about the Scots' Royalist allies, and worked closely with the region's Independents to raise forces against the Engagers (an echo of the Independent–Presbyterian alliance at Westminster). The Independents' efforts to expel the Scots from the northern counties, and the king's efforts to bring them back in, had altered the region's political complexion. By 1648 the north was no longer the bastion of Royalist sympathy it had been five years earlier. Indeed, if it constituted a regional power-base for any group it was the Independents. Like his ill-fated predecessor, Henry VI, Charles discovered that using the Scots to fight his quarrels was likely to lose him the affection of his northern English subjects.

The Failure of Royalist Strategy

Despite the Royalists' plans for a coordinated offensive, the risings occurred in such a piecemeal fashion that they never stretched Parliament's military resources to breaking point. The basic idea, of course, was that all the risings should coincide with the Scottish invasion. But as we have seen, the Hamiltonians were delayed at every turn, and the heat from the Kent and Essex actions, combined with the false hope that London would revolt as it had in 1647, touched off the other insurrections like a string of firecrackers. Poor communications added to the Royalists' coordination problems. Whereas Parliament had a centralised and efficient intelligence network, run from Derby House, the Royalist high command (if it could be called such) was in Paris – and communications across the Channel could be tenuous at the best of times.

The Royalists' defeat in the Second Civil War was down to more than just poor timing, however, and requires explanation. There can be no doubt that their opponents – the Derby House junto – were massively unpopular by 1648. 'This Caball ... at Derby-house', wrote Walker, 'govern by power, not by love, and ... with a military Aristocracy, or rather Oligarchy, rule this Nation with a rod of Iron';[19] while another commentator claimed that 'it is notoriously known that ... the people every where dislike what you are now a doing, and are ready to pull you off those Benches [in Parliament], did not the Army you keep up restrain them'.[20]

The key to the junto's political survival was its absolute control of army finances. The grandees and their placemen on the Army Committee and the treasurers-at-war made sure that the New Model field regiments were paid almost in full during the first half of 1648. While it is true, therefore, that the threat of popular insurrection limited the scope for ruling groups to pursue their own interests, an oligarchic faction with an army at its disposal and the means to pay it could limit the people's freedom of action a whole lot more.

The junto's cause was helped by the fact that its opponents were divided among themselves. The Civil War had created political and religious divisions that penetrated deep into local communities and precluded the emergence of a broad-based campaign of provincial unrest of the kind that had frustrated Charles during the Second Bishops' War. Alienated Parliamentarians in the localities were incapable of overcoming distrust within their own ranks, let alone their distrust of the Scots and Cavaliers. Similarly, the Royalists were deeply divided on the question of a Scottish alliance. One northern Cavalier allegedly declared that 'though they hated ye Scots as bad as the Turkes, yet they would all joyne either with Scot or Turke to suppresse the Independ[en]ts & restore the King'.[21] But other Royalists, it was reported, would have preferred the king to perish than see him restored by Scottish hands. Although this is doubtless an exaggeration, it is clear that a large number of the king's party in England wanted nothing to do with the Engagement or the Second Civil War.

The discord and in-fighting among Royalists in 1648 went right to the top, and prevented them taking advantage of perhaps their biggest coup of the war – the defection of eleven Parliamentarian warships to the king late in May. This mutiny had been sparked off by a combination of material grievances and anger at the Independents' 'overunning, disarming, and plundering [of] the country … as if it were a conquered nation'.[22] For the first time, the king's party had a powerful fleet at its disposal, and Jermyn and the Prince of Wales's other confidants – his 'old presbiterian Counsellors' as Hyde sarcastically called them[23] – knew exactly what they wanted to do with it. Assured by Lauderdale that the Scots were on the march, they were determined to preserve the fleet in order to convey the prince to the head of Hamilton's army. Inevitably, Hyde and the Royalist patriots lambasted this policy. To them it was a self-serving design by the enemies (both Catholic and Presbyterian) of the Church of England, and represented a gross betrayal of the honour and interest of the English nation. They wanted the prince and fleet sent to Ireland with Ormond, or to the insurgents in Wales – in fact to any group loyal to the English crown and church, which in their view excluded the Scots. Although it was the pro-Scots faction, backed firmly by the queen, that won the argument, the seamen were adamant that the prince should remain with them, and there was talk of throwing Lauderdale overboard.

Racked by division and dissent the fleet proved virtually useless. After mounting a short-lived blockade of the Thames estuary, and failing to engage an inferior parliamentarian squadron, it returned to Holland 'full of discontent'.[24] Through factionalism and poor leadership the Royalists had squandered yet another opportunity.

Hamilton's Invasion

The Hamiltonians had dreamed of marching 40,000 troops into England, but widespread opposition to the Engagement and the general war-weariness of Scotland had put paid to that. By early July, Hamilton's army consisted of about 10,000 poorly armed and largely untrained conscript foot, and about 4000 horse, reportedly of good quality. His most experienced troops were 2000 or so New Scots soldiers under Monro's nephew, Colonel George Monro, and an English advance guard under Langdale numbering about 3500. It was the need to support Langdale, who was being hard-pressed in Cumberland by Major-General John Lambert's Parliamentarian forces, that spurred Hamilton to march his ill-prepared army across the border near Carlisle on 8 July, obliging Lambert to fall back into Yorkshire. Aside from a scattering of local forces, the way was clear for Hamilton to strike into the heart of England. However, his army was short of supplies, and in expectation of receiving more men and provisions from Scotland, he made camp in Cumberland for a month. While Hamilton stayed put in the north, Cromwell was able to batter Pembroke Castle (the last rebel stronghold in south Wales) into submission, and to march his New Model troops to join Lambert's men in Yorkshire. Their combined force numbered in the region of 10,000 men.

Although Parliament's recent victories in England and Wales had convinced Cromwell that Providence would favour him against the Scots, the mood at Westminster was less sanguine. With a Royalist fleet in the Thames estuary, and Colchester still holding out against Fairfax, the Independents' enemies in London were growing bolder by the day. Since April, the Common Council had pestered the two Houses for greater autonomy in civic affairs, and for a personal treaty with the king. If the grandees were not to lose their already tenuous grip on the capital they must make some concessions to civic feeling. Consequently, they released those citizens who had been imprisoned after the coup in July 1647, and gave the Common Council greater control over London's military resources. But while this was enough to keep the City fathers broadly in line (for they were as fearful of a Cavalier take-over as most MPs), among Londoners generally, Royalist enthusiasm remained at dangerously high levels.

The crisis in Parliament's relationship with the City came late in July. To MPs already alarmed by Hamilton's invasion came the unpleasant realisation that they were close to losing control of London. During July, Skippon and the Derby House Committee had been raising their own forces in London (having no faith in the City militia), and the Common Council was outraged. Moderate opinion among the citizenry now swung behind the Royalists in condemning this affront to civic autonomy. On 27 July the council issued what amounted to a veiled threat, declaring that if Skippon continued enlisting men it would lead to 'a sudden distemper'. The next day, the Commons faced up to an issue it had been dodging for weeks – whether to agree with the Lords for a personal treaty without any preconditions. The Independent–Presbyterian alliance had insisted that before Parliament talked to Charles he must agree to settle Presbyterianism for three years, relinquish control of the militia for ten, and revoke all his wartime declarations against Parliament. For the more 'rigid' Presbyterians, these three propositions provided a basic guarantee of a godly church settlement; for the Independent grandees it was more of a spoiling tactic, since they were certain that the king would never agree to treat on such terms.

By late July the pressure for an unconditional treaty was becoming so intense that the grandees could not retain the three propositions without further jeopardising their hold on the City. On 28 July, therefore, the majority of them voted with the peace-at-any-price element to sweep away preconditions. But whereas they had been willing to hold the treaty negotiations near London while the three propositions had been in play, without them they insisted that the talks be held on the Isle of Wight, well away from the City Royalists. Well might Marchamont Nedham, the most penetrating of the Royalist pamphleteers, complain that 'this Treaty comes arse-wards into the world'.[25] Even so, in the space of exactly three months, Parliament had gone from overturning the vote of no addresses to sanctioning a full-blown treaty with the king. Scottish intervention and civic brinkmanship were pushing Parliament and the army back onto a collision course.

Preston and Colchester

If MPs had witnessed Hamilton's generalship at first hand then perhaps they would have been less jittery. Although not a complete novice as a general, he was providing an object lesson in how to lose a campaign. Too much the politician, he put not offending Callander, his prickly second-in-command, before strictly military considerations. Thus instead of resolving a dispute over precedence between George Monro and Callander, he posted Monro and the New Scots brigade to guard the border, thereby depriving his army of its most experienced soldiers. Moreover, when he finally began to march his army southwards into Lancashire in mid-August, he allowed his troops to become strung out in a 20-mile-long column with the cavalry well in advance of the foot. Speeding across the Pennines to intercept them was Cromwell's army, but Hamilton, oblivious of the danger, allowed his troops to keep pushing south. On 17 August, as the Scottish foot straggled across the Ribble at Preston, Cromwell descended on the town from the north-east to cut off their line of retreat to Scotland. Langdale and his men bravely held their ground to the east of Preston for several hours, but instead of supporting them, Hamilton was persuaded by Callander to withdraw the Scottish foot south across the Ribble to join up with the cavalry. The Scottish troops were demoralised by this decision to abandon Langdale without a fight, and what began as a tactical withdrawal turned into a disorganised retreat. Cromwell pursued the Scottish army southwards, and gave the infantry a severe mauling near Warrington, whereupon it surrendered. The Scottish cavalry were chased all the way to Uttoxeter in Staffordshire, where Hamilton surrendered on 25 August (Callander escaped to the Continent). Having disposed of Hamilton's main army, Cromwell turned northwards to deal with Monro's brigade and those of Langdale's cavalry who had escaped the débâcle at Preston.

Had the Scots been better led from the start, then things just might have gone differently. Admittedly, Cromwell's troops were more disciplined and better supplied. He also enjoyed home advantage – fighting on English soil and among country people who generally hated the Scots. Yet the Scots were not without a few advantages of their own. They had superiority of numbers, their cavalry was good, and Langdale's and Monro's infantry knew their business. With Hamilton in charge, however, they had stood no chance.

News of Hamilton's defeat convinced the Royalists in Colchester that the game was up, and on 27 August the town surrendered. The siege had been a long and bitter one, and at its conclusion Fairfax had two Royalist commanders executed. The fall of Colchester transformed the situation in London. Relations between the Commons and the City had remained fraught throughout August. The Common Council had not been satisfied with the vote of 28 July, and had petitioned for the king to be allowed to come to London to treat. After Colchester, however, civic defiance crumbled, and early in September the army began to imprison its leading metropolitan opponents.

The Whiggamore Raid

When news of Hamilton's defeat reached Scotland, the south-west of the country rose in the name of the Kirk, and by early September several thousand 'westerners' were marching on Edinburgh. The Whiggamore Raid, as it became known, established a new regime in Scotland that demonstrated an unprecedented willingness to heed the advice of radical Presbyterian ministers. Argyll and several of his aristocratic allies were not without influence in this 'Kirk party'. Nevertheless, the majority of noblemen had been discredited by their association with the Engagers, thus leaving the political stage to the radical Covenanters, who were mostly men of lesser rank with a zeal for moral and social reform.

Driven from Edinburgh and with Cromwell approaching from the south, the Engagers were forced to strike northwards, and in mid-September they seized Stirling. At this point, with a nasty civil war threatening, the Kirk party and the Engagers began negotiating in earnest for a treaty. The Engagers realised that their cause was lost; and the Kirk party did not want to drive them into the arms of the Royalist clans. Above all, the Kirk party was anxious to deter Cromwell from entering Scotland by showing him that they had the situation under control. Whereas they had been happy to exploit Cromwell's victory to seize power in Scotland, they regarded the English 'sectarian' army as only marginally less offensive than the Engagers. On 22 September the new regime at Edinburgh passed an Act excluding all Engagers from political office. But Cromwell was not satisfied that enough had been done to prevent a Royalist resurgence in Scotland, and he marched his army up to Edinburgh. Some of the Independent grandees were hoping that he would conquer Scotland, but he thought that idea 'not Christian'.[26] Before he arrived in Edinburgh, the Kirk party and the Engagers signed a treaty in which both sides agreed to disband and to leave a final settlement to Parliament, which was due to meet in January. With its troops disbanded, the Kirk party relied largely upon Cromwell's army to enforce its will.

Cromwell stayed in Edinburgh for just a few days in early October, during which time he held talks with Argyll. If, as David Stevenson has conjectured, Cromwell secured Argyll's assent to the principle that kings might be tried for their crimes, it was an ominous sign of the way his thoughts were now running.[27] Leaving Lambert and several regiments in Edinburgh to prop up the Kirk party, Cromwell returned to England, his military work in the two kingdoms largely completed.

But though the Engagement was a dead letter in Britain, the Covenant was certainly not. The Kirk party would feel no less threatened than the Engagers had at the prospect of a settlement in England brokered by a triumphant New Model, especially if it involved putting the king on trial. Moreover, the Engagement was not just a British phenomenon. It had helped inspire a Royalist reaction in Ireland, where powerful forces were still intent upon bringing down the New Model and restoring the king. The Second Civil War might have ended, but the War of the Engagement was only half over.

Ormond Returns to Ireland

By consuming Parliament's attention and resources, the Engagement and Second Civil War gave the Confederates an opportunity to revive their military fortunes in Ireland. As one English Parliamentarian dolefully commented, 'if they doe not now their businesse, it must be Gods great mercy to this Kingdome, for here there is little or no care taken of that matter'.[28] The Confederates' treaty with Inchiquin meant that their combined forces numbered around 15,000 men – which was considerably more than Colonel Michael Jones's Parliamentarian garrison in Dublin. The Royalist Confederates could also count upon the support, or at least the neutrality, of the New Scots army (or what remained of it) and pro-Engagement elements among the British forces in Ulster. The only significant Parliamentarian opposition they faced in the north consisted of a few thousand men in Connacht and Ulster under Sir Charles Coote and Colonel George Monck respectively.

Common sense dictated that the Royalists should concentrate their forces against Jones, who was by far their deadliest opponent. But neither Inchiquin nor his soldiers were yet prepared to fight against fellow Protestants. Moreover, the Confederate Supreme Council had become obsessed with Owen Roe O'Neill and his defiance of its authority in refusing to accept the Inchiquin treaty. The armies of Inchiquin, Preston, Clanricarde, and Taaffe were thus deployed in trying to crush O'Neill. However, he was too good a general to risk his few thousand men in battle, and the result was that the Royalist forces spent most of the summer and autumn vainly chasing him around the middle of Ireland. While the Royalists and O'Neill played their game of cat-and-mouse, Jones expanded his sphere of influence around Dublin, and Coote and Monck moved against Parliament's opponents among the Ulster British. The New Scots army, weakened by the loss of George Monro's brigade, and divided over the Engagement, surrendered their garrisons without a fight.

What the Royalist alliance in Ireland needed in order to render it an effective military force was supplies and a treaty with the king, and it looked to Ormond to provide both. Inchiquin's army was living off cats and dogs by mid-1648; and news of Hamilton's defeat and the suppression of the English Royalists sapped its morale still further. As the Royalist position in Britain deteriorated over the summer, the promise that Ormond would return with money from the royal court, and ideally a fleet carrying the Prince of Wales, became about the only thing that prevented Inchiquin's men from deserting *en masse*. The Confederates' position was not much better. On top of the perennial difficulty in supplying its forces, the Supreme Council had to work hard to prevent Rinuccini using clerical censures to rally support among the people. It had one major advantage in the propaganda war, however, and that was control of the Kilkenny presses, which turned out numerous declarations portraying the nuncio as a dupe of the Ulster militants, and accusing O'Neill of trying to alienate the people from their loyalty to the crown. Ruffled by the council's tactics, Rinuccini made the mistake in July of withdrawing to Galway, where Clanricarde's troops were able to cut him off from the rest of Ireland. In a further effort to widen its support base and circumvent the clergy, the council called a General Assembly for 4 September to ratify the projected settlement with Ormond.

Ormond did not arrive in Ireland until 30 September, having been delayed in France by contrary winds and empty promises of money from the royal court and Mazarin. Ormond's presence was enough to steady Inchiquin's troops, at least for a time, but the lord lieutenant faced a much tougher task trying to negotiate a treaty with the Confederates. Although the peace faction was strongly represented in the new General Assembly, those of the Catholic bishops who attended were still determined to establish their church in 'full liberty and splendour'.[29]

Moreover, the collapse of the Royalist cause in Britain undoubtedly encouraged the Confederates to push for better terms from Ormond, since the king himself had no prospect of regaining power without their help. The big sticking point was the issue of ecclesiastical jurisdiction. The assembly insisted that the Catholic clergy be allowed to retain the churches in their possession and to exercise their jurisdiction independently of the king (the right claimed by the Scottish Kirk). To grant such a request, however, would be to impair royal authority precisely where Charles valued it most. More immediately, it would prove entirely unacceptable to the Munster Protestants.

Ormond was now facing the same difficulty that had confronted the Hamiltonians – how to unite groups of differing religious and political persuasion in the royal cause. The only viable basis for building a strong party for the king in any of his dominions was upon loyalty to his person and a desire to use the crown as a bulwark against the aggressive power of the Independents. What typified Charles's adherents during the War of the Engagement was their capacity to put 'civil duties' to the king before all other considerations – or as Inchiquin put it, 'a strong mutual assumption that his Ma[jes]t[i]es service should bee the Center whereat wee should all meet, and whereunto wee should have our cheif regard in all capitulations'.[30] In all three kingdoms, however, but particularly in Ireland and Scotland, there were influential figures who either were unwilling to subordinate their religious scruples to serving the crown, or for whom a particular form of church government was inseparable from their conception of the proper functioning of royal authority. Ormond needed a powerful spur to 'civil duties' if he was to overcome such scruples and salvage the Royalist alliance, and like Hamilton before him he found it in the threatening posture of the New Model Army.

Treaty or Justice

The army's victories at Preston and Colchester came too late to deflect Parliament from its resolve to negotiate with the king. Indeed, to those in Parliament and the country generally who yearned for settlement, fear of an enraged and all-conquering soldiery made them even more desperate for a treaty. The grandees too were resigned to the need for a speedy settlement. Although they had been unhappy with the idea of an unconditional treaty, the ominous stirrings in the army by September made them willing to make the best of a bad job. The war had created a dangerous cocktail of emotions in the soldiers – righteous jubilation in victory, and anger that so many of their comrades had died re-fighting a war they had thought already won. Back in April, with the storm clouds gathering, army officers had held a prayer-meeting at Windsor, where they had vowed, 'if ever the Lord brought us back again in peace, to call Charles Stuart, that man of bloud, to an account for the bloud he had shed'.[31] The grandees' pursuit of a treaty with the twice-defeated Charles flatly contradicted this vow, now consecrated with the blood of more soldiers. Yet only by negotiating a settlement and then presenting the army with a *fait accompli* could the grandees see how to stifle the growing pressure in the ranks for punishing the king and overhauling what Cromwell's secretary termed 'that old job-trot form of government of King, Lords, and Commons'.[32] They were willing to jeopardise their relationship with the army in order to achieve a lasting peace that preserved the fundamental government.

Fear of the army's intentions was heightened by the dramatic re-emergence of their old allies, the Levellers. Buoyed by the army's recent triumphs, the Levellers petitioned the Commons on 11 September, urging MPs to assume supreme authority in the nation, and that rather than treat with the king the House should execute justice upon 'the capital authors' of the civil wars. A few days later, the Commons received the first in a series of radical county petitions that likewise denounced the treaty and decried Charles's wickedness in defying Providence and in defiling the land with innocent blood. These petitions served as a cautionary to all but the radical Independents (who cried them up) of the alternative to an agreement with the king. But for all their menace, it was only by exploiting discontent in the army that the Levellers and Puritan radicals in the provinces could hope to put pressure on Parliament. Consequently, September saw the beginning of a struggle for the hearts and minds of the soldiers – the radicals to rouse them against the treaty; the grandees, by attempting to secure their arrears of pay, to keep them in due obedience to Parliament.

The treaty talks with the king began on 18 September in the town of Newport on the Isle of Wight. Heading Parliament's negotiating team were Northumberland and Saye, whose resolve to conclude a peace was stiffened by the promise of high office in the restored court. The main stumbling block at Newport was basically the same as at Kilkenny – religious jurisdiction. The king could not be persuaded to abolish episcopacy, and with it his supremacy in religion, and establish Presbyterianism for three years as the Hampton Court Propositions required. Yet this was precisely the area where the commissioners had least flexibility, for the more rigid Presbyterians at Westminster would accept nothing less of him. Even Saye, whose dislike of Presbyterianism matched the king's own, was desperate to secure his compliance on this point. If Charles would not budge then the Westminster Presbyterians were prepared to resist a settlement as surely as the radical Independents were.

Another impasse emerged late in October after news reached England of Ormond's proceedings in Ireland. Parliament immediately demanded that the king call off Ormond's negotiations with the Confederates, but Charles procrastinated, for, as he secretly made clear to Ormond, he was pinning all his hopes upon the successful outcome of the talks at Kilkenny. Any concessions he made at Newport would be merely a sham – a way of spinning out time while Ormond united Ireland in his cause. In a challenging re-interpretation of the political manoeuvrings that preceded the regicide, John Adamson has argued that events in Ireland, or at least the perception of them, had a major bearing on English politics during the final months of Charles's life. The fact that only Charles could call off Ormond gave him a strong bargaining position with his captors.[33] The alternative – a Royalist Ireland with a powerful fleet to contest control of the Irish Sea – was a terrifying prospect. Worse still, if he could not be persuaded to renounce Ormond then the army would almost certainly intervene to make him do so. And therein lay the danger for Charles as well. For it was down to the army to subdue Ireland, and the soldiers would be understandably angry if Charles was purposely making their task much more difficult, not to say bloody. Many in the army, including Cromwell, had regarded Hamilton's invasion as a wicked design by the king 'to vassalize us to a foreign nation [i.e. Scotland]'.[34] By threatening to repeat this strategy using the hated Irish, Charles was risking not just his crown but also his life.

Yet whatever the prevailing mood in the army, it was divided on a whole range of issues, from whether to stop the treaty, to what action, if any, should be taken against the king. There were still soldiers who wanted to see Charles restored on moderate terms, and Fairfax hoped to quiet those less charitably disposed towards the king by supporting the grandees' efforts to satisfy the army's material grievances over pay and conditions. His main rival in this struggle to mould army opinion was his second-in-command in Cromwell's absence, Henry Ireton. The last of Ireton's enthusiasm for restoring Charles had vanished with the king's flight from Hampton Court back in November 1647. Ten months and another war later, he was convinced that God had pronounced against

Charles as man and monarch, and that any accommodation with him represented a betrayal of the public interest, godliness, and everything that the army had fought for. He could see no other option in the short term but for the army to force the withdrawal of its enemies in the Commons, as it had in the summer of 1647, and to put the king on trial. However, he could not proceed with this policy without the consent of the majority of officers, and above all of Fairfax. It seems likely, therefore, that Ireton and other radical officers had a hand in that autumn's flood of petitions to Fairfax from regiments and garrisons throughout the country, denouncing the treaty and demanding justice against 'capital delinquents'. Significantly, some of the petitioners vilified Charles not only as the author of Hamilton's invasion but also for his continuing treachery in refusing to disavow Ormond.

Ireton's proceedings in the south were supported by Cromwell in the north. After pacifying Scotland, Cromwell spent several months conducting operations against the last pockets of Royalist resistance in northern England – a task that devolved on him in the absence of the region's commander-in-chief, Lambert, whom he had left in Edinburgh. Despite the importance of Cromwell's assignment in the north, his failure to return to London as soon as possible has been interpreted as a sign of indecision over what course to take against the king. In recent years, however, Ian Gentles, John Morrill and others have re-emphasised Cromwell's reliance upon Providence – the perceived manifestations of God's purpose in the world – as a guide to political action, and have concluded that by the autumn of 1648 Cromwell was convinced that Charles was a 'man against whom the Lord hath witnessed'.[35] Any doubts that he entertained were not about whether the army should try Charles, or at least subject him to a formal reckoning of some kind; they centred instead upon God's will as to how and when the king was to be brought to justice. Far from being an undecided onlooker in army politics, Cromwell was instrumental in rallying soldiers and civilians in northern England behind Ireton's hard-line programme.

Remonstrance and Purge

Ireton's campaign to steel the army for political intervention was given a major boost on 7 November with the convening of the council of officers at St Albans. His revolutionary agenda initially met with strong opposition from Fairfax and other conservative officers, who were keen that the army acquiesce in the outcome of the Newport treaty. Yet as the week progressed and more regimental petitions arrived denouncing the treaty and demanding justice against the king, the advantage gradually shifted towards the radicals. At this critical juncture, with the army poised between revolution and moderation, the king announced his refusal to call off Ormond before the Newport treaty had been concluded. By clinging to his instruments of war in the middle of peace negotiations, Charles seemed to demonstrate what the army radicals had been arguing for weeks – that he could never be trusted.

On 18 November the council of officers approved a lengthy declaration that had been drawn up by Ireton and amended after consultation with leading Levellers (Lilburne and Wildman) and radical MPs. Known as 'the Remonstrance', it was something of a compromise document – a manifesto for revolution designed to appeal to a cross-section of officers as well as their civilian allies. In light of the king's treason against the English people, not least in his continuing reliance upon Ormond 'and his associated Irish Rebells', Parliament was urged to break off the treaty at Newport, and to sanction the king's trial 'for the blood spilt, and other the evils and mischiefs done by him'.[36] At one point the Remonstrance came close to demanding that Charles should be executed, calling for 'exemplary Justice ... in Capitall punishment upon the principall Author and some prime instruments of our late warres'.[37] As to the settling of the kingdom, it proposed the adoption of a new constitution underpinned by a Leveller-style 'Agreement of the People'. Supreme power would be vested in a reformed House of Commons, and the monarchy, if retained at all, was to be elective.

When the Remonstrance was presented to the Commons on 20 November it was fiercely criticised by the army's opponents, who secured a vote to postpone consideration of it for a week in the hope that by then the treaty with the king would be concluded. In fact, Charles did not make his final submissions on the outstanding issues at Newport – episcopacy, Ormond, etc. – until 27 November, whereupon the Commons renewed its order for shelving the Remonstrance and set about debating whether his answers constituted a viable basis for settlement. Convinced that the House was planning to bring the king to London, the army seized Charles at Carisbrooke on 1 December and deposited him in the forbidding stronghold of Hurst Castle, on the Solent. Back at army headquarters in Windsor, Ireton had another round of consultation with Lilburne, after which it was agreed that the army should march on London and either purge the Commons or dissolve Parliament entirely.

One likely source of encouragement for Ireton and his allies was the Whiggamore raid in Scotland, which provided a timely illustration of how Parliaments could be forcibly purged and new elections called.

By 2 December the army had established its headquarters at Whitehall and soldiers thronged the city streets, and yet still the majority of MPs refused either to debate the Remonstrance or to abandon the treaty. News of Charles's removal to Hurst Castle reached Westminster on 4 December, provoking a lengthy argument in the Commons on whether the king could be trusted to keep his agreements. The debate lasted until 8 o'clock the next morning (the 5th), when it was voted that the king's final answers from Newport constituted a viable basis for settling the peace of the kingdom. For most of the grandees it came down to whether they disliked the army's agenda more than they distrusted the king, and on this they were probably divided, although no peer entered his dissent when the Commons' vote passed the Lords. But it made little difference to the army. The only question now for Ireton and his allies was whether to purge the Commons or dissolve Parliament. Under pressure from the Levellers and radical MPs, who feared that a dissolution would devolve too much power upon the army, Ireton agreed to a purge.

On the morning of 6 December, Colonel Thomas Pride and his men, assisted by the radical MP Lord Grey of Groby, arrested 40 or so members as they attempted to enter the Commons. More members were denied entry the following day, so that in all about 100 MPs were either imprisoned or secluded in 'Pride's Purge', and many others (including most of the grandees of both Houses) decided to abandon their seats in fear or protest. The purge's victims were a mixed bag, but most either were prominent opponents of the army or had supported the treaty, particularly in the 5 December vote. The handful of peers who still attended the Lords were left untouched – the army hoping to use their prestige and personal influence to help bring the king to trial. The purge, like the Remonstrance, made plain the army's desire for a final reckoning with Charles, and although he was slow to realise the danger of his predicament, the same could not be said of Ormond and the Confederates.

The Second Ormond Peace

Late in November, the Confederate commissioners who had been sent to Rome almost a year earlier, Nicholas Plunkett and Bishop French, returned to Kilkenny. The two men's report on their mission to consult with the pope was eagerly awaited by all parties. Substantial aid from Rome would increase the Confederates' military options and strengthen their hand in the negotiations with Ormond. Likewise, a clear papal line on religious concessions would be crucial in shaping the attitudes of both clergy and laity to a peace settlement. To the relief of the peace faction, Plunkett and French reported that the pope had effectively washed his hands of Ireland, having failed to offer any practical guidance as to the treaty, or to invest further papal funds in the Confederate cause. Bishop French also hinted (falsely) that influential figures in the Vatican disapproved of Rinuccini's latest excommunication. The nuncio's campaign against the treaty was finished.

By exposing how little the church militants could now offer the Confederates, the commissioners' report re-affirmed the need to subordinate religious scruples to civil allegiance. Nevertheless, when the negotiations resumed in December there seemed to be no getting around the vexed question of church property and jurisdiction. Ormond could not concede ground on this point without losing Inchiquin and his army or exceeding his authority from the king. Equally, the Confederates were obliged to press their demands or else risk a damaging split in their own ranks. The deadlock was only broken late in December when news reached Kilkenny of the New Model's Remonstrance and its intention of putting the king on trial. Realising the grave threat to both Charles's crown and his life, the Confederates declared their willingness to accept Ormond's assurances that the Catholic clergy would not be disturbed in their churches or jurisdiction until the matter was resolved in a 'free' Parliament in Ireland once the king had been restored. The bishops were still reluctant to concede on the issue of jurisdiction, but dropped their opposition when they realised that the assembly was determined 'to rest satisfied however they should declare'.[38]

The treaty between Ormond and the Confederates was signed at Kilkenny Castle on 17 January 1649. The Second Ormond Peace was far more generous to the Catholic Irish than its predecessor. The most significant of the Catholic gains in 1649 were the free exercise of their religion, the removal of all impediments to their participation in the Irish Parliament, and the right of those dispossessed by the Ulster plantation to petition Parliament for redress. This last concession was probably intended to persuade O'Neill and his followers to join the Royalist majority, as some Ulster Gaels had already done. But O'Neill would not accept the treaty unless it was endorsed by Rinuccini – and the nuncio would have no further dealings with the Confederates once they had put themselves under the power of the 'heretic' Ormond. Late in February the nuncio departed Ireland for the Continent.

The Second Ormond Peace marked the end of the Association of Confederate Catholics. Supreme power within Royalist and Catholic Ireland now passed to Ormond and 12 Catholic 'commissioners of trust'. The treaty provided for a 17,000-strong Royalist army under the overall command of Ormond, who was confident that with a little assistance from abroad it would speedily reduce all of Ireland to the king's authority and be 'ready powerfully to assist any designe that may be for his restauration in both, or either of the other [kingdoms]'.[39] Besides the king himself, the only power that could now prevent the Royalists conquering all of Ireland was the New Model Army.

The Denbigh Mission

After Pride's Purge it seemed that nothing stood between the army radicals and their desire for swift and exemplary justice against the king. Yet December was to witness at least one attempt to strike a deal with Charles that would have preserved both his life and possibly his crown. Not until early January, five weeks after the purge, was legislation passed establishing a court to try him; and a further two weeks went by before the trial itself got under way.

Although the Remonstrance and purge had suggested that the king's trial was imminent, in fact all that Ireton had succeeded in doing was to unite the officers behind a policy of removing their enemies from Parliament and ending the Newport treaty. Like their civilian allies, the officers remained as divided as ever on how to proceed against the king and to settle the government. It should also be emphasised that the purge reflected the army's fear of Charles as much as its desire for justice against him. It was with growing alarm that the army had watched Parliament's vain attempts to persuade the king to halt the ominous proceedings in Ireland, where he was threatening to become more powerful than at any point since 1640. The purge allowed the army to pressure Charles directly, and for most of the officers he was still worth negotiating with, if only to prevent Ormond turning Ireland into a Royalist fortress. The king may have been defeated in England and Scotland, but with Ireland effectively his to command he remained a force to be reckoned with – and both he and his captors knew it.

The only advocates of trying the king without further ado were Ireton and a few other militant officers, and they were too isolated at this stage to seize the initiative. Even their closest civilian allies, the Levellers, refused to endorse proceedings against the king until a new constitution had been put in place to prevent a military dictatorship. Ireton therefore spent much of his time in the weeks following the purge arguing with leading Levellers and officers over the terms of a revised 'Agreement of the People'. A more moderate strand of opinion in the army was represented by Cromwell, who had arrived back in London on the evening of Pride's Purge. Cromwell's mind is never easy to read, and no two historians put precisely the same construction on his actions (or, more often, his inaction), but it seems that he was resolved upon bringing the king to public account for his crimes, if necessary by putting him on trial, but was still willing to contemplate a punishment that fell short of Charles's outright deposition. In other words, he had not entirely abandoned the idea of a negotiated settlement. In this he enjoyed the backing of Fairfax and the small caucus of Derby House peers that had continued to sit in the Lords after the purge.

John Adamson has recently argued that the desire of Cromwell and the grandees to continue negotiating with the king was quickened by two key developments.[40] The first of these was the return to London in mid-December of Parliament's admiral, the Earl of Warwick. The biggest security worry facing the new regime at Westminster was not internal unrest but the king's formidable naval strength. If the fleets under Ormond, the Confederates, and the Prince of Wales went unchecked they could impose an embargo on English trade and facilitate an Irish invasion. Parliament and the army were therefore desperate to keep Warwick and the navy on side; and this, it was widely believed, meant proceeding cautiously against the king or else risking another mutiny among the seamen. Warwick was prepared to acquiesce in the purge, but only on the understanding that a further effort be made to bring Charles to terms, and that 'exemplary justice' be confined to the likes of Hamilton. The second development was the arrival a few days later of news that the Confederates had concluded a commercial treaty with the Dutch – which amounted to a naval alliance with Europe's greatest maritime power. The possibility of war with the Dutch made it even more vital to reach agreement with Charles, for only with his blessing would a Royalist–Confederate–Dutch axis ever materialise.

Late in December the Earl of Denbigh went to Windsor Castle, where the king was then being held, to present him with a deal worked out by the Derby House peers and probably Cromwell. The evidence suggests that their main demands were that Charles surrender his negative voice; that he consent to the perpetual abolition of episcopacy; that he renounce any compliance with the Scots as to the settlement of England; and that he call off Ormond and the Prince of Wales. It is not clear what was to happen if Charles agreed to these terms. One possibility is that he would be put on trial (as a gesture to satisfy the army) but then acquitted and allowed to reign as a puppet monarch. But Charles rejected the Denbigh mission – apparently expressing confidence that his Irish subjects would come to his rescue. As one old courtier observed: 'He hath a strange conceit of my Lord of Ormonds working for him in Irland; he hangs still upon that twigg, and … will not be beaten off it.'[41] Whether or not he really believed the Irish would rescue him, he was convinced that his restoration was only a matter of time because he could not conceive that his enemies would hold firm in the face of the military threats from abroad, or that they would dare to execute their anointed sovereign.

Trial and Regicide

Charles's rejection of the Denbigh mission made his trial unavoidable. On 1 January 1649, the purged House of Commons (which would become known as 'the Rump') passed an ordinance establishing a high court of justice to try the king. When the Lords rejected the trial ordinance, the Commons voted itself the supreme power in the nation and invested its own acts with the force of law. Despite talk of Charles's treason, there was no consensus as to the preferred outcome of the trial or the king's position in the new constitutional order that must follow it. The possibility was raised by Cromwell and others of deposing Charles and settling his youngest son, the Duke of Gloucester, on the throne as a titular monarch. But given the prevailing view that the king could be intimidated into submission, regicide was widely considered imprudent. It risked a mutiny in the navy, the anger of the Dutch and other foreign powers, and would be to exchange a king in their power (Charles) for one outside it (the Prince of Wales). At this stage, perhaps only Marten, Chaloner and a few other doctrinaire republicans favoured regicide. Killing the king would be a big step towards the creation of a 'free commonwealth' – a regime that would satisfy their republican principles as well as their desire for power. Certainly if a puppet monarchy was retained, then they would be outside the charmed circle pulling the strings.

The ordinance for the high court of justice appointed 135 trial commissioners – mostly radical army officers and MPs – although fewer than half that number attended the court's preliminary sessions between 8 and 19 January. While the commissioners busied themselves with gathering evidence against the king and appointing the trial officials, further efforts were made by the Derby House peers to broker a settlement based upon Charles's disavowal of Ormond. According to Adamson, the crucial issue for the peers, and possibly for Cromwell too, was not the king's guilt for causing the first two wars against Parliament, but whether he would act to prevent the third that now threatened from Ireland. The mood of uncertainty and expectation at Westminster was heightened on 20 January, when the army presented the Commons with the revised version of the 'Agreement of the People'. Lilburne had already washed his hands of the document, believing that only mass subscription by the people would force Parliament to accept it, and he was probably not surprised that the officers acquiesced in the Commons' decision to lay the 'Agreement' aside until after the trial (and in fact permanently, as it turned out).

The Levellers' defeat was overshadowed by the opening of the king's trial in the Great Hall at Westminster on 20 January. There is a tendency in much of the literature on the trial to regard Charles's execution as more or less inevitable. But in hindsight, the only fixed point in the whole process was his obduracy. References in the charge read out at the beginning of the trial to his current 'evill designes' involving Ormond and the Prince of Wales offer a clue as to the court's true purpose.[42] For if the trial managers had indeed already settled upon regicide, then to dwell upon his current 'mischiefs' was a major tactical blunder. Charles might justly be condemned for the first two wars, but if he condescended to avert a third then a capital sentence against him would seem merely vindictive. In fact, there is every indication that the trial was simply a formal continuation of the carrot and stick policy adopted towards Charles since the purge. This would explain the heavy regal symbolism in the court's ceremony and paraphernalia; and why he was allowed the ministrations of no less a cleric than the Anglican bishop of London, William Juxon – the idea being to bring home to Charles the possibility that he could still enjoy at least the trappings of kingship if he came to terms. Likewise, it was probably no accident that his guard was composed of pro-regicide soldiers, whose shouts of 'execution' served as a reminder of what he could expect if he remained obdurate.

The court's halting progress, as Sean Kelsey has emphasised, was symptomatic of the contingent nature of the trial proceedings.[43] At least half a dozen times during the first three days of the trial – 20, 22, and

23 January – the lord president of the court, John Bradshaw, asked Charles to plead to the charge. On each occasion he refused to do so, demanding to know by what authority he was being tried. Yet still the court would not pronounce him contumacious and proceed to sentence. The commissioners spent 24 and 25 January examining evidence against the king – which in itself was a futile exercise, but it gave the trial managers time to re-assess their options and attempt to heal the growing divisions among the commissioners. The pressure to halt the trial was by now intense, and was taking its toll on the less regicidal of the king's judges. In London and across the country, Presbyterian ministers denounced the trial and inveighed against the terrible sin of king-killing. The Scottish Parliament protested 'in confident and lofty language', insisting that Scotland too had an interest in the king. And the arrival of ambassadors from Holland to mediate for the king was another 'cooling card'. But by this stage, the only person with both the desire and the power to stop the trial was Fairfax, and he lacked the political acumen to challenge Cromwell and Ireton.

By 26 January, the commissioners had agreed on a death sentence. Yet the next day, before the trial resumed, they instructed Bradshaw that if the king acknowledged the jurisdiction of the court, or indeed offered anything worth their consideration, they should withdraw and debate the matter. It is hard to construe these contradictory impulses of the court as anything but a device by the trial managers to maintain unity among the commissioners and at the same time take a final gamble on their policy of 'bargaining with menaces'.[44] With death staring him in the face, Charles was to be given one last chance. What exactly the trial managers had in mind if he did enter a plea is impossible to say. But presumably their intention was to establish some kind of a dialogue in the hope of grinding him into submission. In the event, Charles denied the court's jurisdiction again by asking for an audience with the Lords and Commons. His request met with sufficient support among the commissioners to oblige the court to adjourn for half an hour, during which the hard-liners browbeat their wavering colleagues. Yet when the court resumed Charles was given two further opportunities to plead to the charge. He refused, however, and Bradshaw was left with no alternative but to proceed to sentence. Fifty-nine of the trial commissioners, including Cromwell, Ireton, Marten, and Chaloner, signed the death warrant. These were the regicides.

The familiar picture of Charles during his trial, as passive victim or noble martyr, is romantic fiction. His conduct in Westminster Hall was consistent with his abiding preference for coercion over conciliation. In refusing to recognise the court's authority he was signalling his refusal to forswear the use of Scottish and Irish arms against his English enemies. In effect, he was playing out the hand he had acquired in signing the Engagement – convinced to the last that no one would dare strike down God's anointed. But as Adamson has pointed out, his 'strategy of brinkmanship' contained a fundamental flaw.[45] The various parties conjoined in Ormond's alliance were held together primarily by loyalty to the person of Charles I – remove him and the whole ramshackle structure would be undermined. In light of his intransigence, therefore, regicide became a matter of cold necessity.

A similar set of calculations applied to Charles's relationship with the Scots, and probably explains the high proportion of northerners among the regicides. The king's imperviousness to demands that he abjure the Scots raised the spectre of another Scottish invasion of northern England. The trial managers had been at pains to emphasise that Charles was being tried as king of England and Ireland, and they evidently hoped (vainly, as it turned out) that severing his head would likewise sever the union of crowns and thus finally exorcise the threat of covenanting confederalism. These politic considerations aside, Charles's refusal to renounce his perceived design to 'vassalize' the English to the Celtic nations probably removed any lingering doubts in the minds of Cromwell and other regicides that the providential moment for justice against 'that man of blood' had finally arrived.

Charles was beheaded on 30 January on a scaffold erected outside the Banqueting House in Whitehall (Hamilton followed him to the block a few weeks later). His death settled remarkably little as far as relations between the three kingdoms were concerned. The Rump still had Ireland to contend with, and it is hard to see how the post-Preston entente between the New Model and the Kirk party could have endured, whatever the outcome of the trial. The transformative effects of trial and regicide were felt first and deepest in England. The court and its sentence symbolised, in Kelsey's phrase, the 'civic' character of the new political order, and were thus a means of wrenching the revolution from the hands of the Levellers and their army allies. In repudiating the court, Charles had not just jeopardised national security, he had also pulled at the makeshift barricade that his judges had erected against constitutional chaos and further military intervention. In the end, only his blood could seal the authority of the new regime.

Epilogue and Conclusion

The Conquest of Ireland

In the months after the regicide the Rump completed the constitutional revolution it had begun early in January 1649. The House of Lords and the monarchy were abolished, and a Council of State was established in place of the Derby House Committee. The Rump's top priority after putting its own house in order was the reconquest of Ireland. In April 1649 the assessment was raised to £90,000 a month to help finance an invasion force under the command of Cromwell. In 1649 alone the Rump would spend over half a million pounds on the Irish expedition – this compares with the Confederates' annual revenue of about £70,000 at the height of their power in 1645–6. Cromwell embarked for Ireland in August 1649 with 12,000 New Model veterans, a large train of siege artillery, and a war chest of £100,000.

The regicide excited such horror in Ireland and Scotland that most Scottish and Anglo-Irish leaders in Ulster joined Ormond's royalist coalition. An alliance of ex-Confederates, Protestant Royalists, and ex-Parliamentarians was bound to be fragile, however, and needed victories to hold it together. Above all, it had to capture Dublin and the other major ports still in Parliamentarian hands in order to deny Cromwell's invasion force a secure bridgehead. Ormond apparently had the men for the task – 13,000 by May. What he lacked was money to pay his troops, and, crucially, the decisiveness to make the most of his short-lived advantage. Instead of launching an all-out assault against Dublin before Michael Jones could be reinforced from England, he frittered away the spring and summer mopping up outlying garrisons. His attacking options were further limited by Parliament's control of the sea-lanes around Ireland (a Dutch–Royalist naval alliance having failed to materialise), and by Owen Roe O'Neill's continuing defiance of his authority. The renegade general demanded a reversal of the Ulster plantation and full Catholic religious liberty before he would commit his 4000 troops to the coalition – terms that Ormond could not possibly grant without losing his Protestant support. Inchiquin and Clanricarde thus spent much of 1649 harrying O'Neill when they could have assisted Ormond against Dublin. By the time Ormond had readied his army for a final assault on the city, it was too late. Jones, who had been reinforced from England in May and June, sallied out of Dublin on 2 August and routed the Royalists at Rathmines, inflicting 4000 casualties.

Rathmines was the decisive battle of the War of the Engagement in Ireland, just as Preston had been in Britain. Cromwell was assured a secure landing-base near Dublin, and the royalist coalition was demoralised and divided beyond repair. Inchiquin's men deserted in droves after the battle, many joining Cromwell to fight against their former allies. O'Neill's decision, after Rathmines, to join the Royalist coalition was a case of too little too late. Already a sick man, he died that autumn, and his Ulster army was destroyed by Sir Charles Coote the following year. In March 1650, Kilkenny fell to the New Model, and in August the Catholic leadership disowned Ormond, who withdrew with Inchiquin to France in December. Even before the last Protestant Royalists had laid down their arms, the Parliamentarians had abandoned any pretence of fighting to restore English liberties in Ireland and were waging instead a full-blown war of religion and conquest. The Catholic leadership replaced Ormond with Clanricarde, who himself fled into exile after the fall of the last major Catholic stronghold, Galway, in May 1652. The Parliamentarians lost more soldiers to disease (Ireton and Jones among them) and combat in Ireland than the New Model had in all its previous campaigns. But given Cromwell's able generalship, English superiority in matériel, and the steady disintegration of the Royalist coalition after Rathmines, the conquest of Ireland was never in much doubt.

Of all the splits within the anti-Parliamentarian interest in Ireland, perhaps the most damaging in terms of preventing a Confederate or a Royalist–Confederate conquest in 1642–7, and of undermining the Royalist coalition before Rathmines, was not that of Protestant versus Catholic but between confederate peace and clerical parties. The peace party would not countenance the creation of a unified military command under the Confederates' most capable general, Owen Roe O'Neill; and the clerical party consistently blocked a settlement with Ormond's Royalists on terms that were practical given the realities of three-kingdoms politics. Ethnic differences among the Irish were largely overlaid by a complicated political struggle between the pre-Rising ins (peace party) and outs (clerical party) over the terms for assisting the king, particularly as they related to the distribution of power – civil and ecclesiastical – and land in post-settlement Ireland. Had one side in this struggle succeeded in crushing the other – as members of both parties advocated – then some kind of unified Ireland would probably have emerged and been able to assist the king in Britain in 1648, or perhaps deter a Cromwellian invasion in 1649. An Ireland in which the anti-Parliamentarian forces continually fought among themselves was incapable of doing either.

The cost of defeat after eleven gruelling years of war was very high. Ireland's population fell by over a quarter during the period 1641–52, with most of these losses occurring after 1649 from plague epidemics and an economic breakdown brought on by the Parliamentarians' refusal to tolerate Catholicism or to grant the Irish secure title to their estates. The invasion left the Rump owing almost £2 million in pay to its troops, which it recouped partly by a massive expropriation of Irish land. Ireland by 1652 was as thoroughly devastated as parts of Germany after the Thirty Years War, and would take years to recover. The cause of Catholic religious liberty and political equality under the crown was lost forever.

The Defeat of the Covenanters

The regicide destroyed the fragile entente between the Kirk party and the army junto in England. Anxious not to provoke England's new rulers, the Covenanters had made clear their opposition to killing the king, but had tacitly conceded the legitimacy of trying him. The Rump's leaders had apparently thought the Kirk party too weak to raise any serious objections to their severing the regnal union. They received a nasty surprise early in February 1649, therefore, when the Covenanters proclaimed the Prince of Wales as Charles II, king of Great Britain (i.e. Scotland *and* England) and Ireland. There is no evidence that the English wanted to 'obtrude' their republican government upon Scotland, as some Scots believed, and therefore the Covenanters' attempt to revive the union of crowns in defiance of Westminster might seem deliberately provocative. Yet the Kirk party could have no assurance of its own long-term survival, or that of Scotland as an autonomous kingdom, without a restoration of monarchy in all three kingdoms. Both the appeal of monarchy among the Scottish people, and the threat of military encirclement by an uncovenanted English regime, were simply too great to ignore. Nevertheless, before the Kirk party would allow Charles to assume the crown, he was required to take the Covenants of 1638 and 1643, and agree to the establishment of a covenanted uniformity throughout his domains. In other words, it was to be settlement 'at the old rate', with Charles II, like his father, reduced to a mere figurehead.

Ormond's defeat in Ireland persuaded Charles that a deal with the Covenanters represented 'the only probable human means to recover our other kingdomes'.[1] His overtures to the Scots were encouraged by Argyll (who aspired to the role of kingmaker and principal power behind the Scottish throne), pro-Scots royal counsellors such as Lord Jermyn, and that minority in the English Covenant-engaged interest prepared to defy the Rump. After much wrangling the king agreed to all that the Kirk party asked of him, although with a manifest ill-grace, and embarked for Scotland in June 1650. Yet even though Charles had no intention of honouring his promises to the Covenanters, the policy of a Scottish alliance was strongly opposed by anti-Presbyterian factions at court. The Royalist patriots looked to a revival of the king's party in England on the back of Ormond's hoped-for victory in Ireland or a Royalist uprising in Scotland under the Marquess of Montrose – a doomed venture that ended in Montrose's execution by the Covenanters in May 1650.

The threatening turn of events in Scotland prompted the Rump to recall Cromwell from Ireland early in 1650. The Council of State decided that the best form of defence was attack, and as Fairfax was reluctant to lead an invasion of Scotland he was replaced as commander-in-chief by Cromwell. In July 1650, Cromwell crossed the Tweed with 16,000 troops and a large artillery train. His expedition was supplied with food and munitions by a fleet of 140 ships, at an overall cost to the English taxpayer of £1,200,000. The Scottish army under David Leslie was almost twice the size of Cromwell's. But as with the Royalist forces at Rathmines, the effect of divided counsels and loyalties at the top sapped military effectiveness on the ground. July and August witnessed heated dispute between Covenanter purists and more moderate figures such as Argyll over the composition of Leslie's army. Victory for the purists resulted in the purging of 4000 'malignant' officers and men – most of them veteran soldiers. Even the king was ordered to depart the camp on the grounds that his presence was encouraging 'carnal confidence' in the troops, rather than godly zeal. Although disease and supply shortages had taken their toll of the New Model by the end of August, the accustomed unity among and between the officer corps and the ranks held firm. On 3 September, at the battle of Dunbar, Cromwell's 11,000 troops fell upon Leslie's unprepared and ill-disciplined 20,000, killing or taking prisoner over half of them for the loss of a mere 20 English soldiers. The Kirk party fled northwards to Stirling on news of the defeat, leaving Cromwell to seize Edinburgh unopposed.

In the aftermath of Dunbar the Covenanting interest split along the old fault line between the radical Presbyterians and those such as Argyll who had tried to reconcile the cause of perfecting Scotland's Reformation with the exercise of parliamentary authority and the maintenance of the established social order. The purists in the Kirk party formed their own political movement and army centred upon Glasgow and the radical south-west, and bid defiance to both Cromwell and their former colleagues at Stirling. The military wing of this Western Association was destroyed by the English in December 1650, but their allies in the Kirk continued to agitate against any compromise with a malignant and untrustworthy king. Some Covenanter purists even regarded the English Independents as more agreeable masters than an unregenerate monarch, and surrendered to Cromwell. The majority of Covenanters, however, recognised that with most of southern Scotland now in the invaders' hands, the national interest must take precedence over religious purity. In December 1650, therefore, the Kirk grudgingly acceded to the recruitment of malignants. A power struggle among the Stirling Covenanters between the nobles and men of lesser rank hastened the inevitable resurgence of the Royalist interest. The Covenanters had lost so much ground by mid-1651 that Royalist Highland clansmen had begun to enlist in the king's army. The final act in the disintegration of the Covenanting interest occurred in July, when the purists in the Kirk formally separated from their more moderate colleagues. Unity in religion, the Presbyterians' last comfort, was gone for good.

The distracted and divided state of Scottish counsels left the military initiative entirely with the English. In July 1651, Cromwell sent a force across the Firth of Forth, which succeeded in cutting off the Stirling government from all hope of reinforcements from the north. Cromwell had deliberately left the way clear for a Scottish invasion of England, calculating that the Scots could be brought to battle more easily on English soil than loose about the Highlands – and with 14,000 English troops closing in from the north and east, the king and his Scottish followers had no choice but to accept the wager being offered them. Charles and his army crossed into England early in August, hoping, as Hamilton had three years earlier, that the country people would rally to their cause. But the will to resist Parliament and the army had been crushed during the Second Civil War. Royalist attempts to foment uprisings in the localities in 1650–1 had either stalled because of loathing for the Scots, or been suppressed. Once again, a policy of allying with the Covenanters had sapped the resolve of the king's party in England. Indeed, nothing was more calculated to boost support for the Rump from all sections of English society than a Scottish invasion.

The Scots penetrated as far as Worcester before fatigue and unrest in the ranks forced the king to call a halt. Cromwell, who had hurried south in their wake, had an army of 31,000 men by late August, outnumbering the Scots by almost three to one. Militia regiments had streamed into his camp from all over England, undeterred by the fact that their taxes had risen to a staggering £157,000 a month. On 3 September, the first anniversary of Dunbar, Cromwell's huge army rolled over the Royalist lines around Worcester, chasing the king's troops through the city streets, and killing or capturing 10,000 of them. Charles escaped to the Continent, but most of the Scottish nobles with him were killed or taken. Foremost among the political casualties of the defeat at Worcester were the pro-Scots Royalist clique at court and in Paris. Sir Edward Hyde and his Royalist patriots would dominate the king's counsels until the Restoration and beyond. Back in Scotland, the majority of leading men quickly made their peace with the English; though Argyll held out until August 1652 before making his submission. It was to take the New Model several years to conquer the Highlands, but Lowland Scotland had been completely subdued by the end of 1651. What had begun back in 1637 as a rebellion to prevent Scotland's reduction to the status of an English province had ended in precisely that fate.

The Scots were left nursing the consequences of two failures – first, to secure Scotland against her more powerful southern neighbour by forging some kind of closer union between the two kingdoms; and second to stop squabbling among themselves long enough to prevent the Cromwellian conquest. Victory for the Independents in the English Civil War had made it necessary for the Scots to impose a British settlement by force, but this required a degree of domestic unity that they simply did not possess. The most debilitating division in this respect was that between the radical mainstream under Argyll and the pragmatic Royalists/Covenanters under Hamilton. Most of the issues on which these two factions were split – the relationship between Kirk and state; the scope and limits of royal prerogative, etc. – were subsumed in a long-running quarrel over how best to sustain their respective power-bases and preserve Scotland's autonomy within the Stuart realm. Whereas Argyll's party favoured a confederal settlement based upon the two kingdoms' Parliaments, the Hamiltonians pushed for a strengthened regnal union centred upon the crown and a reconstructed, British court. It is impossible to accord primacy to any one determinant of allegiance in this conflict, although the degree of susceptibility to an apocalyptic and evangelical interpretation of the Covenanting cause must rank high on the list. Whether it was possible at any point for the more powerful faction – which by early 1647 was clearly the Hamiltonians – to destroy their weaker rivals and hence confront the English Independents without an enemy in their rear, is also hard to say. Hamilton's brother, the Earl of Lanark, apparently thought that it was. And certainly the radical Covenanters were militarily vulnerable after Inverlochy, as Mauchline Moor revealed only too clearly. But Scotland's political leaders, like Catholic Ireland's, never pushed their quarrels to a resolution, and thus left their country vulnerable to the Cromwellian onslaught.

Scotland as a whole did not suffer the same degree of material devastation that Ireland did during the wars of the three kingdoms. Nevertheless, the cost of financing and equipping countless military expeditions, and the destruction wrought by the fighting in 1644–7 and 1648–51, brought ruin to several sectors of the Scottish economy, while plague epidemics, famine, and warfare literally decimated the population. Economic recovery was slow. It took several decades for Scotland to regain the level of prosperity it had enjoyed in the 1630s. What proved impossible to salvage from the military disasters of 1648–51 was the Scottish national myth of the never-conquered people. With it too went the apocalyptic vision of the Scots as God's standard-bearers in a British crusade against Antichrist.

The Triumph of Westminster

Despite the many difficulties facing the Rump in the aftermath of the regicide, it was in a far stronger position than the ruling groups in the other kingdoms. With the army's help, the Rump's leaders had achieved a thorough conquest of their people and polity – a feat unrivalled by their counterparts in Scotland and Ireland. The English were unique among the peoples of the Atlantic Archipelago in enduring a sustained *civil* war – the issue of which was not finally decided until Pride's Purge and the regicide – which meant that victory for a particular interest, when it came, was virtually complete. As we have seen, the Covenanters and Confederates failed to achieve a similar resolution of their own internal conflicts. This is not to say that the Rump was devoid of faction-fighting – far from it. But none of these factions were so fundamentally at odds with each other (as the Independents and Scottified Presbyterians had been in 1645–8, for example) that they would resort to armed force against their rivals.

The army junto's victory was rendered more conclusive by the nature of English nationhood. The English were a people knit together partly by shared reverence for national institutions, above all Parliament. There was no authority in England by 1649 to rival that of Parliament, which embodied the continuities of law and magistracy 'even across a divide so deep as regicide'.[2] Only the Levellers, with their ideas about law paramount and natural rights, had developed a coherent appeal to supra-parliamentary authority; which may partly explain why it was their supporters in the army who mounted the only serious domestic chal-lenge to the fledgling Commonwealth – a challenge that Fairfax and Cromwell quickly suppressed. In general, control of Parliament and its army ensured the Rump's leaders a degree of compliance, or at least acquiescence, from the English people that the Kirk party, with all its dominance of the Scottish Parliament and army, could never hope to command from 'the Scots'. Moreover, the Rump's unprecedented victo-ries against the Irish, Scots, and later the Dutch, seem to have refreshed the link in popular (and certainly literary) imagination between Parliament and a sense of national pride and destiny.

The lack of profound ethnic and religious animosities among the peo-ples of England and Wales also contributed to the decisiveness of the army junto's triumph. The Independents did not have to overcome a powerful domestic bloc united on the basis of ethnicity or religion against the kingdom's laws and governing institutions. Even supposing the Welsh or Cornish defined themselves primarily in ethnic terms (which is debatable), they were 'jointed in' to the English state, not resentful outcasts from the political nation. The English, for their part, did not regard the Welsh and Cornish as racial enemies, which precluded the possibility of the Civil War developing into a prolonged ethnic conflict. Nor was there a major division within the kingdom over the fundamentals of religion. The wars in Ireland and Scotland, that pitted Gael against *Gall* and Presbyterian against Catholic, featured a degree of ethnic and confessional hatred that was unknown in England. It is sig-nificant in this respect that the influence wielded by the clergy was much greater in Confederate Ireland and Covenanter Scotland than in England. There was no equivalent in English politics to the Irish Catholic bishops or the leading ministers of the Kirk.

Two main factors tended to push religious issues and divisions to the fore at Westminster and Oxford (or wherever the Royalist grandees happened to congregate after 1645). The first was the king's scrupulous attachment to his supremacy in religion and to an inclusive Anglican church – themselves issues with profound implications for the exercise of temporal power. The second was the intervention of the Covenanters. Thus, the Saye–Pym group's attempts in 1642–3 to portray the struggle against the king as a war of religion were intended mainly for a Scottish audience. Likewise, the Presbyterian grandees' opposition to toleration and demand for a 'rigid' Presbyterian church settlement stemmed largely from their military reliance upon the Scots. Left to their own devices, the grandees of both parties at Westminster would probably have settled for the 'lame Erastian Presbyterie' that so offended the Covenanters. The grandees' fundamental quarrel – indeed the fundamental quarrel among the leaders of all three kingdoms – centred upon the terms for the king's restoration and their own position within a redefined Caroline imperium. Civil War politics at the centres of power was, to borrow John Adamson's phrase, 'restoration politics'. It was this struggle to shape the post-Restoration order that linked the 'moments of climacteric' within and between the three kingdoms.

Viewed from the localities or the army camps, the English Civil War does indeed bear some of the hallmarks of a war of religion. Yet English religious loyalties were so closely bound up with ideas about 'liberties' and the structures of good government that it seems unwise to single out any one of these as the prime motive for the majority of active participants in the war. On the other hand, there clearly were powerful groups in Ireland (Rinuccini and the nuncioists) and in Scotland (the purists in the Kirk party) that drew a sharp distinction between divine and civil ordinances, and prioritised obedience to the former. The confessional partisanship of the Irish nuncioists – which was inspired by European Counter-Reformation practice – stands in marked contrast to the legalist–constitutionalist approach to temporal and ecclesiastical affairs that prevailed in England.

Although the direction and to some extent the ethos of politics at Westminster changed under the Rump, the basic political structure did not. The House of Lords was gone, and the grandees were somewhat less grand and somewhat more inclined towards religious Independency and sectarianism. Nevertheless, a good deal of public business was still thrashed out by small cabals of leading politicians, whose backroom decisions were then rubber-stamped on the floor of the House. The pilots of the Rump used executive committees and control of public revenues to steer the ship of state, just as their predecessors in the Long Parliament had. Their power was built upon that of the Independent grandees. Indeed, it was the administrative and fiscal innovations introduced or made possible by leading Parliament-men in the mid-1640s that laid the foundations for the English financial and military revolutions of the later seventeenth century, and with them Britain's emergence as a world power.

Notes

Preface

1. C. Russell, *The Causes of the English Civil War* (Oxford: Clarendon Press, 1990), p. 27.
2. J. Adamson, 'The English Context of the British Civil Wars', *History Today*, XLVIII (Nov. 1998), 23–9.
3. J. Adamson, 'Eminent Victorians: S. R. Gardiner and the Liberal as Hero', *Historical Journal*, XXXIII (1990), 656.

Chapter 1   Society, War, and Allegiance in the Three Kingdoms

1. W. Dunn Macray (ed.), *Clarendon's History of the Rebellion and Civil Wars in England* [hereafter cited as Clarendon], 6 vols (Oxford: Clarendon Press, 1888), vol. I, pp. 145–6.
2. R. Cust and A. Hughes, 'Introduction: After Revisionism', in R. Cust and A. Hughes (eds), *Conflict in Early Stuart England* (London: Longman, 1989), p. 21.
3. M. Stoyle, *Loyalty and Locality: Popular Allegiance in Devon during the English Civil War* (Exeter: Exeter University Press, 1994), p. 241; M. Stoyle, *West Britons: Cornish Identities and the Early Modern British State* (Exeter: Exeter University Press, 2002), ch. 3.
4. P. Gaunt, *The British Wars, 1637–1651* (London: Routledge, 1997), p. 8; J. Morrill, *Revolt in the Provinces: The People of England and the Tragedies of War, 1630–1648*, 2nd edn (London: Longman, 1999), p. 178.
5. N. Canny, 'Irish, Scottish and Welsh Responses to Centralisation, c.1530–c.1640', in A. Grant and K. J. Stringer (eds), *Uniting the Kingdom? The Making of British History* (London: Routledge, 1995), pp. 153–6.

6. I. D. Whyte, *Scotland's Society and Economy in Transition, c.1500–c.1760* (London: Macmillan, 1997), p. 71.
7. J. Scally, 'Counsel in Crisis: James Third Marquis of Hamilton and the Bishops' Wars, 1638–1640', in J. R. Young (ed.), *Celtic Dimensions to the British Civil Wars* (Edinburgh: John Donald, 1997), pp. 18–19.
8. W. Makey, *The Church of the Covenant, 1637–1651: Revolution and Social Change in Scotland* (Edinburgh: John Donald, 1979), p. 30.
9. G. Burnet, *The Memoires of the Lives and Actions of James and William, Dukes of Hamilton and Castleherald* (London, 1687), p. 46.
10. A. I. Macinnes, *Charles I and the Making of the Covenanting Movement, 1625–1641* (Edinburgh: John Donald, 1991), pp. 183, 201.
11. Ibid., pp. 183–4.
12. C. Russell, *The Fall of the British Monarchies, 1637–1642* (Oxford: Clarendon Press, 1991), pp. 27, 43–4, 60–2, 203.
13. Ibid., p. 126.
14. J. Peacey, 'The Outbreak of the Civil Wars in the Three Kingdoms', in B. Coward (ed.), *A Companion to Stuart Britain* (Oxford: Blackwell, 2003), p. 297, and in forthcoming publications.
15. J. Howell, *Mercurius Hibernicus* (Bristol, 1644), p. 2.
16. A. I. Macinnes, 'Regal Union for Britain, 1603–38', in G. Burgess (ed.), *The New British History: Founding a Modern State, 1603–1715* (London: I. B. Tauris, 1999), pp. 53–4.
17. A. Clarke, 'The Genesis of the Ulster Rising of 1641', in P. Roebuck (ed.), *Plantation to Partition: Essays in Ulster History in Honour of J. L. McCracken* (Belfast: Blackstaff Press, 1981), pp. 40–1.
18. M. Ó Siochrú, *Confederate Ireland, 1642–1649: A Constitutional and Political Analysis* (Dublin: Four Courts Press, 1999), pp. 24–6.
19. T. Carte, *The Life of James Duke of Ormond* [hereafter cited as Ormond], 6 vols (Oxford: Oxford University Press, 1851), vol. V, p. 281.
20. D. Stevenson, 'The Century of the Three Kingdoms', in J. Wormald (ed.), *Scotland Revisited* (London: Collins and Brown, 1991), p. 111.
21. G. Burgess, 'Was the English Civil War a War of Religion? The Evidence of Political Propaganda', *Huntington Library Quarterly*, LXI (2000), 201.

Chapter 2   The Outbreak of the English Civil War

1. J. Hexter, *The Reign of King Pym* (Cambridge, Mass.: Harvard University Press, 1941).

2. J. Adamson, 'Parliamentary Management, Men-of-Business and the House of Lords, 1640–49', in C. Jones (ed.), *A Pillar of the Constitution: The House of Lords in British Politics, 1640–1784* (London: Hambledon Press, 1989), pp. 21–50.
3. Clarendon, vol. II, pp. 393–4.
4. *Mercurius Aulicus*, no. 15 (9–16 Apr. 1643), p. 190.
5. Clarendon, vol. II, p. 507.
6. British Library, London [BL], Harleian Manuscript [MS] 164, fo. 264r.
7. BL, Harleian MS 165, fo. 93r.
8. M. Kishlansky, 'The Emergence of Adversary Politics in the Long Parliament', *Journal of Modern History*, XLIX (1977), 617–28.
9. C. Walker, *The Mysterie of the Two Juntos* (London, 1647), p. 7.
10. BL, Harleian MS 164, fo. 327v.
11. Ormond, vol. V, p. 3.
12. S. R. Gardiner, *History of the Great Civil War, 1642–1649*, 4 vols (London: Windrush Press, 1987), vol. I, p. 95.
13. Clarendon, vol. II, p. 443; vol. III, p. 10.
14. D. Laing (ed.), *The Letters and Journals of Robert Baillie* [hereafter cited as Baillie], 3 vols (Edinburgh, 1841), vol. II, p. 34.
15. D. Stevenson, *The Scottish Revolution, 1637–1644* (Newton Abbot: David and Charles, 1973), pp. 263–4; J. Young, *The Scottish Parliament, 1639–1661: A Political and Constitutional Analysis* (Edinburgh: John Donald, 1996), p. 58.
16. Clarendon, vol. II, pp. 405–8.
17. *Historical Manuscripts Commission* [*HMC*], *Hamilton Manuscripts* (London, 1932), p. 63.
18. Ibid., p. 66.
19. Bodleian Library, Oxford [hereafter: Bodl.], MS Carte 4, fo. 83r.
20. P. J. Corish, 'The Rising of 1641 and the Catholic Confederacy, 1641–5', in T. W. Moody, F. X. Martin, and F. J. Byrne (eds), *A New History of Ireland, III: Early Modern Ireland, 1534–1691* (Oxford: Clarendon Press, 1976), p. 298.
21. P. Lenihan, *Confederate Catholics at War, 1641–49* (Cork: Cork University Press, 2001), p. 134.
22. D. Cregan, 'The Confederate Catholics of Ireland: The Personnel of the Confederation, 1642–9', *Irish Historical Studies*, XXIX (1994–5), 490–509.
23. Ormond, vol. V, p. 287; M. Ó Siochrú, *Confederate Ireland, 1642–1649: A Constitutional and Political Analysis* (Dublin: Four Courts Press, 1999), p. 7.

24. Ó Siochrú, *Confederate Ireland*, p. 19.

25. R. M. Armstrong, 'Protestant Ireland and the English Parliament, 1641–1647' (Trinity College Dublin, Ph.D. thesis, 1995), p. 106.

26. I. Roy, 'The Royalist Army in the First Civil War' (Oxford University, D.Phil. thesis, 1963), pp. 345, 347.

27. Clarendon, vol. II, p. 222.

28. Roy, 'The Royalist Army', pp. 78–9.

29. Baillie, vol. II, p. 80.

30. *HMC, Portland Manuscripts* (London, 1891), vol. I, p. 87.

31. BL, Harleian MS 164, fos 399v–400.

32. BL, Harleian MS 164, fo. 122v.

33. *Mercurius Aulicus*, no. 32 (6–12 Aug. 1643), p. 425.

34. *To the Honorable… Commons House in Parliament Assembled: The Humble Petition of the Lord Mayor, Aldermen, and Commons of the Citie of London in Common Councell Assembled* (London, 1643).

35. *Mercurius Aulicus*, no. 32 (6–12 Aug. 1643), p. 434.

36. S. R. Gardiner (ed.), *The Constitutional Documents of the Puritan Revolution, 1625–1660*, 3rd edn (Oxford: Oxford University Press, 1906), pp. 267–71.

Chapter 3   The Wars of the Three Kingdoms

1. Bodl., MS Clarendon 29, fo. 92.

2. W. Fiennes, *Vindiciae Veritatis* (London, 1654), p. 41.

3. Clarendon, vol. III, p. 300.

4. Ormond, vol. VI, p. 38.

5. Bodl., MS Carte 11, fos. 491–2.

6. J. Adamson, 'The Triumph of Oligarchy: The Management of War and the Committee of Both Kingdoms, 1644–1645', in C. R. Kyle and J. Peacey (eds), *Parliament at Work: Parliamentary Committees, Political Power and Public Access in Early Modern England* (Woodbridge: Boydell Press, 2002), pp. 116–17.

7. For the Presbyterian alliance, see M. P. Mahony, 'The Presbyterian Party in the Long Parliament, 2 July 1644–3 June 1647' (Oxford University D.Phil. thesis, 1973).

8. D. Evance, *The Noble Order, or the Honour which God Conferr's on them that Honour His* (London, 1646), p. 41.

9. J. Adamson, 'The Peerage in Politics, 1645–49' (Cambridge University, Ph.D. thesis, 1986), p. 125.

10. K. Lindley and D. Scott (eds), *The Journal of Thomas Juxon* [hereafter cited as Juxon], *1644–1647* (Camden Society, 5th series, vol. XIII, 1999), pp. 63–4.

11. D. Underdown, 'The Parliamentary Diary of John Boys, 1647–8', *Bulletin of the Institute of Historical Research*, XXXIX (1966), 156.

12. M. Kishlansky, *The Rise of the New Model Army* (Cambridge: Cambridge University Press, 1979).

13. Baillie, vol. II, pp. 491–2.

14. Hull City Archives, Hull Letters, L383.

15. Adamson, 'The Triumph of Oligarchy', pp. 122–4.

16. C. Walker, *The Mysterie of the Two Juntos* (London, 1647), p. 7.

Chapter 4   *Anglia Rediviva*

1. J. Morrill, *Revolt in the Provinces: The People of England and the Tragedies of War, 1630–1648*, (2nd edn (London: Longman, 1999), p. 190.

2. M. Perceval-Maxwell, 'Sir Robert Southwell and the Duke of Ormond's Reflections on the 1640s', in M. Ó Siochrú (ed.), *Kingdoms in Crisis: Ireland in the 1640s* (Dublin: Four Courts Press, 2001), p. 238.

3. Bodl., MS Nalson IV, fo. 212v.

4. H. W. Meikle (ed.), *Correspondence of the Scots Commissioners in London, 1644–1646* (Edinburgh, 1917), p. 129.

5. R. Scrope and T. Monkhouse (eds), *State Papers Collected by Edward Earl of Clarendon*, 3 vols (Oxford, 1767–86), vol. II, p. 308.

6. Ibid., vol. II, p. 263.

7. J. Adamson, 'Strafford's Ghost: the British Context of Viscount Lisle's Lieutenancy of Ireland', in J. Ohlmeyer (ed.), *Ireland from Independence to Occupation, 1641–1660* (Cambridge: Cambridge University Press, 1995), pp. 128–59.

8. A. Williamson, 'Patterns of British Identity: "Britain" and its Rivals in the Sixteenth and Seventeenth Centuries', in G. Burgess (ed.), *The New British History: Founding a Modern State, 1603–1715* (London: I. B. Tauris, 1999), p. 154.

9. T. Ó hAnnracháin, *Catholic Reformation in Ireland: The Mission of Rinuccini, 1645–1649* (Oxford: Oxford University Press, 2002), p. 229.

10. T. Ó hAnnracháin, 'Rebels and Confederates: The Stance of the Irish Clergy in the 1640s', in J. R. Young (ed.), *Celtic Dimensions to the British Civil Wars* (Edinburgh: John Donald, 1997), pp. 96–111.

11. Bodl., MS Carte 63, fo. 413r.

12. J. Bruce (ed.), *Charles I in 1646: Letters of King Charles the First to Queen Henrietta Maria* (Camden Society, LXIII, 1856), pp. 22–3.
13. Baillie, vol. II, p. 362.
14. Juxon, p. 104.
15. T. Edwards, *The Second Part of Gangraena* (London, 1646), p. 212.
16. Bruce, *Charles I in 1646*, pp. 36, 38.
17. Ó hAnnracháin, *Catholic Reformation*, p. 162.
18. J. Lowe (ed.), *Letter-Book of the Earl of Clanricarde, 1643–47* (Dublin: Irish Manuscripts Commission, 1983), p. 292.
19. National Archives of Scotland, Edinburgh [NAS], Clerk of Penicuik Manuscripts, GD18/3110. I am grateful to Sir John Clerk of Penicuik for permission to publish extracts from this manuscript.
20. Bruce, *Charles I in 1646*, pp. 40, 41.
21. S. R. Gardiner, *History of the Great Civil War, 1642–1649*, 4 vols (London: Windrush Press, 1987), vol. III, p. 114.
22. *To the Honourable the House of Commons … the Humble Remonstrance and Petition of the Lord Major, Aldermen, and Commons of the City of London* (London, 1646), p. 3.
23. Bodl., MS Clarendon 28, fo. 5r.
24. Bodl., MS Tanner 59, fos. 325–6.
25. Scrope and Monkhouse, *State Papers Collected by Edward Earl of Clarendon*, vol. II, p. 339.
26. S. E. Hoskins, *Charles the Second in the Channel Islands*, 2 vols (London: Richard Bentley, 1854), vol. I, p. 432.
27. Ibid., vol. I, pp. 434–5; Scrope and Monkhouse, *State Papers Collected by Edward Earl of Clarendon*, vol. II, p. 326.
28. Ibid., p. 340.
29. Hoskins, *Charles the Second in the Channel Islands*, vol. I, p. 445.
30. Bruce, *Charles I in 1646*, pp. 51, 80.
31. C. Walker, *An Appendix to The History of Independency* (London, 1661), pp. 8, 10.
32. Juxon, p. 138.
33. Meikle, *Correspondence of the Scots Commissioners*, p. 220.
34. T. Chaloner, *An Answer to the Scotch Papers … Concerning the Disposal of the King's Person* (London, 1646).
35. National Library of Wales, Aberystwyth [NLW], Wynnstay manuscripts, 90/16. I am grateful to Lloyd Bowen for this reference.
36. NAS, Hamilton manuscripts, GD 406/1/1951.
37. Ibid., GD 406/1/2147.

38. J. G. Fotheringham (ed.), *The Diplomatic Correspondence of Jean de Montereul*, 2 vols (Publications of the Scottish History Society, XXIX, XXX, 1898, 1899), vol. I, p. 364.
39. NAS, Hamilton manuscripts, GD 406/1/2024.
40. D. Stevenson, *Revolution and Counter-Revolution in Scotland, 1644–1651* (London: Royal Historical Society, 1977), p. 79.
41. NAS, Hamilton manuscripts, GD 406/1/2103.
42. NLW, Wynnstay manuscripts, 90/16.

Chapter 5   The Rise of the New Model Army

1. M. Mendle, 'Putney's Pronouns: Identity and Indemnity in the Great Debate', in M. Mendle (ed.), *The Putney Debates of 1647: The Army, the Levellers, and the English State* (Cambridge: Cambridge University Press, 2001), pp. 126–7.
2. S. R. Gardiner (ed.), *The Constitutional Documents of the Puritan Revolution, 1625–1660*, 3rd edn (Oxford: Oxford University Press, 1906), p. 269.
3. A. H. Williamson, *Scottish National Consciousness in the Age of James VI* (Edinburgh: John Donald, 1979), pp. 142–3, 146.
4. BL, Browne papers, uncat.: Sir Edward Nicholas to Sir Richard Browne, 17 Jan. 1647 new style.
5. A. Sharp (ed.), *The English Levellers* (Cambridge: Cambridge University Press, 1998), pp. 77–84.
6. P. Baker, 'The Origins and Early History of the Levellers, *c*.1635–*c*.1647' (Cambridge University Ph. D., forthcoming).
7. Bodl., MS Tanner 58, fo. 46r.
8. I. Gentles, *The New Model Army in England, Ireland, and Scotland, 1645–1653* (Oxford: Blackwell, 1992), p. 149.
9. *Journal of the House of Lords*, vol. IX, p. 115.
10. *HMC, Egmont Manuscripts* (London, 1905), p. 368.
11. Ibid., p. 367.
12. M. Ó Siochrú, *Confederate Ireland, 1642–1649: A Constitutional and Political Analysis* (Dublin: Four Courts Press, 1999), pp. 127, 141, 249, 267; T. Ó hAnnracháin, *Catholic Reformation in Ireland: The Mission of Rinuccini, 1645–1649* (Oxford: Oxford University Press, 2002), pp. 172–4.
13. Ó Siochrú, *Confederate Ireland*, p. 157.

14. Baillie, vol. III, p. 27; J. Adamson, 'Strafford's Ghost: The British Context of Viscount Lisle's Lieutenancy of Ireland', in J. Ohlmeyer (ed.), *Ireland from Independence to Occupation, 1641–1660* (Cambridge: Cambridge University Press, 1995), pp. 147–50.
15. T. Thompson and C. Innes (eds), *The Acts of the Parliaments of Scotland* [*APS*], 12 vols (Edinburgh, 1814–75), vol. VI, i, p. 764.
16. J. Adamson, 'Strafford's Ghost' [ch.], p. 149.
17. *A Declaration of the Engagements, Remonstrances, Representations... from His Excellency Sir Tho: Fairfax, and the Generall Councel of the Army* (London, 1647), p. 8.
18. Bodl., MS Clarendon 29, fo. 195v.
19. *Declaration of the Engagements, Remonstrances, Representations*, p. 11.
20. Bodl., MS Clarendon 29, fo. 195v.
21. Ibid., fo. 229r.
22. NAS, Hamilton manuscripts, GD 406/1/10808.
23. *Declaration of the Engagements, Remonstrances, Representations*, p. 27.
24. Ibid., p. 64.
25. Gardiner, *Constitutional Documents of the Puritan Revolution*, pp. 316–26.
26. Bodl., MS Clarendon 29, fo. 92r.
27. Juxon, p. 161.
28. *Memoirs of Sir John Berkley* (London, 1699), p. 34.
29. Juxon, p. 165.
30. G. Burnet, *The Memoires of the Lives and Actions of James and William, Dukes of Hamilton and Castleherald* (London, 1687), p. 320.
31. Bodl., MS Clarendon 30, fo. 168r.
32. *HMC, Portland Manuscripts*, vol. I, p. 433.
33. *HMC, Egmont Manuscripts*, p. 472.
34. Ibid., p. 483.
35. Ó hAnnracháin, *Catholic Reformation*, pp. 195–6.
36. J. Morrill and P. Baker, 'The Case of the Armie Truly Re-Stated', in Mendle (ed.), *Putney Debates*, pp. 103–24.
37. C. H. Firth (ed.), *The Clarke Papers*, 4 vols (Camden Society, 2nd ser., XLIX, LIV, LXI, LXII, 1891–1901), vol. I, pp. 383, 417.
38. Gardiner, *Constitutional Documents of the Puritan Revolution*, pp. 347–53.
39. Adamson, 'Strafford's Ghost', pp. 148, 149.
40. D. Underdown, *Pride's Purge: Politics in the Puritan Revolution* (Oxford: Clarendon Press, 1971), p. 88.

Chapter 6   The Second Civil War and the English Revolution

1. Baillie, vol. III, p. 46.
2. C. Walker, *The Compleat History of Independencie* (London, 1661), part 1, p. 157.
3. D. Underdown, 'The Parliamentary Diary of John Boys, 1647–8', *Bulletin of the Institute of Historical Research,* XXXIX (1966), p. 155.
4. *Mercurius Pragmaticus,* no. 12 (13–20 June 1648), sig. Mv.
5. Walker, *Compleat History of Independencie,* part 1, p. 79.
6. J. G. Fotheringham (ed.), *The Diplomatic Correspondence of Jean de Montereul,* 2 vols (Publications of the Scottish History Society, XXIX, XXX, 1898, 1899), vol. II, p. 407.
7. S. R. Gardiner (ed.), *Hamilton Papers. Addenda* (Camden Society, 2nd ser., LIII, 1895), p. 30.
8. Baillie, vol. III, p. 35.
9. *HMC, Hamilton Manuscripts,* p. 72.
10. *APS,* vol. VI, ii, p. 24.
11. Clarendon, vol. IV, p. 296.
12. Ormond, vol. VI, p. 561.
13. Bodl., MS Carte 22, fos. 83r–v.
14. *Journal of the House of Commons,* vol. V, p. 552; *Journal of the House of Lords,* vol. X, p. 247.
15. M. J. Braddick and M. Greengrass (eds), 'The Letters of Sir Cheney Culpeper, 1641–1657', in *Seventeenth-Century Political and Financial Papers: Camden Miscellany, XXXIII* (Camden Society, 5th ser., VII, 1996), p. 339.
16. D. Underdown, *Pride's Purge: Politics in the Puritan Revolution* (Oxford: Clarendon Press, 1971), pp. 96–7.
17. S. R. Gardiner (ed.), *The Hamilton Papers* (Camden Society, 2nd ser., XXVII, 1880), p. 198.
18. R. Ashton, *Counter Revolution: The Second Civil War and its Origins, 1646–8* (New Haven, Conn.: Yale University Press, 1994), p. 147.
19. Walker, *Compleat History of Independencie,* part 1, pp. 141, 145.
20. *A Letter from an Ejected Member to Sir Jo: Evelyn* (London, 1648), p. 15.
21. Bodl., MS Clarendon, fo. 310r.
22. J. R. Powell and E. K. Timmings (eds), *Documents Relating to the Civil War, 1642–1648* (London: Navy Records Society, 1963), p. 354.
23. Bodl., MS Clarendon 30, fo. 271v.
24. Bodl., MS Clarendon 31, fo. 243v.
25. *Mercurius Pragmaticus,* no. 16 (11–18 July 1648), sig. Qv.
26. C. H. Firth (ed.), *The Clarke Papers,* 4 vols (Camden Society, 2nd ser., XLIX, LIV, LXI, LXII, 1891–1901), vol. II, p. 52.

27. D. Stevenson, *Revolution and Counter-Revolution in Scotland, 1644–1651* (London: Royal Historical Society, 1977), p. 124.
28. Bodl., MS Clarendon 31, f. 110v.
29. M. Ó Siochrú, *Confederate Ireland: A Constitutional and Political Analysis* (Dublin: Four Courts Press, 1999), p. 187.
30. Bodl., MS Carte 22, fo. 641v.
31. W. Allen, *A Faithful Memorial of that Remarkable Meeting of Many Officers of the Army of England, at Windsor Castle* (London, 1659), p. 5.
32. *HMC, Leybourne–Popham Manuscripts* (Norwich, 1899), p. 8.
33. J. Adamson, 'The Frighted Junto: Perceptions of Ireland, and the Last Attempts at Settlement with Charles I', in J. Peacey (ed.), *The Regicides and the Execution of Charles I* (Basingstoke: Palgrave, 2001), pp. 36–70.
34. W. C. Abbott, *The Writings and Speeches of Oliver Cromwell*, 4 vols (Cambridge, Mass.: Harvard University Press, 1937–47), vol. I, p. 691.
35. I. Gentles, *The New Model Army in England, Ireland, and Scotland, 1645–1653* (Oxford: Blackwell, 1992), pp. 277, 283–5; J. Morrill and P. Baker, 'Oliver Cromwell, the Regicide and the Sons of Zeruiah', in Peacey (ed.), *The Regicides*, pp. 14–35.
36. *A Remonstrance of his Excellency Thomas Lord Fairfax... and of the Generall Councell of Officers* (London, 1648), pp. 26, 61.
37. Ibid., p. 64.
38. Ó Siochrú, *Confederate Ireland*, p. 197.
39. Ormond, vol. VI, p. 596.
40. Adamson, 'The Frighted Junto', pp. 40–7.
41. *HMC, De L'Isle and Dudley Manuscripts* (London, 1966), vol. VI, p. 578.
42. J. G. Muddiman, *Trial of King Charles the First* (Edinburgh: W. Hodge, 1928), p. 79.
43. S. Kelsey, 'Staging the Trial of Charles I' in Peacey (ed.), *The Regicides*, pp. 84–5; 'The Trial of Charles I', *English Historical Review*, CXVIII (2003), pp. 583–617.
44. Adamson, 'The Frighted Junto', p. 57.
45. Ibid., p. 61.

Epilogue and Conclusion

1. D. Stevenson, *Revolution and Counter-Revolution in Scotland, 1644–1651* (London: Royal Historical Society, 1977), p. 165.
2. S. Kelsey, *Inventing a Republic: The Political Culture of the English Commonwealth, 1649–1653* (Manchester: Manchester University Press, 1997), p. 202.

Index